P9-CDA-022

A TERRORIST'S CALL TO
GLOBAL JIHAD

DECIPHERING ABU MUSAB AL-SURI'S
ISLAMIC JIHAD MANIFESTO

Edited by Jim Lacey

NAVAL INSTITUTE PRESS
Annapolis, Maryland

Naval Institute Press
291 Wood Road
Annapolis, MD 21402

© 2008 by The United States Naval Institute
All rights reserved. No part of this book may be reproduced or
utilized in any form or by any means, electronic or mechan-
ical, including photocopying and recording, or by any information storage and retrieval system, without permission in
writing from the publisher.

Library of Congress Cataloging-in-Publication Data
A terrorist's call to global jihad : deciphering Abu Musab al-
Suri's Islamic jihad manifesto / edited by Jim Lacey.
    p. cm.
 Includes bibliographical references and index.
 ISBN 978-1-59114-462-5 (alk. paper)
  1. Terrorism—History. 2. Terrorism—Religious aspects—
Islam. I. Lacey, Jim, 1958–
HV6431.T5356 2008
363.325—dc22
                                        2007045299

Printed in the United States of America on acid-free paper

14 13 12 11 10 09 08   9 8 7 6 5 4 3 2
First printing

Contents

Preface   v

Introduction   vii

Chapter 1   **The West's Great Assault**   1

Chapter 2   **The Status of Muslims Today**   30

Chapter 3   **The Sharia Rulings for This Situation**   48

Chapter 4   **The Resistance Begins**   55

Chapter 5   **The Islamic Awakening: A Summary of the**   63
             Course of the Islamic Awakening (1930–2001)

Chapter 6   **Armed Jihadist Experiences in the**   101
             Late Twentieth Century

Chapter 7   **The Intellectual and Doctrinal Foundations**   160
             of the Jihadist Movement

Chapter 8   **Sharia-based Political Decision Making**   171
             of the Movement

Chapter 9   **Media and Incitement in the Call to Resistance**   189

             Index   197

Preface

T he Joint Forces Command continues to sponsor research designed to further explore the jihadi movement. The corpus of this work and collected insights from the knowledge base that provide researchers and analysts a better understanding of an enemy that has openly called for the destruction of the United States and its allies as well as the principles on which our civilization rests, including individual liberty, rule of law, and free and fair trade.

Though there has been much commentary since the start of the global war on terrorism on the importance of understanding the current jihadi threat, to date an insufficient level of disciplined research has been devoted to understanding thoroughly the jihadi adversary and its network. This condensed translation of al Qaida veteran Mustafa bin Abd al-Qadir Setmariam Nasar's (aka al-Suri, The Syrian) 1,600-page *Call to Global Islamic Resistance* provides researchers an opportunity to further understand the enemy.*

The commander of the U.S. Joint Forces Command, Gen. Lance Smith, and the director of the Joint Center for Operational Analysis, Gen. James Barclay, have strongly supported the ongoing Terrorist Perspective Project (TPP). The object of the TPP is to understand the "mind" of the jihadi movement in a way that allows joint warfighters to get inside the terrorists' decision cycle, or what U.S. Air Force strategist John Boyd called the enemy's Observe-Orient-Decide-Act decision cycle, or OODA Loop. The TPP aims to study how the adversary views the conduct of its operations and context for how it conveys these strategies across its network. Indeed, the concept that the center of gravity of al Qaida may be a network rather a particular person, place, or strategy is a notion that requires not only further analysis but also a different kind of analytical framework. This is the first serious attempt to examine the context and character of this new and dangerous adversary through his own lens and to avoid the mirror imaging that often leads to faulty intelligence analysis.

This study revealed that an al Qaida veteran, Mustafa bin Abd al-Qadir Setmariam Nasar, more commonly known as al-Suri (The Syrian), was receiving considerable attention within jihadi circles. His 1,600-page *Call to Global Islamic Resistance* began appearing on an ever-increasing number of jihadi Web sites and was repeatedly hailed as the blueprint for the rebirth of the jihadi movement. In this work, al-Suri reveals the beliefs and history of the jihadi movement as they themselves understand it. But, more important, he lays out the current state of the jihad and a strategy designed to overcome what he sees as America's strengths.

Recognizing that 1,600-page document of densely written "jihadi thought" would deter all but the most dedicated analyst, Joint Forces Command has produced this condensed version and translation of al-Suri's work that captures the essence of his thoughts. Where appropriate, we have also removed most of the repetitive theological justifications undergirding these beliefs.

Our intention is to make available this translated work to enable the larger community of public and private analysts, academics, and strategic thinkers to conduct further analysis and collaborative exchange. Our goal is enable researchers to help us collectively better understand the significance of Al-Suri's masterwork and to gain insights on the trends that this document might reveal in the jihadi movement.

Decades ago the world ignored Adolf Hitler's *Mein Kampf* and Vladimir Lenin's *What Is to Be Done*, with tragic consequences. Today, the jihadists have presented the world with a work of similar importance, which we ignore at our own peril. It is in this mind-set that the U.S. Joint Forces Command offers this primary research document.

Editor's Note: The editor has elected to use "al Qaida" as the preferred spelling for the international terrorist group discussed in this book; other recognized English spellings of the group include al-Qaida, al-Qa'ida, al Qaeda, and al-Qaeda.

Introduction

In November 2005, Pakistani counterterrorism forces kicked in the door of a nondescript apartment in Quetta, Pakistan, where one of the world's leading terrorists, Abu Musab al-Suri, was hiding with a friend. So ended an international manhunt for the man often referred to as al Qaida's mastermind. Before his capture, al-Suri had chalked up a long list of murderous activities. He was currently under indictment for his roles in the 2003 Madrid train bombings and was a prime suspect in the planning and direction of the 2005 London bus bombings. Before these events, al-Suri had come to the attention of Western intelligence agencies many times over the past two decades and was often under surveillance as he steadily moved up the terrorist ranks, until finally becoming a top aide to Osama bin Laden. By the time of his captured, there was a $5 million American reward on his head, and next to Osama himself, he topped all of international terrorism's most-wanted lists.

Born, Mustafa Setmariam Nasar in Aleppo, Syria, probably in 1958, he adopted the nom de guerre Abu Musab al-Suri when he entered the jihadist movement as a member of the Muslim Brotherhood in the early 1980s. Forced to flee when Syrian dictator Hafez al-Assad viciously crushed the Brotherhood's attempt to overthrow him, al-Suri fled to Afghanistan to join the jihad against the Soviet occupation. He remained there through most of the 1980s and later claimed that this is when he first met Osama and became a member of al Qaida.

After the Soviet withdrawal, al-Suri left the chaos of Afghanistan behind and moved, first to Spain and then to London, where he continued to work on the fringes of the jihad movement. He found work as a journalist and became the prime mover behind a couple of jihadist periodicals, most of them vocally supporting the mass exterminations of entire villages and towns by Islamic groups in Algeria. He also found time to work as a go-between for Western news agencies and Osama and was responsible for setting up several interviews with the al Qaida leader. Peter Bergen of CNN, who al-Suri escorted on a visit to Osama, said of him, "He seemed to be a very intelligent guy, a very well informed guy, and a very serious guy. . . . he was certainly more impressive than bin Laden."

Before he left Spain, al-Suri managed to establish several sleeper cells, one of which was instrumental in assisting in the logistical support for the 9/11 attacks. In fact, Western intelligence sources report that a close associate of al-Suri traveled from al-Suri's training camp in Afghanistan to Spain and met with Mohammed Atta, the leader of the 9/11 attacks, just a few weeks before he was to kill thousands of Americans.

While in London, al-Suri began writing numerous books and pamphlets dealing with the history of the jihad movement, the movement's beliefs, and also doctrinal manuals, which became how-to guides for budding jihadists. Over time, he became recognized as the movement's premier strategic thinker and became well known for his uncompromising dedication to violence as the only means of attaining Islamic goals. After 9/11, he stated, "I would have advised selecting international flights so that the planes could have been loaded with weapons of mass destruction. Attacking America with such weapons is difficult . . . but it is becoming a necessity."

Suspected by British authorities of participation in the 1995 Paris subway bombings and also of establishing sleeper cells in England and other European countries, al-Suri was briefly detained and then, upon his release, fled to Afghanistan. There he linked up once again with Osama, who had recently established himself there after being thrown out of the Sudan. Upon al-Suri's arrival in Afghanistan, he swore allegiance to the Taliban leader, Mullah Omar, and renewed his close ties with the leaders of al Qaida.

In Afghanistan, al-Suri established his own training camp for budding jihadists and began lecturing throughout most of the other training camps. He also began assisting in experiments with a variety of chemical weapons he planned to use against Western targets, particularly government leaders. His most prized pupil, who later became his closest associate, was the vicious killer Abu Musab al-Zarqawi, who until he was killed in June 2006, was the leader of al Qaida in Iraq. Zarqawi burned his way into the

consciousness of most Americans through his videotaping of the behead-
ings of innocents his organization had kidnapped. In fact, during most of
2005 and 2006, al-Suri was believed to be often at Zarqawi's right hand,
helping to plan operations against Americans in Iraq and also providing
ideological guidance for the movement.

While still in Afghanistan, al-Suri cemented his position as al-Qaeda's
leading theorist, and it was during this time that he began writing his masterwork, *The Call to Global Islamic Resistance*. This manifesto has been
referred to as a combination of Adolf Hitler's *Mein Kamp* and Vladimir
Lenin's *What Is to Be Done*. Since its publication in 2005, it has attracted
substantial media attention and is available for download, in Arabic and
on dozens of jihadist Web sites. It is through this book that al-Suri hoped
to make a lasting contribution to the ongoing jihad.

The Call to Global Islamic Resistance is much more than a typical piece
of jihadist literature, though it does have its full share of hate mongering
and does not stint on its calls for the destruction of Western civilization.
However, when you write a 1,600-page tract, you can cover a lot of ground,
and al-Suri does that. His work is unusual among other jihadist works for
taking an unstinting look at not only the movement's successes, but also
its failures over the last few decades. For instance, while he glories in the
spirit behind 9/11, he also blames it for the catastrophes that have befallen
the jihadi movement since that date. In fact, al-Suri plainly states that the
jihadi movement is on the verge of extinction and that unless it changes its
entire method of operation, its days are numbered.

In fine detail, he lays out the mistakes jihadi movements have made
and continue to make that present them as easy targets for counterterrorism attacks. He then goes on to explain how jihadi groups must change
their methods of operation and organization to avoid being caught up in
what he calls "The American Crusade against Islamists." As such, his
treatise provides a detailed how-to guide for the new al Qaida he hopes
will arise from the ashes of the first.

However, al-Suri concerns himself with much more then practical operations. As the movement's leading theorist, he laments that
new jihadis are entering the movement without the proper instruction
in Islamic doctrine. For him, someone who kills in the name of Islam
without understanding the principles of Islam (that permit him to kill)
is not a proper jihadi. Like the communist cadres that fought in the Cold
War, being willing to fight is not enough. The fighter must also be properly

indoctrinated in the ideology of the group so that he is fighting and dying for the right reasons.

Al-Suri identifies the American-led global war on terrorism as the key reason for this shortcoming, claiming that there was plenty of time for proper indoctrination in the Afghan training camps, but that was all ruined by the American onslaught. Moreover, he professes concern that so many of those who were qualified to instruct newcomers on the history, tradition, and ideology of the movement have been killed in recent years, leaving a void of qualified instructors. One of his clearly stated reasons for writing *The Call to Global Islamic Resistance* was to make up for this deficiency and to present new jihadis a clear and thorough history of the movement and of the ideology that underpins it. As such, it constitutes an important window into contemporary jihadist thought and the historical evolution of jihadi movements.

For too long, analysts and even the general public have observed the jihadi movement from the outside and tried to understand it from our own perspective. Too often our own biases have gotten in the way of accurately interpreting what we see. This misinterpretation of the movement's ideas, goals, strategies, and plans has led policymakers not only to underestimate the enemy, but also to advocate policies that are, at best, inappropriate. In the end, the final defeat of global Islamic terrorism requires that we fully understand our enemy, and al-Suri's work gives us a rare chance to do that by seeing our enemy through his own eyes.

Al-Suri informs us that:

- We have severely underestimated how much damage we have done to Islamic terror groups.
- Most of the world's terror groups were too concerned with their own survival and local issues to buy into the global al Qaida movement.
- The jihadi movement makes up a miniscule portion of the greater Islamic community. It particularly disturbs al-Suri that jihad has only enlisted the active support of fewer than one in a million Muslims.

Finally, he unintentionally lays out numerous pathways for those waging the global war on terror, which could potentially lead to the movement's demise before it becomes a multigenerational conflict.

Unfortunately, only the most dedicated individual has the will or can make the time to read three-quarters of a million words of jihadi literature. For that reason, I have created this volume, which I hope captures the essence of al-Suri and will spare the reader over a thousand pages of useless meandering. One may well ask, what is lost when an editor cuts 600,000 words from a manuscript, and that is a fair question. By far, the largest amount of deletions are the thousands of quotes from the Qur'an and medieval Islamic scholars that al-Suri uses to underpin the Islamic legality of his pronouncements, ideas, and principles. My assumption was that the general reader is much more concerned with what the average Islamic terrorist believes then what perversions of Islamic scholarship are being used to justify murder and wholesale slaughter.

Moreover, al-Suri wrote this book over a long period of time and often under what could at best be called trying conditions. Probably because of this, he often loses focus and repeats long passages of material he related earlier. Most, but not all, of this repetition has been removed. The repetition that remains is where I judge that al-Suri was repeating himself for the sake of emphasis and I considered it important that this emphasis not be lost. Finally, al-Suri spent hundreds of pages detailing his version of world history from the rise of Ancient Rome through the twentieth century. As a "unique" version of history, it was interesting. However, it did not add much to our knowledge of the current jihad, so it was deleted.

To ensure I got as much of the critical essence of al-Suri into this work as possible, I presented my draft to several experts who have been heavily involved over the past years in studying the jihadist movement. They were told that they could have me add anything they thought important from the original, but for every word they placed in the book, they had to remove one. I was determined to keep this work at a reasonable length for the average reader, but I also wanted to make sure I captured the true essence of the man the *Washington Post* called "The most dangerous terrorist you never heard of."

CHAPTER 1
The West's Great Assault

A t the onset of the twenty-first century, the Islamic *ummah* is enduring American-Zionist, Crusader-Western invasions, helped by the
cooperation of hypocritical governments that control the Arab and
Islamic world.

Many jihadist cadres have been destroyed, and a large number of their
bases have vanished because of military attacks conducted by this alliance of infidels and hypocritical Arab and Islamic governments. This has
placed the continuity of the jihadist movement—and its ability to preserve its purity—under threat.

Likewise, the Islamic awakening is enduring an intellectual decline
as a result of the efforts of hypocrites among the *ulama* and the defeatists
within its leadership. This decline threatens both the core group and the
Awakening's masses, just as it also threatens the creed, identity, and existence of the *ummah*.

The American war of ideas and the attack on our educational system
began in the first decade of the twentieth century. The continuation of
this assault on the foundational principles of the *ummah* may eventually lead to the *ummah*'s destruction. There is a need to preserve the religious, intellectual, and cultural identity of the *ummah* and to sustain the
thoughts of the Islamic awakening and particularly its jihadist vanguard.

I believe that, because of these circumstances, jihadist nuclei will be
strewn about with no common ideology or identity to unite them—except
the goal of repelling the Crusader assault.

It is possible that our enemies will note the disarray arising from these
disparate centers of Muslim resistance and will exploit these mistakes to

cripple the jihad and drive a wedge between the jihadist resistance and its audience within the *ummah*, thereby forcing the jihad along the path of dispersion and defeat.

Because of the continuous fall of martyrs from the leadership and the destruction of cadres who had been prepared methodologically over a long period of time, the majority of our current resistance and jihadist groups lack an educational, political, legal, and intellectual paradigm that can serve as a reference for them. They have no means to properly prepare new cadres or a fixed foundation to help settle their disputes.

For these reasons, I have written this book, so that it will be, with God's permission, used as an aid and a guide.

This book contains a summary of the legal, political, intellectual, and methodological foundations on which the jihadist movement was raised from its birth and throughout its long journey.

It also includes a history of many jihadist experiences and a summary of the valuable lessons drawn from them, so that the next jihadist generation can be built on these lessons and benefit from them. These are lessons and experiences we have paid for with the pure blood of our brothers.

The book also contains a summary of the struggle between the centuries-long struggle between the Muslims and the *Rum* through the centuries, particularly the modern-day *Rum*—the Americans and the Europeans. They have conspired over the past two centuries to drive Muslims away from their faith, which they realize is the reason for Arab power and glory.[1]

The information I present forms an intellectual foundation for the mujahid, which will give him an understanding of the course of this current conflict, its roots, and the enemies' method of managing it. It also contains, for the mujahideen and resistance fighters, information about the preferred means of resisting invasive Crusader campaigns.

This book gives everyone resolved to a life along this luminous path a comprehensive education that will qualify him for the jihadist way of life. It also provides him with information I hope will aid him in work that is acceptable to God in the End of Days.

I hope that this book contains between its covers and in its chapters a comprehensive intellectual, political, and legal guide that will serve as a reference for the leadership of the jihad. I view it as a foundation delimiting the movement and also an axis for engagement between the different jihad groups, whose throngs I see forming in the womb of a generous *ummah*.

The modern Crusader-Jewish, American-led campaign against the Arab and Islamic world has clearly announced its goals: total elimination of the civilizational, religious, political, economic, social, and cultural existence of Muslims. The [George] Bush administration has announced its plans for the next decade:

1. Transforming the political map of the Middle East and the Arab-Islamic world; that is, transforming the ruling systems and reconstructing, replacing, or forming them anew.
2. Redrawing the map of certain countries, encouraging fractiousness as well as localized, religious, ethnic, and political strife.
3. Destroying cultural- and identity-based resistance movements and reconstituting the social fabric by removing the religious, intellectual, and moral foundation of the region and reshaping this foundation on the basis of Western thought, specifically American-Zionist thought.
4. Hegemony over the sources of wealth in the region, particularly oil and gas, mineral resources, and other agricultural and livestock resources, so as to pump them through the arteries of the invaders and the Zionist entity implanted in the heart of the region.
5. Transforming the region into a market for liquidating imperialist products via so-called partnership and free trade agreements in the Middle East.

Numerous media sources have revealed that America, with Britain and Israel behind her (along with all of the NATO and European nations rotating in America's orbit), has sought to use all its military, strategic, economic, and media might to realize these objectives.

In short, the world is witnessing Western civilization's most insolent, malevolent, barbaric attack in history. The West is following the leadership of a gang of Crusader, would-be Zionists in the American administration. However, it is also known that this "Third Crusader Campaign" is a malicious continuation of the two campaigns that preceded it—the first during the eleventh and twelfth Christian centuries, and the second spanning from the seventeenth century until the middle of the twentieth century.

We stand before a military invasion armed with the newest military instruments and scientific technology, supporting the most destructive strategic plans. They use tanks to implement programs for social, religious, and cultural transformation, for replacing the Islamic faith, and fragmenting the Arab and Muslim identity. They plan programs for reshaping our societies that include intellectual and cultural elements, educational changes, and media programs they hope will reshape everything, including the Friday sermon in the pulpits of Muslim mosques.

In short, the hole has grown wider than the patch, and we need to step back and contemplate the methods we can use to confront this campaign. These methods must be much more then empty, superficial, or spastic reactions. We are facing an overwhelming disaster, which is reaching its tragic apex. We must understand that for the first time in Muslim history, and possibly the history of all colonized people resisting invasion, that the colonizer has focused his attack, using all of the instruments of power on the gigantic fifth column planted within Arab and Islamic societies.

The American attack today depends—and we must accept this agonizing reality—on complete cooperation from the overwhelming majority of the current Arab rulers. These rulers, because they think this is how they can best defend their own interests, cooperate with the plans of the American colonizers. They follow American leadership and make war against the religion of the people and against the jihadists. What's more, these rulers have mobilized all of their security, media, and controlling apparatuses to annihilate all seeds of resistance to the American invasion. This begins with the suppression of any form of association established for nonviolent change, demonstration, or opposition, and ends with the killing, imprisonment, and banishment of anyone who argues for the formation of resistance groups, especially the seeds of armed and legitimate jihad.

If only the calamity ended with the ruling systems' alliances with the invading enemy. However, the calamity is much worse because a considerable segment of Arab and Islamic societies has been transformed intellectually, culturally, and politically so that they are also willing to assist the occupiers. This is the case even if some of these societal elements are part of the opposition to the apostate ruling systems. In places like Iraq and Afghanistan, opposition movements present themselves as even more prepared than the current ruling systems are to serve the American cause.

At the hands of our countrymen, who have names like our own, who wear our clothes and speak our tongue, services are offered to the colonizer to assassinate her *ummah*, defeat her religion, kill her sons, and wipe out all elements of civilization. These collaborating groups are not confined to intellectual movements, nor to specific ethnic or religious groups. Within this vile column are those who claim a variety of identities, beginning with so-called Islam and continuing with every color of secularist and political demon in our lands.

It is a disaster that many of the good Islamic *ulama*, as well as party and organization leaders, have begun to sell the notion of prostration and our inability to wage war. The enemy media has convinced them to sell the idea of peaceful coexistence, intercivilizational exchange, and peaceful dialogue and mutual understanding with colonizers who devastate us day and night with smart bombs and rockets and who destroy us with armies composed of our stupid sons. All this is proclaimed under the pretense of moderation, or wisdom.

Thus are God's religion and its clear commands abandoned. It is commanded that we wage jihad against this assault, that we fight the enemies of God with all available means and all of the strength we can muster, and that we resist them until the last spark of life. But the battle cries of the noble ones are suppressed. Muslim demonstrations are beaten down under the batons and tear gas canisters of the fear forces—otherwise known as the "security forces." They are crushed under most vile fatwas presented by the Sultan's battle-shirking *ulama*, who are the missionaries of prostration, shame, and destitution.[2]

Nothing now remains in the field resisting the Crusaders apart from a few pure hearts and here and there weak brigand cells that are bleeding martyrs, most often for no gain. If conditions remain as described above, there is no doubt that we are threatened. I do not mean that we are threatened with extinction, because God proclaimed for his *ummah* longevity, triumph, and victory. But we are threatened with conquest, hardship, and pain. We are faced with hunger, fear, killing, humiliation, and destitution. It is, therefore, necessary that a jihad-waging group of noble elite step forward and present methods for arousing resistance and to awaken the *ummah* to join the fight against the enemies of God.

Axes of the Resistance

I believe—and this consideration would be obvious to anyone—that the size of the elite resisting the invading enemies is a frighteningly small segment of the *ummah*. This is not only caused by the viciousness of the enemy attack, but also by the decadence and the individual acceptance of colonialism and defeat within the *ummah*. I believe that in order to engage in this long-lasting war, it is necessary to devise a multifaceted program that will give birth to the seeds of the resistance in the *ummah*.

In the end, successful jihad will only happen within an *ummah* where the fighting creed is firmly established and clarified. This must happen to attain the "revolutionary jihadist climate" that will spontaneously give rise to instruments of resistance. I think that the problem of creating this climate is too great for just the shoulders of the jihadist elite alone, especially since this elite faces near extinction as a result of global struggle against terrorism that America is leading. Through America's exploitation of the events of September 2001, this assault has gone beyond the destruction of numerous cadres and jihadist groups around the world. It has also destroyed part of the Islamic awakening, which has supported the jihad. With that in mind, I believe it is the obligation of the believing elite to work toward three aims:

The Religious-Cultural Aim—Setting in place programs for preserving religious identity and preserving the pure defining intellectual, cultural, and social elements of the Arab and Islamic people.

The Political-Intellectual Aim—Setting in place programs for stimulating political activism, local organizations, and civil society organizations as well as encouraging peaceful media activities that nourish the intellectual and cultural existence of the Arab and Islamic *ummah*.

The Military Aim—Setting in place programs and methods for training in the fighting jihadist creed and for preparation in its educational and spiritual facets. Also, setting up programs for training in the essential military sciences, so as to enable the immediate implementation of a "global Islamic resistance" that will confront America within our Arab and Islamic lands and then in her homeland.

1. Military work and armed jihadist action are the things that will compel the enemy into retreat and lead this *ummah* to victory. Without military resistance, the influence of all peaceful work, however important, will be scattered to the winds. As long as the infidel-Zionist-Crusader-invading colonizer is perched on our chests and in our lands, the entire *ummah* will remain guilty and responsible before God for not sufficiently repelling the enemy. Violent jihad is as an individual duty obligatory on every Muslim. All the *ulama* have said this, and it becomes even more pressing now that the attacker has entered our abode.

2. Armed jihad does not arise from a vacuum and will not transform into the desired magnitude until a revolutionary jihadist climate exists to

give rise to it. This means we must invest great effort in a variety of nonfighting fields—proselytizing, media, education, and defining elements of our religion. It also means broadcasting the Islamic creed and the laws of the sharia, which will fill the heart of the believer with assuredness that militancy is a sharia obligation.

3. Political movement awareness constitutes—along with the religious conviction—the necessary foundations in the mind of the individual Muslim for moving into active fighting.

4. Fearlessness in jihad and armed action in the confrontation with America and her allies is undertaken by only a small percentage of the *ummah* that possesses resoluteness, conviction, and desire compelling it to direct action. Whereas there is a large part of the *ummah* that is convinced of the need for confrontation, its resoluteness on this matter has yet to reach the point of being classed as the highest Islamic obligation.

5. If the elite does not undertake the work of thwarting the enemies' programs for destroying our civilizational structure, then they will become extinct at the hands of the enemy's military effort. The *ummah* will not produce a replacement, but will melt away under the enemy's media and educational barrage.

6. Preserving the religion and the defining elements of our civilization requires a plan of action that forces adherents to conduct clandestine dissemination and education. This kind of positive educational work multiplies the seeds of the resistance and provides the fuel of the revolution. Mosques and religious schools must play a large role in this area, just as religious education and study circles in peoples' homes play an important role. There is also an important role for women and female missionaries inside the family and the home to ensure that the younger generations adhere to their faith and culture.

7. Those employed in the political, media, intellectual, and cultural fields are able to disseminate the idea of civil resistance and its justifications. They are also able to defend our jihad both inside and outside of the country. Likewise, writing, protesting, and other works of civil resistance are works that are permissible under the "false democracy" of colonialism, and this can be used by our supporters safe from penalty or accusations of terrorism.

There are two very important observations concerning the field of nonviolent civil resistance, whether in religious, political, or intellectual work:

First, it is never permissible, and illegal according to the sharia, to join the governing apparatus under the pretext of "peaceful resistance and service to the faith." Employment in any governing, parliamentary, executive, or judicial apparatuses is impermissible.

Second, it is never permissible for an individual working in the civil resistance and the political and media mission to commit the crime of slander against the jihad, the mujahideen, and the Muslim resistance fighters under the pretext of deflecting suspicion away from himself so as to continue his work.

This is because the object of his existence and the justification for his work is the creation of a climate for jihad and support for the resistance. How will resistance be born and continued if the most prominent Islamic missionaries, intellectuals, leaders, and literati within the *ummah* take it upon themselves to slander the jihad and the mujahideen and destroy the good reputation of the resistance and the resistance fighters?

At this moment, the jihadist media should avoid slandering those working in the field and, moreover, should avoid accusing them of shirking battle and of lacking jihadi spirit—even if this were true of the bulk of them.

Levels of the Resistance

Participation in the resistance and confronting the enemies of God passes every individual on three levels:

Islamic Religious Sentiment—Produced by the larger idea of religion, and the natural inheritances of honor and nobility a person feels. It is a natural reaction to the condition of occupation and injustice, the destruction of glory, and the rending of the threads of our religious, civilizational, and national dignity at the hands of the colonizers.

The Will to Fight—This is the foundation that produces the capability for jihad. Will is a determination in the mind, heart, and soul to embark on an action. The stages of embarking on jihad and fighting are will, preparation, dispatch. The will to fight is formed after the maturation of the religious sentiment and the solidifying of the fighting conviction. The formation of the fighting will is aided when the jihadist is made aware of the enemy's hostile works, injustices, killing, and destruction. Then will the man carry weapons and resist.

The Jihadist Creed—This does not arise except through education and instruction. It is the foundation for the jihad's most important operations.

The jihadist creed presents the pillars and doctrine of the movement. The creed serves to clarify intentions and tells us that he who fights is on the path of God, because he who dies in this instance is a martyr. The jihadist creed tells a man his obligation as well as the rules and requirements of the life he is embarking. With the jihadist creed and its pillars the jihadist idea is implanted in the soul of the mujahid, along with complete awareness built on knowledge of God's sharia.

Without the jihadist creed, our work will be thwarted and the path to God will deteriorate. The path will be blocked with fighters who met with misfortune on the road and the underbrush of the dead, imprisoned, and frightened. The jihadist creed is the guarantor for rooting the mujahid will in the face of deceptive media storms and the temptation and deviation the enemies introduce.

It is necessary for those working in the field of resistance, jihad, and direct military action against the enemies of God to have their own *ulama*, intellectuals, and literati as well as their own media tools. This is needed to animate the sentiments of the believers and turn them by way of jihadist propaganda toward fighting as well as to cultivate and instill in them a jihadist creed that will enable younger generations to continue the resistance.

The bitter reality must be mentioned, that tens of millions of loyal Muslim youths continue to face these gloomy, unjust conditions resulting from the tragedies imposed on the *ummah*. These youths are humiliated, confused, and impotent! They waver in religious sentiment and swallow losses and bitterness, then commit unpraiseworthy acts in reaction. This sentiment has not been transformed into a fighting will—except with an insignificant few hundred here and there, or perhaps a mere ten individuals in some Arab and Islamic countries.

Indeed, it is unfortunate that from the time of the rise of the American occupation of the Arabian Peninsula—where they landed publicly in 1990 and remain until today, nearly thirteen years later; where hundreds of thousands of American, English, and European soldiers revel within her territory and hundreds of thousands of their civilians hang around with their families, overseeing economic pillage—the number of jihadist operations has only been a slight few, in which the American losses did not exceed a few dozen. In addition to the troops of their allies, the Americans have spread in our Arab and Islamic region around 1.5 million American troops, which they call "Central Command."

How could such an occupier deceive a nation that contains the holiest of holy sites and that forms the very heart of their homeland? This is truly a rare phenomenon in the history of colonialism and the colonizers of mankind!

The greatest disappointment is the fact that an Islamic state was realized in Afghanistan in the days of the Taliban, which was wide open for six years so that training camps and fighting regiments were set up and the opportunity for jihad under the banners of the sharia was set in place. Despite this, the number of those who entered jihad did not exceed fifteen hundred mujahideen, among which only three hundred came with their families. This is one millionth of a percentage of the *ummah*! Even more harmful was the fact that not a single Muslim scholar migrated to Afghanistan during this time, let alone any famous ones. (I promise you that the imaginary al Qaida numbers American intelligence disseminated in the media are invented so as to realize their goals. And, I vouch for the numbers I have stated as one of those who has field expertise from this period.)

If we compare this situation with the size of the jihadist bands Muslims created in both their ancient and recent history, we would find that the present condition of the *ummah* begs for defeat. But there are signs of hopefulness in segments of the *ummah*, which require efforts to bear their fruits and they are transformed into a useful "global Islamic resistance." For the sake of this objective, I composed the contents of this book. This book was composed and this missionary call was implanted for the sake of answering this question:

> *How do we confront the new world order? How do we confront our enemies in a post–September 11 world? How do we resist the American-led third Crusader campaigns?*

For the Sake of the Third Generation of Mujahideen

I believe a jihadist generation is being born today; created by the events of September [9/11/2001], the occupation of Iraq, and the apex of the Palestinian intifada. Through all of this the *ummah* has stood as a spectator to the jihadist sacrifice because of the silence of its *ulama* and the suppression by its rulers. If we look at past experiences, such as launching of the jihad in the mid-1960s, we note that two whole generations of jihadists have arisen. First, there is the generation of the founders—or the first gun burst—that lit the torch of jihadist thought and initiated the move-ment's first experiences. Most of this generation died on the luminous path and was followed by a second generation, which followed the course from the beginning of the 1980s until the end of the twentieth century,

Then, for those passionate about the jihadist duty, the doors of jihad swung wide open in Afghanistan. Afghanistan was the place where the second generation of jihadists was born. The school of the Arab Afghans was a remarkable experience through which the jihad launched its cadres to various quarters of the Islamic world, notably participating in the Bosnian and Chechen arenas.

Then came the events of September 11, when the second generation entered the "furnace of trial." The third millennium was inaugurated with frightening sacrifices, which destroyed most of the cadres, leaders, and their bases—of which only a small group escaped death or imprisonment.

I believe, in short, that it is the obligation of the third generation to digest the essence of this experience, so as to pass on theories of action to continue to fight the jihad in enormously difficult circumstances. Being one of those who remains from the second generation, I am enjoined to write this book to aid all who follow in our footsteps. The book is meant to help whoever has the confidence to follow on the path of jihad, a path that is smeared with the blood of tens of thousands of martyrs. The coming jihadist generation must know its roots and must digest the experiences of its forebears. The coming jihadist generation must build on these lessons so that it becomes a natural link in the chain formed by the journey of the glorious caravan toward the desired Islam, which is returning the rule of God to this earth. Knowledge has become the most important weaponry in this age, and the ignorant cannot lead in this struggle, however loyal to the obligation they may be.

My Story

By way of field experience during this crucial period of the modern jihadist movement, I lived the jihadist experience in Syria in the field from 1980 and was a member of the military leadership of the Muslim Brotherhood during the events of Hama in 1982.[3] I was also with the Arab jihad in Afghanistan against the Soviet Union and in the field from 1988 to 1992. I was involved with the sad and bitter jihadist experience in Algeria through my media work with the Algerian *Ansar al-Jihad* in London (1993–97), until we were forced to leave because the leadership was taken over by deviators, as I have explained in my book, *My Personal Testimony on the Jihad in Algeria 1989–1996*.

I then took to the field for the last jihadist experiences, the most important of which was in the last decade with the Taliban and the Afghan Arabs in Afghanistan (1996–2001). Before this, there were numerous sanctuaries for me, particularly in many Arab, Islamic, and European countries. These experiences provided me with a chance to interact with different segments of the Islamic awakening and to get to know most of the movements, organizations, and the leadership of the modern jihadist movement. I do not mention these things here to boast, but rather, so that the reader might know that what he reads is the result of long and varied field experiences and that he give them their due weight.

I internalized the bitter jihadist experiences, and I was able, by virtue of my position, to learn about a number of other incredible experiences through the narrations of friends who participated in them. I then compared these with what I learned about the history of modern revolutions and tried to include all of this into the book—to present theories of action that will be helpful to us on our coming journey.

Despite my determination to avoid it, I was delayed in writing this book by the arrogant attack spearheaded by America and its allies. Perhaps the greatest benefit to come from the delay in producing this work is that my ideas within it have matured. Recent events have increased my conviction in the need for a vicious resistance, necessitated by the barbaric and arrogant attack. Another benefit from this delay is that the book's publication has come in the furnace of the trial whose climax we are living at the moment. To understand the stages of crystallization of the ideas in this book, it would helpful to discuss their sequence. The book was undertaken in progressive stages over the course of fourteen years, from the end of 1990 to the end of 2004. Its final form began to take shape in 2002, and I've overseen its completion now at the end of 2004.

The First Stage: Pakistan (1990–91)

The congregation of Arab mujahideen present in Afghanistan and the Pakistani border areas, particularly their capital Peshawar, from 1987 to 1992, reached its apex in 1990 and included without a doubt every faction within the Islamic awakening. This congregation witnessed a psychological earthquake for the Arab mujahideen as a result of the American-led coalition's descent upon the Arabian Peninsula under the guise of liberating Kuwait. This was clearly only a disguise for the new arrogant Crusader campaigns—led by America, Western Europe, and the Jews into the Muslim heartland.

This earthquake struck the whole Arab and Islamic *ummah*, including its religious and political leaders. This time, the Christians had entered the land of the two holy sites and had surrounded the Arabian Peninsula—the heartland of Islam—by land, sea, and air. They had deployed within it nearly one million soldiers; more than half of them American. A number of Arab and Islamic governments such as Saudi Arabia, the Gulf countries, Pakistan, Turkey, Syria, Egypt, and Morocco were significant participants as well. There is no room for doubt that the Islamic *ummah*, its holy sites and resources and, in particular, its oil resources, were the desired goal of this Crusader-Jewish wave of direct military occupation. It is an occupation that has as its final goal to comprehensively eliminate the civilizational existence of Muslims.

A few months following this earthquake, at the beginning of 1991, another earthquake came with the disclosure of a possible peace settlement with the Jews. This settlement entailed the sale of what remained of Palestine and the sacred sanctuary under phony designations such as reconciliation, normalization, and peace between the Arabs and the Jews. This tidal wave that was inaugurated with the Madrid conference in 1991, in which Israel and the countries of the Arab land (Egypt, Syria, Jordan, Lebanon) participated, in addition to the Palestine Liberation Organization. At this conference, the majority of Arab and Islamic states ostensibly lent their support to this perfidious course of surrender. One of the most important long-term effects of this political earthquake was that the people of the Arab and Islamic *ummah* went along with it, even as the dangerous facts were exposed, such as:

- The Islamic *ummah* faced direct military occupation for the purpose of taking control of the holy sites (Mecca, Medina, and Jerusalem) for the sake of the Jewish occupation of Palestine.
- Oil—the Muslim treasury—was pillaged for the sake of the Western social and cultural needs.
- Political occupation became firmly established through the Arab and Islamic governments and organizations, which was crowned by the

launching of Desert Storm or "the liberation of Kuwait." This assault was aimed at the *ummah* for the purpose of subjugating it under the broad banner dubbed "the new world order," which meant, in short, the subjugation of the *ummah* to the American-led Crusader-Jewish will.

All Arab and Islamic countries, without exception, participated in supporting this campaign. The apostate governments that had entrenched the infidel systems in their countries gave all possible aid, support, and logistical services to the occupation forces. They also supported them through their media apparatus; indeed, many of them participated militarily, whether actually or symbolically, to secure their presence and inclusion in this campaign against Islam and Muslims. They did this to prove that they were a crucial element in this new world order, through warring against their people and their correct faith, betraying their core concerns, selling off their resources, and surrendering their holy sites. It is clear that the prevailing religious structure in Muslim lands is essentially bankrupt and collapsed and is unfit for confronting this attack.

The worst thing is that the majority of those who are called Sunni *ulama*, the luminaries among them and their most distinguished jurists, all joined in the media aspect of these Crusader campaigns. They endowed this campaign with sharia legitimacy and approved it. Indeed, the biggest hypocrites among them considered that the American entry into the Arabian Peninsula was the greatest blessing God could give to his *ummah* and that it deserved prostrations of gratitude! Sheikh Abu Bakr al-Jaza'ri expressed this, and he is a member of the Council of Senior Ulama in Saudi Arabia!

They distorted the true picture so as to transform it from a Jewish-Crusader occupation of Muslims to a picture of legitimate support from loyal Islamic and non-Islamic nations for the land of *tawhid* [Saudi Arabia] and the "legitimate" government of Kuwait, which had been swept away by a tyrannical, infidel enemy who coveted blood, wealth, and dignity [Iraq]. The final insult came at the Mecca conference of 1991. The Saudi government invited approximately four hundred scholars to this conference, including the most prominent *ulama* in the Islamic world, and official and unofficial religious organizations in every Arab Muslim country. In addition, the majority of the leaders of Islamic movements, including the Muslim Brotherhood, Sufi, Salafi, Tablighi, and reformist organizations, were in attendance. A statement from these scholars, leaders, and symbolic figures said these invading forces were legally protected guests, and a fatwa was issued making it illegal to attack them.

Anyone who fought against them were considered transgressors against the Muslim's protected people, and their punishment was to be either killed, crucified, or their hands and feet were to be cut off on opposite sides. Indeed, they claimed that the aggressors against these legally inviolable ones (the Crusader-American forces) would not inhale the fragrance of paradise!

Unfortunately, because of organizational weakness, the armed jihadist organizations that rejected this situation and called for jihad against the Americans and their allies were unable to offer a solution to this catastrophe that had befallen Muslim lands. Our confrontation with the Americans was confined to poorly distributed statements in countries, far removed from the *ummah*.

In the midst of these earthquakes, while following the news and analyses concerning what had occurred and what was taking place, the beginnings of these ideas started to take shape for me. These circumstances motivated me to think about the multiple dimensions of what was taking place, and the means of confronting it. It was clear from the performance of the awakening faction and the Islamic jihadist movements that these groups had adopted programs, methods, and goals that had little to do with confronting the coming crisis.

The program of the Muslim Brotherhood and its likes centered around the idea of parliaments, winning elected office, finding a common denominator with governments, and seeking out platforms that didn't conflict with the new invaders of the region. Or else there were plans for partial, gradual reform, all of which revolved in the regional orbit of different groups. Personal and party interests became mixed up with the interests of Islam. The interests of Salafist movements became concentrated on debates over creed and Islamic jurisprudence, giving the appearance that these problems were closer to their concerns than studying the issues of the coming invasion and the infidel nature of Muslim rulers. As for those affiliated with the apolitical groups such as the Sufi and the reformist schools, their intellectual structure and the nature of their concerns are far removed from these battles, and they found ways to appease the governments and those behind them.

During those days, I had the first inklings of the ideas I would organize in this study. All of the basic principles that constituted the basis of my thinking then became clear to me. They are:

1. The Desert Storm war is the beginning of the transformations brought on with the emergence of the new world order. These invasions brought to light the true enemy who had been hiding behind our governments— Crusader America and its vanguard of NATO nations with Israel behind them. It also made clear that persisting with limited battles with Arab governments would not bring success

2. The coming global war between Muslims and their enemies requires a system for global confrontation, a system that is global in its thinking and methods of confrontation, not the system that exists today.

3. The system for combating terrorism that America and Europe proposed over a series of security conferences in recent years makes it clear that their confrontations with the jihadist and fundamentalist Islamic movements have shifted to the international level. It is also clear that this transition will lead to the termination of all prior jihadist work methods, from association, to financing, to communications, to organizational activities.

4. The official religious establishment and a large portion of the *ulama* and their religious institutions are unflinchingly poised to become a part of the new world order. More clearly, they are poised to join the enemy, having officially chosen to go along with their infidel governments that function within the new Crusader-Jewish campaign. These religious organizations will undertake the intellectual and religiously justified termination of any jihadist resistance project.

5. The other schools of the Islamic political awakening, particularly the political parties, will explain away the situation, because they are also a part of the world system. They are also a part of the enemy, whether they intend it or not, and exist under the guise of gradualism and slogans that would not even convince animals of their benefit and justifications.

6. I believe that the remaining jihadist organizations and their remnants, such as those emerging in Egypt, the Levant, and elsewhere, and those already in existence or beginning to build themselves up like most of the emerging jihadist organizations and rotations from North Africa, established themselves on foundations remote from battlefield developments. They will be consumed by the flames of the new security measures for combating terrorism.

The Islamic awakening has been bankrupted, and the majority of its parties and leaders will soon be in the trenches of the enemy, whether out of conviction after having deviated, or pragmatically, so as to secure themselves a place in the new world order. The other choice is jihad and confrontation, but they shirk this option. As for us, the mujahideen, we have perhaps two or three years until the stoppage of our movement and the dissolution of our activities by the security forces. As I see things, there is no way to avoid this future except by focusing on a radical and comprehensive transformation of our military methods, propaganda methods, and our organizational structure.

Even in Afghanistan a small group of us outside the organized framework of the leadership could see the catastrophe approaching. However, our ideas were insufficiently clear to convince the others to undertake an internal revolution in the our methods and organization. In time, it was proven that the armed endeavors of the jihadist movements that were carried out on the basis of sectionalized-secret-pyramidal frameworks can only lead to failure and annihilation. This is because they were unable to prevent the global transformation that took place with the launching of the new world order, and because they did not understand its political and security dimensions and their impact on the jihadist movement.

The leadership and its supporters—the cream of the *ummah* at that time—did not possess the requisite strength of motivation, loyalty, and dedication to avoid their fate, whose signs were apparent to those who could observe them. At that time, I was unable to present very many of my thoughts, save a few lectures at the Al-Nour Media Center. Among the most important lectures delivered in the summer of 1991 is one titled, "The Balance of Power in the New World Order." In essence, I said the balance of power in the next conflict will take the following form:

The New World Order vs. The Armed Jihadist Movement

Crusaders commanded by America + Zionist Jewry + the apostate governments in Muslim lands + the deviant and rebellious Sunni sects + the official religious structure of the Sunnis + the Islamic democracy movements in the awakening

vs.

The armed jihadist organizations, the vanguard of the *ummah* in the confrontation

I followed this up with a series of studies and dialogues focused on the necessity of revolution against the hypocritical Sunni *ulama* structure. Unfortunately, this structure has acquired sanctification, even from a large segment of the armed members of the jihadist movement! This persisted even when these *ulama* announced themselves at the side of [Norman] Schwarzkopf, the commander of Desert Storm, and expressed the view that the mujahideen are sowing dissent and corruption for his soldiers and Marines.

It was clear that the distance to the desired transformation was vast and that a new aggression against the *ummah* was required to aid the majority in understanding and comprehending what was occurring. Then, the destruction I warned about came to early fruition when the winds of Desert Storm landed in the form of a security sweep against the Afghan Arabs in Pakistan, most of whom were deported to their home countries. Those who were unable to return to their countries scattered to other corners of the world, and the great mujahideen congregation in Pakistan decreased from tens of thousands to several hundred who went into hiding. The volleys of the Crusaders continued until they reached their peak in reaction to the shock waves of September 11.

The Second Stage: Madrid (1991)

The storm descended, and thousands of those who stepped forward for jihad in Afghanistan were scattered to every corner of the earth. Most returned to their home countries to face security sweeps, interrogations, and imprisonment. Fugitive mujahideen who had been accused in their home countries of belonging to armed jihadist organizations were distributed among various temporary sanctuaries. The fugitives then took on a new identity, under a new term created by the West, "Afghan Arabs."

A short time before this I had made a gradual return to Madrid, Spain, where I had resided two years earlier. There I composed a study considered the basis for a large portion of the ideas in this book. It was called "A Call for the Sake of Establishing the Global Islamic Resistance." It was a concise study of around forty pages. My objective was to transmit the ideas in this book to as many Arab mujahideen as possible. Because of their experience as armed jihadists, I considered them more worthy and capable of acting on the ideas in the book. I later discovered their incapacity to follow through. Though they had undergone advanced military training, they had not been given the necessary religious, methodological, intellectual, and political guidance.

A summary of the ideas contained in that pamphlet are as follows:

- A demonstration of the Muslim condition and situation, particularly during the Gulf War (Desert Storm), a rebuttal of the claims concerning the legitimacy of the Crusader descent into the Muslim heartland, the Crusader campaign as a justification for the call to jihad, and a rebuttal of those who claimed that Saddam Hussein is a kind of champion in their confrontation with the Crusaders.

- Establishing that the strength of the jihadist movements and organizations is not sufficient for confronting the global Jewish-Crusader campaign. What is needed is to convince the whole *ummah* to support the jihadist mission and to make it into a global Islamic resistance, facing down the global Crusader-Jewish attack.

- Establishing that the call to the *ummah* must rely on general Islamic ideas and the sort of message that is sympathetic to jihad—not on details of creed, intellectual niceties, and complicated jihadist legal theories—even though these are without a doubt all correct. For this purpose, the call to liberate the holy places was chosen as a slogan for the call to resistance. I also called for fighting the external enemy [America] as opposed to jihad against the local Arab rulers, because the people would not understand why they were also the enemy because of the services rendered by the audacious Sunni *ulama*.

- Awarding economic jihad its legal legitimacy, which was absent from the Jihadists' platform and remains absent.

- Calling the youths and the Muslim masses to practice individual resistance, so that the resistance does not depend on a pyramidal, cell-based organization and structure where the arrest of some of its members leads to the annihilation and arrest of all its members. This is a system that is not an organization in the traditional sense of the word. Every Muslim will fall under one designation, the global Islamic resistance. The actions of this collective maximize the benefit, so that the arrest of one does not lead to the arrest of all, because there is no connection between any of them. This was the essence of my strategic military thinking.

- Identifying the objectives of the enemy that are sensitive to attack. These are their physical presence in our countries, in other countries outside their homeland, and in their homeland (in that order). In particular, this means the political, military, missionary, economic, cultural, and tourist presence in our country, especially of the Jews, America, Great Britain, Russia, all of the NATO countries, and any country standing with them in the attack against Islam and Muslims.

- A summary of the sharia evidence proving that shedding the blood and destroying the possessions of all citizens and interests of these countries is approved by God.
- Commissioning the jihadist organizations, groups, and individual Muslims who had previously undertaken military training and combat practice to begin turning the wheel of the resistance. Also, calling all people to the methods of civil resistance, from paramilitary to religious and political propaganda works to preparing books and slogans, so that all segments of the *ummah* would participate in the jihad.
- Calling the mujahideen to form small, self-financed brigades, funded by the plundered loot of the enemy. Also, calling on wealthy Muslims to finance and support those who desire jihad.
- Calling all mujahideen to seek out and destroy the external enemy in our lands, in addition to seeking out the prominent apostate Muslim rulers and the top tier of their helpers. Also, urging that the confrontation with governments not be transformed into an open war, as happened in previous experiences. One should only confront the army and local security forces when defending one's self from death or capture.
- Criticizing the hypocritical *ulama* and the symbols of the Islamic movements who have gotten on board with the new world order. Also, calling on Muslims to renounce them and congregate instead around the *ulama* of the mujahideen, and calling on this rare breed of *ulama* to lead the popular resistance in every Muslim country.

I returned to Peshawar at the beginning of 1991 to distribute this book in secret among the mujahideen there. Because of the dangerous ideas in the book, no one would oversee its distribution in the Arab homes, guest houses, and institutions in Peshawar apart from four brothers. We distributed around one thousand copies that had been printed in secret.

It wasn't long before the portents of the security storm increased, and the congregation began its departure from Peshawar. I then left to take up residence in Granada, the last Muslim refuge in al-Andalus [Spain].

The Third Stage: London (1996)

It was the end of 1996, and I had already plunged headlong into supporting the jihad that had broken out in Algeria in 1994. I had settled in London and established a media cell for the Armed Islamic Group in Algeria (GIA). Jihad in Algeria took many turns, which, after the martyrdom of its leadership, led in the end to the GIA being led by a few deviant igno-ramuses who embraced no clear doctrine of jihad. This was exactly what the intelligence services hoped would happen and led to the group's failure and dissolution in 1996.

The issue that connects my experience with the Algerian jihad and the ideas in this book is the shock we felt in London over the success of authorities in aborting the Algerian jihad. This was accomplished by controlling its leadership and penetrating its security. It was also because of Algerian jihad's isolation caused by its participation in the massacres of Muslim civilians. This defeat happened despite the jihadists' dazzling military and popular successes and despite the greatest possibilities of success ever offered to a jihadist movement in the modern era.

This experience was a cruel lesson and convinced me that there is no benefit in localized jihadist attempts that cannot withstand global cam-paigns against so-called terrorism. Through 1997 I spent long hours con-versing with the cream of the jihadist elite from the Afghan Arab cadres and jihadist organizations resident in London. We evaluated the reasons for the repeated armed jihadist failures in the modern era.[4] We organized an informal club and held several meetings to compare the failures of these campaigns with the military successes of the vanguard jihadist campaigns in Bosnia, Chechnya, and Afghanistan.

Our meditations are the basis of this book. They are ideas I carried with me when I departed for Afghanistan after it appeared clear to me that the early signs of a severe security storm against jihadists in Europe was nearing. I determined that the West's demons would not grab hold of me in London.

The Fourth Stage: Afghanistan (1997–2001)

I began my migration to Afghanistan in August 1997 and remained there until we were expelled by force in December 2001. I migrated to Afghanistan for a number of reasons, the most important of which were:

- Sheikh Osama bin Laden and the cream of his personnel's relocation to Afghanistan and their embrace of the idea of confrontation with America.
- His call to the Islamic *ummah* to fight the Americans under the banner of "expelling the polytheists from the Arabian Peninsula."
- His embrace of ideas very close to those that had matured for me.

In bin Laden's embrace of jihadist principles I saw a real opportunity to move the confrontation in the right direction. God had granted him to us as a symbol for enabling this confrontation, and I wanted to participate in this confrontation that would be launched from Afghanistan. It became clear to me that Afghanistan would become for the second time the destination for jihadists along the path of God. Because the Taliban established a state offering us refuge and security, I imagined that a proper jihadist society would soon be constituted in Afghanistan, which compelled me to be present.

As I had expected, the jihadist groups, the leaders of the Afghan Arabs, the jihadist organizations, and a number of individuals flocked to Afghanistan. This phenomenon flourished during the years 1998–2001, and it was apparent that what I labeled "the second phase of the Afghan Arabs" had begun. This bunch embraced their work and gave new hope to the jihadist circles and their supporters in the Arab and Islamic world. This congregation became the hope of the *ummah*, indeed, its greatest hope.

Through various meetings and discussions in which I explained most of the ideas in my book to numerous leaders of the jihadist movement, it became clear that the majority of them were focused on their own goals and not on the wider jihad. It also became clear that they were not ready for any radical transition of their thinking. The way of thinking they left Afghanistan with in 1990 was still dominant among them!

This old way of thought involves "establishing secret sectionalized organizations whose aim is to spark popular revolutions, or fomenting actions so as to sweep away governments in their countries and establishing Islamic governments on their ruins." These organizations aspired only to establish operations for training in secure sanctuaries for their cadres escaping from the global assault against terrorism. The larger battle against the Crusader-Jewish assault did not seem to have major practical import for these organizations, except as concerned wider sympathies with Muslim issues.

Osama bin Laden and al Qaida were unable to budge these organizations, nor could bin Laden convince the majority of the youths who arrived in his camps that the battle against America had begun. This remained true up until the September crashes. America's reaction convinced everyone to abandon their own goals and devote themselves to warring against the United States. I saw many of the older brothers begin to demonstrate comprehension and conviction in the ideas outlined in this book. It appeared to me that the one group that was undertaking strategic actions similar to my own convictions was Sheikh Osama bin Laden's al Qaida organization and his deputy, Abu Hafs. These two believed that the time of local and regional organizations had passed and would be inappropriate for the coming stage. They believed that the duty was to mobilize the *ummah* toward confrontation with the external enemy [America], with a focus on expelling them from the Arabian Peninsula, incorporating this into the struggle against the Jews concerning Palestine and al-Aqsa, and repelling the American assault against all Muslims.

Then, after studying all of the available courses for action, I founded a camp and a group, working independently like all of the other fourteen Arab organizations recognized by the Taliban. I worked directly with the commander of the faithful [Mullah Muhammad Omar], and began broadcasting my ideas. Among the most important items were recordings that dealt with the ideological and strategic perspective jihad, which were recorded and distributed in mujahideen centers These were, in chronological order:

- "The Muslim Condition: Crisis and Exit," in seven cassettes (ninety minutes)
- "Jihad Is the Solution, but Why? How?" in twenty-one cassettes (ninety minutes)
- "The Global Islamic Resistance," in ten cassettes (ninety minutes)
- "The Brigades of the Global Islamic Resistance: The Call—the Way—the Method," recorded on six video cassettes (three hours), or approximately sixteen hours.

The most important of these lectures in terms of explaining the call and the path are the video cassettes, recorded on August 20, 2000. The most wide ranging as regards intellectual propositions and sharia political considerations are the lectures "Jihad Is the Solution," recorded in September 1999.

Despite my efforts, the crashes of September and the toppling of the
Taliban changed the condition of the Arab mujahideen. This happened
before my ideas could be implemented. But I believe that this outcome was
a faithful demonstration that my ideas are a necessity. I am certain that
establishing a new methodology and approach to this global confrontation
will, if God permits, give us victory.

We now enter the present, where the final touches of this book were
applied in our lovely mountain hiding place.

The Fifth Stage: Pakistan (2002–2003)

The crashes of September 11, 2001, and the stinking American response
and Crusader-Western attack coordinated with world Jewry along with
the powers of apostasy and the hypocritical governments in our Arab and
Islamic world filled me with conviction concerning the necessary method
of confronting this global war. This war began with America's steerage
of the new world order and progressed until it exploded in the events of
September 11; which showed that every populated place on earth is an
arena for war against Islam. This attack is founded on the Crusader-Jewish
concept of the clash of the civilizations that America had embraced, with
the West stumbling behind it.

I was struck by the frankness of Jeffrey Steinberg, [a columnist who
writes about Middle East issues for Lyndon Larouche's publications], a
journalist and political analyst from the American Democratic Party, in
an interview with Syrian satellite television in July 2002. His comments
can be summed up as follows:

- There is a catastrophe coming to America and mankind because of the
  policies adopted by the Republican Party under [George] Bush's leadership, which include launching the clash of civilizations on the basis of
  the philosophies of [Henry] Kissinger, [Samuel] Huntington, [Richard]
  Nixon, and others.
- They build their ideas on the principle of white Christian racial hegemony over the colored peoples of the earth, and they consider that
  the time has come to erect a global empire under the leadership of
  America.
- They have planned this out so as to stop the industrial progress of
  developing countries, and to spread disease through ethnic cleansing
  so as to kill off more than 80 percent of nonwhite peoples on earth!

He cited the feelings of hysteria against America in other countries and concluded his comments by noting that there was a catastrophe coming as a result of Bush's policies, which will soon destroy America and the world, perhaps in a week or in a year. What is important is that it is coming soon.

The struggle shifted after the invasion of Afghanistan, and then Iraq, in 2003. This shift occurred as the enemy imposed itself on the battlefield, defending its interest and allies, while destroying and fragmenting most if not all of the jihadist organizations. Because of this tyrannical campaign and the proven jihadist incapacity to face down the attack, there is no need to convince remaining cadres and jihadist entities of the necessity for transforming our methods.

Here is the world filled with oppression and injustice under the guidance of America and its Jewish masters; and here are the alienated believers and mujahideen, fugitives in the land with no refuge, fleeing with their religion from one village to the next, exactly as Mohamed did. The earth is filled up with oppression and injustice, and events are tumbling toward the appearance of the Mahdi [Muslim messianic figure]. He will emerge to lead the confrontation and fill the earth with justice. At present, the choices before us are limited to patience, steadfastness, sacrifice, resoluteness, progress in belief, and advancing toward the trenches. But the obligation of jihad from the past to the present, and the continuation of the fight for this religion is always with us—this is a command fixed within our religion. We have no choice but to establish a comprehensive global Islamic resistance to this attack.

The successful attack of the nineteen martyrs against the heartland of the infidel and the tyrannical abode, America, which hit her in the heart of her economic and military structure, was by any measure an historic and monumental action. Ignoring the crashes themselves and the nature of the confrontation that ensued afterward, particularly in Afghanistan, I say that Sheikh Osama bin Laden's confrontation set the battle on its right course by forcing the confrontation between us and our true, eternal enemy—America.

What connects the September crashes with the ideas in this book is that there is a war established and imposed on us by our enemy that, in accordance with the requirements of our religion, we are obliged to fight. Defensive jihad has become a duty incumbent upon all Muslims. As God said, "Slay them wherever you catch them, and turn them out from where they have turned you out; for persecution is worse than slaughter."

If we are to confront them, we have two choices. We can enter the battle according to the expectations of the enemy, scattered and exhausted, and waste our energies in conflicts with the apostate rulers and the hypocritical, accursed, and ignorant ones, which is what we did for more than thirty years in failed and costly campaigns. Or else we can orient the battle toward the primary enemy and the prime mover of all our local enemies, and by this I mean the evil trinity, Israel-America-Europe.

There is no doubt now that confronting these enemies is the most appropriate thing to do. The battle against the Jews, America, and Europe is obligatory, and we must bear its consequences, as the poet remarked: "If there is no escape from death, then it is shameful to die a coward." [Line from tenth-century poet al-Mutannabi—which the author misquotes. The original said: "If there is no escape from death, then from incapacity you will die a coward."]

In short, the price of war against the Jews, America, and Europe will be great, because the *ummah* continues to sleep and shirk battle. This price will be great because of the growth of love for worldly things and the hatred for death has advanced within the *ummah* and because the reliance of the majority of *ulama* on the friendship of their rulers has expanded. But the price does not scare the *ummah*'s youths.

Sheikh Osama did well in choosing the nature of the battle and defining the enemy. As I see it, he was correct in his chosen method for opening the struggle, just as the executors of the September attacks did well in producing the lightning explosion that initiated the battle with an overwhelming attack that inflicted massive losses on the enemy. Still, I believe that the Islamic *ummah*, with all of its energies, is still absent from the battle, despite the fact that it is the one most affected by this jihad and its instruments. I also believe that an important field of confrontation remains out of play, because the true field is Muslim lands, where the Jews, Christians, and their apostate and hypocrite helpers have descended.

There remains before us much work to be done in proselytizing, sermonizing, and rousing the believers, so as to set the implementation of the battle in its correct place and retake the initiative that America claimed after the events of September and in whose hands it remains. Whatever the opinions and positions within the Islamic and jihadist ranks concerning the events of September, it is indisputable that they have created a new reality. We now face an American attack that we must confront. Turning attention away from this reality to waste time blaming each other, and arguing about events is dangerous. The battle has become a battle of destiny, whether we are engaged in it or not.

The Sixth Stage: (2003–2004): The American Occupation of Iraq and the Zionist-Crusader Campaign against the Middle East

Then the well-known advance by the Americans and their allies, the British, occurred, whereby they implemented a plan similar to what they did in Afghanistan. They were able within a short timetable to destroy the Iraqi army and dissolve that country's unity. They entered Baghdad, whose fate it was to fall for a second time under the toe of the new Mongols of the modern day Rum, who were no less barbarous than their predecessors who had advanced with Hulagu.[5]

The most important reasons for the American triumph in Afghanistan/Iraq:

- Reliance on support from local collaborating powers.
- Isolating the target country from its neighbors and neutralizing these neighbors or else relying on them as a launching point for logistical services.
- Reliance on overwhelming air and missile superiority to destroy targets.
- Preparedness to commit massacres of civilians so as to realize their military goals.
- Bypassing the international community and every dissenting voice and subjugating the latter to American programs by enticement, coercion, or inattention designed to make America the sole power on earth.
- Transforming the Muslim people into mere impotent witnesses to the events, after their rulers and *ulama* had prohibited Muslims from the arena of conflict.

America's victory in Afghanistan and its annihilation of the Taliban's and jihadist military forces, and likewise its victory in Iraq, was followed by a military advance on all anticipated centers of resistance to America's imminent or eventual presence. Among the most important of these was the destruction of the Kurdish Ansar al-Islam organization's bases near the Iranian border. The Americans employed there the same method used to destroy the al Qaida and Arab mujahideen bases in Tora Bora in Afghanistan, aerial bombardment and precision-guided missiles, with local collaborating Kurdish militias to annihilate those mujahideen who remained on the ground. Likewise, there was the destruction and razing of the jihadist organization bases in Jabal Hatat in Yemen, relying on the Yemeni army and security forces for aerial bombardment before the Yemeni advanced on their bases.

America followed this method in every known center where mujahideen hostile to it congregated. Additionally, America relied on methods of pursuit that helped round up other secret jihadist organizations and cells in a number of places with the cooperation of local security apparatuses, as occurred in Saudi Arabia, Morocco, Indonesia, and several countries in East Asia.

The conclusions I reached from these events can be summed up as follows:

- Open confrontation with America or any of its military allies is impossible as long as America can maintain complete dominance by using its overwhelming technological capabilities and gain the help of the collaborating powers who conduct its administration on the ground.
- After the Americans established regionwide security coordination, it became impossible for secret organizations to confront the domestic security apparatuses of collaborator governments. This is particularly true of groups following the traditional methods of localized units with a cellular and pyramidal structure.
- Since there is no escape or alternative to resistance, the sole method for confrontation that presents itself in light of this situation is war by secret bands of disconnected cells that are both varied and abundant.

At the conclusion of this introduction, I will say that many of the jihad paid an exorbitant price. The commander of the faithful in Afghanistan, Mullah Muhammad Omar, and the faithful Taliban jihadists paid the great price so as to safeguard their integrity and carry out their duty to preserve Islam and Muslims and not surrender to the enemy's threats. Al Qaida gave a number of its men as a price for initiating the conclusive round, and Sheikh Osama and his aides paid the enormous price, taking their share of death, imprisonment, and expulsion. Many of the cadres of the jihadist organizations in Afghanistan were killed defending the Islamic emirate and in the resistance to the indiscriminate American assault on Afghanistan. Toward what end? And for what return? And why all of this suffering?

The goal was to awaken the drugged and sleeping *ummah* that is absent from the field of jihad and to set it face to face with this obligation. I am convinced that victory is in the hands of God, and the primary prerequisites for this are working to transform this confrontation into an *ummah*-wide battle after the *ummah* has been ignited by the jihadist elite. Yes. We are passing through the most difficult of circumstances and are living the climax of affliction. The best of our brothers have been killed and the rest of us have been banished or seized by the treacherous foxes of apostate governments in the service of America.

I say to all who inform about us to America and her allies: "Go back to them, and tell them we shall come to them with such hosts as they will never be able to meet: we shall expel them from our lands in disgrace, and they will feel humbled." Fate has previously ordained: "God has decreed: 'It is I and my messengers who must prevail,' for God is strong and mighty."

Chapter 1. The West's Great Assault
1. The *Rum* was how the Arabs referred to the Byzantine Empire, and it now is used to generically describe an "enemy of the Arabs."
2. The term "Sultan" is must often used to refer to Arab rulers who supposedly support American policies.
3. Hamma, a city of ten thousand, was obliterated by the Syrian military when it became a hotbed of Islamic jihadi sentiment.
4. Morocco 1963, Syria 1965, Egypt 1965, Turkey 1970, Algeria 1976, Syria II the long experience of 1975–82, Egypt II 1981, Libya 1989, Algeria II 1990–96, Libya II 1994–96.
5. When the Mongol leader Halagu departed Baghdad, he left behind a pyramid of five hundred thousand skulls of those he had slaughtered.

CHAPTER 2
The Status of Muslims Today

I t is possible to summarize the status of Muslims today under three primary headings.
- Loss of religion from the majority of Muslims;
- Loss of worldly power for the great majority of Muslims;
- The enemies' control and tyranny over all aspects of Muslims' lives.

Departure of Religion

The *ummah* has nearly lost all of the elements of its religion, and that is evident in the breakdown of religious life and its corruption among most Muslims. It is also evident in the corruption of the *ummah*'s condition and the loss of sanctity, the most important of which is the absence of governance according to God's sharia. The rule of Islam has been gradually wiped away, beginning with the weakness of the Abbasid Caliphate at the end of the third Muslim century [approximately AD 913]. The kingship fell apart and was replaced by sultanates, kingdoms, and emirates, which depended on subjugation and dictatorship, and within which goodness and corruption were intermixed.

The caliphate changed gradually into a nominal symbol more than a system of law and governance. Government was pushed further away from God's perfect sharia because of the inclinations of kings and the deceit of the *ulama*, leading to corruption throughout all aspects of Muslims' lives. This continued until the Tartars' invasion of the eastern portion of Muslim territories, when they overthrew the caliphate in the center of its own home. This occurred after the Crusader attacks of the Romans and European Christian kings had been initiated and were able to establish Crusader colonies on the shores of al-Sham. This deterioration reached its climax when Baghdad fell into the hands of the Tatars in 1258.

Then an anomalous awakening took place, and for a limited time, with the establishment of the Ottoman government, the new caliphate was able to restore its prestige as a centralized government. Then the occupying European countries pounced on the caliphate, and the Jews conspired against it to reach Palestine, so that the combined enemy forces were able to overthrow the Ottoman Caliphate in 1924. This was followed by the fall of all the Muslim countries to occupation by the Crusader European countries led by England, France, Russia, and others.

During the time of occupation, secular schools were established in Islamic lands. These spread among the educated class of society under the care of the colonizer, who was happy to establish political parties, personalities, and a ruling family to which it arranged the handoff of authority at the end of the colonial stage, or what was called then "independence." This occurred so that the tyrants in all Muslim countries could rule with other than what God laid down.

Most Muslim governments proclaimed to rule by other than what God laid down, indeed, most of them declared the Islamic sharia unsuitable for rule in the modern age! They even blame the current backwardness of Muslims and their problems on the sharia itself! And that is how the constitutions were laid down and written and how laws were fashioned that conflict with God and His apostle.

In many Islamic nations, the rule of sharia has been removed from the constitutions' texts, and in some they retained the title and mixed it with obviously polytheist elements, according to the slogan, "the sharia is the primary source for legislation," thus making it a source in addition to other sources. At the same time, some countries claimed like Saudi Arabia that "the sharia is the only source for legislation," but this has influenced Saudi Arabia to set up civil or specialized or issue-oriented courts, or whatever they named them, alongside the sharia courts, all of which are ruled by laws and legislation, derived from Europe's legislation.

And there is no doubt that the situation we are in stems from this great disaster, which is: We live by rules other than what God laid down. His laws have been replaced by those of our own traitorous apostate rulers, and their clientage to the Jews and Christians' occupation of the three holy sites in the Muslim faith is a continuing insult to the *ummah*.

- Mecca the revered, within which is the Ka'aba and the al-Haram mosque;
- Medina the illuminated, within which is the Mosque of the Apostle of God;
- Jerusalem the noble, within which is the al-Aqsa mosque, which is the original direction marker for Muslim prayer.

Contrary to popular belief that Jerusalem was the first of the holy sites to be lost—in the year 1967—and Mecca and Medina and put under the authority of the Americans and their Crusader coalition in the 1991 Gulf War, in reality Mecca and Medina were lost and were put under Christian authority long before then. That is, the British Empire had occupied much of the Islamic world since the beginning of the sixteenth century and had spread its direct control to the Arabian Peninsula.

Britain became aware of Arabia's desire for self-rule and to escape the centralization of the Ottoman Caliphate. So Britain carried out a malicious deception to control these territories. It did so with the cooperation of their greatest agent, Abd al-Aziz Al-Saud, the founder of the current Saudi government. In 1898 the British colonial ministries seized control under the oversight of their new envoy and agent, Abd al-Aziz Al-Saud, who had just turned twenty years of age. Britain provided him with military support and British gold, and his advisers urged him to take advantage of the Wahabi missionary call and the enthusiasm of its missionary mujahideen.

The British signed an agreement with Abd al-Aziz guaranteeing his dominion over that country under the new name instituted by Britain, "The Kingdom of Saudi Arabia." And with that, Britain guaranteed the throne for Abd al-Aziz Al-Saud and his children after him in return for its continued influence over the country. Since that time, Mecca and Medina have been under British control, until the Americans inherited the Saudi throne, the peninsula's oil, and the guardianship of Mecca and Medina after World War II. After that, the Saudis received support from their new masters, the Americans, and they gave them their allegiance with the same ease they gave it to their predecessors—the British.

The Saudis' sins since then have been many:

- Agreement to the English plans for Zionist migration to Palestine;
- Absence of an objection to ceding Palestine to the Jews;

- Agreement to the Balfour Declaration, which promised the Jews a state in Palestine;
- Helping stop the revolution against the Jews in 1936, which was the first step toward losing Jerusalem;
- Through a conspiracy in 1967, helping Israel occupy East Jerusalem— within which are the Dome of the Rock and the al-Aqsa mosque;
- Participation in the Madrid Peace Accords in 1991 for normalization with the Jews.

All this came after they had decreed it permissible for the Crusader, European, and American armies to enter the Arabian Peninsula under the pretext of having to confront the danger of Saddam Hussein!

Anyone looking into the condition of the 1.25 billion Muslims today will find that the majority of them possess only a superficial form of the religion. He will find that those who practice religion among the people of Islam today are few, and that these few devote themselves to distorted creeds that contain nothing of what the ancestors of this *ummah* and its earliest flock practiced beyond the superficial pledge of faith. The breakdown of the Muslim creed has proceeded gradually since the second Muslim century. The ordeals and deviations continue to gradually overtake it through the corruption of the kings and the debased interpreters of this religion.

But the masses have forgotten God and thus forgot who they really are. Most of them began to worship the governments, or money, or their own desires, or the satellite channels, and television screens, which they watch at night, and believe every poison shoved in their heads. America and the West, their culture and ideas, have become the god of the times, worshipped, sanctified, and believed in by the people more than they worship God. The role of fashion, symbols of art, magazines, and the stars of the big and small screen have become the model for imitation and following. And there is no longer among them any association to the people of Islam except by name and by adhering to a few traditions with religious roots.

So, if you were to review the world of money and business and people's livelihood, you would find most of them unconcerned whether they received their livelihood through legitimate or illegitimate means. You would also find dealings in usury permissible and people taking each other's money through invalid means, cheating, trickery, selling donations, and the banking system. These market dealings are based on religiously impermissible principles, let alone how they spread bribery, corruption, stealing, deception, and looting.

If you were to examine the media, from satellite dishes and television screens to radio stations, Internet networks, international information, newspapers, and magazines to forums and educational centers, and so forth, you will see that most of it is the source of demons' gateway to humanity. Its very foundations are based on impermissible actions and abominations, from music, singing, entertainment, nudity, commingling of the opposite sexes, fornication, and prostitution programs to the spread of filth and corruptive thoughts and scandalous Western-style clothes.

The social and moral life of most Muslims is no longer founded on the basis of Islam: modesty, shame, truthfulness, loyalty, compassion, and cooperation in devotion. So, the life of most Muslims is based on hypocrisy and lies, gossip and defamation, enmity among relatives, disagreement and disregard, jealousy and lying, as well as cheating and illegitimate gain. All of this, let alone the spread of female uncovering, to the point where the veil has become a rarity, just as the life of commingling with women who work among men in every field has led to the spread of corruption and filthy perversity, and marital infidelities and the spread of fornication and of divorce. This is besides the problems of tourism and nude beaches, filthy clubs and immoral coffee houses, shameless nightclubs, crazed centers of entertainment, and the spread of alcohol and drugs and casinos and all kinds of *haram*.

As far as the cultural and intellectual life, it is imported from East and West, along with philosophies built on atheism and secularism and denial of this *ummah*'s religion and its identity and origin in all fields of thought, culture, literature, and art. And then there is America today, pursuing us with plans to change our systems of education, media, and religious study in every aspect. It also fabricates for us programs for cultural transformation that extend to every field, such as language, history, religion, culture, and all of our religious components.

As for the political life, it is the most fertile field for corruption and remoteness from religion. Political parties, movements, and groups based on beliefs and thoughts opposed to Islam have spread. Democracy and its Western model have become a religion that is believed in, and for its sake blood flows in riots and at the voting booths. As for the political parties that are called "Islamic," their political programs are built on a mixture of

Islamic and Western democratic foundations mixed with some religious foundations to call them "Islamic programs" and "Islamic parties."

The minority striving in God's path, confronting God's enemies so as to correct these conditions and to push away this ordeal, have become alien within that faithful band. Its condition has become one of alienation. The twentieth century has passed, and we have entered the twenty-first century to find that most people act as if they are preparing to follow the Antichrist.

Loss of Worldly Blessings

The overwhelming majority of the 1.25 billion Muslims live a life of poverty. This is because of their poor material condition in addition to religious corruption and remoteness from their God.

The Arabian Gulf region contains the largest oil reserve known on earth, and the second most important reservoir is in the Islamic republics of Central Asia. There is another petroleum lake in southern Sudan and the Horn of Africa and a third one extending from Egypt to Algeria. In fact, the Islamic world owns a tremendous strategic reserve of mineral resources; and if we add to that the agricultural and zoological fortunes abundant to these regions, in addition to transit rights for an area, which contains three of the five most important international naval straits and passageways (the Strait of Hormuz, Suez Canal, and Gibraltar), we see that the Islamic world is spectacularly rich.

As we considered all of this, we should be amazed at how Islamic countries often top the lists of poverty, ignorance, and illiteracy in the world! And the overwhelming majority of people in this region, including the people of the OPEC-member oil states, live below the poverty line. This, despite the fact that economic statistics published by the centers for international studies point toward unimaginable fortunes that exceed limitations and astonish the observer.

How was that agreed upon?! That the people of the richest spot on Earth are the world's poorest people! The astonishment will fade away if we look at the mythic historic plundering machine operated by the West and its various governments, led by America, the European NATO countries, and Russia. They are the Christian enemy marching on us today, since oil finances their wars that kill our children's spirits with our own money and the fortunes of our treasury. Put simply, they take it and they massacre us with it! They take our oil to run their planes, their fleets, and their tanks that come to kill our women and children and so that the profits can return to their people so they can live a life of luxury.

The fortunes are being stolen from their very source because they are extracted by foreign companies that supervise extraction, marketing, and trade and that manage the international banks where the returns come to rest. This completes the cycle of robbery from beginning to end!!

The robbery begins with contracts made with the treacherous government and extends to falsifying the amount of oil extracted. Finally, our resources are stolen by limiting the price of oil and marketing it worldwide at the cheapest of prices. We know that the true price of one barrel of crude oil is $260 per barrel. This at a time when the price of one barrel of crude oil throughout its history has never exceeded $45 and has fluctuated most of the time in the $20 range, sometimes going below $10! All of this because the masters of the international exchanges that deal with commodity prices are Jews and leading Crusader capitalists!

Then comes the last stage of stealing, when our country's share of the profits is transferred to Western banks to turn into electronic numbers and zeros in the accounts they run their economy with and do not permit our governments to withdraw from it except in limited and calculated amounts. Most of what they let us withdraw goes toward buying industrial materials, weapons, and our necessities from their industrialized world, and they impose any price they desire for that material!

As for the majority of the mineral fortunes, it is stolen in the same way. It is not manufactured or used locally, which wipes out our chance to build an industrial infrastructure. So, the local work force is only good to be lifters from the mines to the ports of exportation!

The sorrows of robbing the Muslim treasury and their fortunes does not end at its theft, for the greater problem is that most of our riches are stolen by a handful of pharaoh rulers! We know that the oil and gas fortunes of the Gulf states—whose revenues exceed $1 billion daily—are divided by the ruling and sovereign families whose numbers do not exceed tens of princes. In the Gulf states, their numbers do not exceed a few hundred princes, kings, and their elder children. They are dividing the Islamic *ummah*'s fortune among themselves. For example, the daily expenditures for Prince Sultan ibn Abd al-Aziz, the second deputy to the king of Saudi Arabia, reach three million dollars daily. These sums of money cover services in their castles extending from the coasts of America to

Europe and East Asia, providing entertainment, prostitution, gambling, and corruption.

Rulers of the remaining countries in the devastated Islamic world aspired to this as well. Thus, the sons of kings and presidents, their ranking officials, their army commanders, and their intelligence institutions took charge in dividing the countries' fortunes, countries in which most individuals from Islamic nations practically live below the poverty line. The heart breaks for this and the forehead sweats for it.

This is how people have donned the clothes of humiliation and defeat. So that now, bitterness and feelings of helplessness control most of the people, particularly toward their rulers and generally between each other. Fear is now the clothing worn by most Muslims since the softening of their fighting spirit. People fear their rulers, and every weak person fears those who are stronger than him. They live in police states where the executioners are artistic in the ways of torture and governments spend a large part of their budgets to build prisons. Terror controls all classes of society; the employee fears the manager, the teacher fears the tattling student, the driver fears the traffic police, the citizen fears the intelligence agents, the protester fears the crackdown, the Friday preacher fears spies among those praying, and the traitor ruler fears America.

They fear because many Muslim countries are exposed to genocide from the Western occupier. Daily reports tell stories of massacres, which during the last two decades alone reaped hundreds of thousands of Muslims in Bosnia, Chechnya, Kosovo, Kashmir, India, the Philippines, Afghanistan, Iraq, Palestine, Lebanon, Somalia, Indonesia, Nigeria, Burma, Eritrea, Iraqi Kurdistan, and others.

Indeed, organized killing campaigns and starvation struck millions of children, as occurred in Iraq. America was not content with the killing of over three hundred thousand persons during Desert Storm. They engaged in ten years of siege, which killed more than 1.5 million children by malnutrition and lack of medicine. The racial eradication and ethnic cleansing operations against Muslims would require volumes of books to detail.

In all those regions devastated with wars and aggression of Christian, Hindu, and atheist and other infidel gangs and governments, Muslim women were not safe from their ugliest violations and assaults. Indeed, it has reached a scary level in some afflicted regions such as Bosnia, where human rights organizations recorded more than fifty thousand rape cases against Muslim women. These violations also take place at the hands of

governmental police systems and the men of the intelligence organizations who carry out aggression against women in their prisons, which no
one sees or punishes.

They also impose on us their economic strategy programs, which are
controlled in detail by the International Monetary Fund [IMF], so that
our lands do not reach self-sufficiency for primary food products such
as wheat, sugar, rice, and others. For example, the IMF forbade Sudan
from reaching self-sufficiency with wheat after al-Basheer took over rule.
When the government insisted, the IMF threatened to cut off assistance.
America then enticed Sudan by supplying them with ten years' worth of
wheat through interest-free loans and with quantities of food grants in the
form of gifts with nothing in return! The purpose was clear: to turn the
fertile land into a wasteland not good for agriculture, as our fighters could
not compete with America's "free" gifts. It is enough for us to know that
Egypt, which used to supply the Roman Empire with wheat, lives today
on the American wheat reserves sufficient to supply Egypt with three
months' worth of bread.

Indeed, for the collaborators, subjugation to Western interests has
come to encompass the field of debauchery and entertainment, through
the importing of Muslim women for the entertainment of the colonizing
soldiers who invade our lands. This occurred and was mentioned by some
media, concerning the use by American and Western forces during Desert
Storm of hundreds of prostitutes from several Arab countries presented
with the agreement of these countries' governments, for entertaining the
American and Western forces during breaks from the battles . . . and while
they are liberating Kuwait! Indeed, this new system of subjugation is a
new invention to return the rule of slavery in a contemporary style fitting
to the genius mentality of the culture they call the American European
white race.

Our governments are stripped of their own will for the benefit of the
colonizing enemy's will, particularly Americans and Europeans. No trade
contracts, no armament regime, no system for transferring authority, and
no democratic elections or military coups can occur without the hidden
but apparent master's oversight (America and its allies). For example, Hafiz
al-Assad passed away in Syria in 2000, so U.S. secretary of state Madeline
Albright—the Jewess—attended and oversaw the transition of power. She
did not leave the region until she announced in a press conference, with

complete disrespect, that America was comfortable with the transfer of power in Syria!

Similarly, King Faisal was killed in Saudi Arabia when he did not follow through some of his positions concerning what his father had promised by way of allegiance to [Franklin D.] Roosevelt aboard an American battleship.

Similarly, there is the assassination of the Pakistani president Ziya al-Haq and American supervision of the coup that brought in Pervez Musharraf to oversee the toppling of the Taliban.

In sum, those who would stand against this—the jihadist core—were, over the decades, broken down and scattered. Those remaining pioneers are on the desolate roads of migration, scattered and alienated, living through the greatest manhunt known to the history of mankind.

The Status of Muslims Today in the World after September 11, 2001

If we wanted to generalize the statement on the status of Muslims today after September 11, 2001, we would say that their condition has worsened and persisted under all the things I have mentioned above—starting from losing their religion and their world and ending with the enemy's dominion over them. In the loss of their religion, the governments' insistence and their excuses for replacing the sharia as well as the fighting of Islam has increased, as did the occupation of holy sites. The wave of belief corruption and spread of dissent intensified the madness of debauchery and deviation, as a result of the ferocity of the media attack and the spread of satellite communications aiming at corrupting our politics. The estrangement of believers, jihadists, and the enjoiners of good and forbidders of evil has increased because of the fierceness of the security attack.

America's program calls for full occupation of the Arab world. However, it is worth shining the light on what happened to Muslims after September 11, 2001. The most important of which are:

* Destruction of the Islamic Emirate in Afghanistan—In the midst of international silence and open disloyalty by Arab and Islamic governments, the takedown of the Taliban government was completed in December 2001 via an American military attack. With that, the abortion of the only honorable attempt to establish the Islamic government since the fall of the Ottoman Caliphate was completed.

- Attempt to Eliminate the Core of the Jihadist Organization—The establishment of the Islamic emirate and the rule of the Taliban caused what remained of the core of the jihadist movement to return to Afghanistan for refuge. America took the events of September 11 as a pretext, and the destruction of the Islamic emirate as a means for realizing its goal to butcher what remained of the core of this jihadist movement.

- By way of savage aerial bombardment, and the damaging attacks of the Afghan apostates who toppled the Islamic government, America and her allies inflicted grave tolls of wounded and dead against the Arab mujahideen as well as those from Central Asia and Pakistan. The Pakistani government, under the leadership of Musharraf, contributed a frightening portion to the slaughter, because they killed many mujahideen in Pakistan and imprisoned hundreds and delivered them to the Americans, despite the help some of our righteous Pakistani brothers who rescued whoever they could from those who fled through Pakistan and Iran and who were able to help gather themselves after the crushing battles.

- This assault on Afghanistan was accompanied by a fierce assault and cooperation between America and Russia to eliminate the mujahideen in Chechnya, which succeeded to a great degree.

- America followed up this campaign with an attempt to wipe out the armed jihadist pockets in the Philippines, Yemen, and the Horn of Africa, and wherever else it could after having cut the primary thorn in Afghanistan.

The Americans have eliminated the majority of the armed jihadist movement's leadership, infrastructure, supporters, and friends, by means of both covert and overt assassinations, kidnappings and imprisonment, and transferring the detainees to the American Guantanamo prison in Cuba or its prisons scattered across the globe.

They are attempting to completely eliminate the Islamic political and social awakening under the pretext of combating terrorism and uprooting the fundamentalism that composes its incubator. Indeed, the campaign has encompassed all things Islamic and related to Islam: Muslim charitable and humanitarian organizations, social organizations, trading companies, Islamic banks, groups, parties, even nonusurious Islamic banks! Indeed, the affliction has even reached ordinary people, who have been reached by the American attack because they are wealthy Muslims who are prey for the young American bird.

All this occurs through exploitation of their campaign to combat terrorism. The beginnings of this campaign are in the gradual plan to eliminate the Islamic and Arab communities in the West. America and all European countries have enacted laws to combat immigration and political asylum, or rather, unofficial rulings permitting the seizure and detention of foreigners, stripping their citizenship if they were citizens, canceling their official residency if they were residents, and detaining them for indefinite periods without accusations. These unofficial laws are far worse than the unofficial rulings enacted by the revolutionary military governments of the third world. And even the most deeply rooted democracies such as Britain, the Scandinavian countries, and France are not innocent of this.

In light of this, there is the frenzied media wave directed from the Jewish- and Crusader-controlled media via television, newspapers, films, and all other media outlets. Similarly, the racist crimes increased to the point where one statistic in Europe mentioned that in 2002 racist attacks against Muslims grew after September 11 by 66 percent over the previous year. During the week I put the final corrections in this book, in November 2004, twenty mosques and Islamic centers were burned in Holland over the course of ten days!

America has compelled every nation in the world through enticement and threats, with all possible means, to join its campaign to combat terrorism. Their ambassadors, diplomats, and security officials have traveled the world securing security pacts and policing agreements here and there in every corner of the globe. America has compelled Arab and Muslim governments to cooperate fully with the campaign under threat of military assault.

Similarly, America has ignored all the opposition voices of the human rights organizations, international bodies, or prominent personalities, despite the large number of those who oppose its transgressing of international law and human rights, its mistreatment of prisoners and detainees, its heedlessness and killing of civilians during military operations, and the historic scandals of its prison in Guantanamo. It ignores all of this opposition, paying no heed to its sources, whether they come from Muslim lands, Europe, allied countries, or even from inside America.

America used the occupation of Iraq as the beginning for redrawing the map of the region. This squares with America's greater plan to control Central Asia by launching their forces from Afghanistan and Pakistan. America proffered feeble justifications for the sake of occupying Iraq as an entry point for marching on the Middle East, beginning with the necessity of toppling Saddam and ending with the elimination of Iraq's weapons of mass destruction.

The last conferences of the Arab and Islamic summit in the post–September 11 world clearly demonstrated our current situation. For instance, the famous Arab summit in 2002 advocated embracing Saudi crown prince Abd al-Aziz ibn Saud's initiative offering complete normalization of relations with Israel in exchange for Israel's withdrawal from the lands it occupied in 1967. Israel's response was to invade the West Bank and reoccupy it and to carry out extensive massacres of the administrative and security infrastructure of the Palestinian Authority as well as the infrastructure of the Palestinian organizations.

The Organization of the Islamic Conference Summit that followed even welcomed a new Afghani delegation of apostates and collaborators appointed by America and supported similar resolutions, including:

- Support for the Saudi initiative for normalization with the Jews and condemning the futility of fighting the Jews, without any quid pro quo;
- The abandonment of Palestine and Jerusalem, and the failure to present any serious project to retake them;
- Support for the American campaign to combat terrorism and emphasizing that the Islam represented by the apostate rulers of more than fifty-two Islamic states rejects "violence and terrorism," which is the new global term for jihad and the right of resistance!

Furthermore, Arab and Islamic countries, especially Turkey, Pakistan, the Gulf states, and Jordan, have put their lands, seas, skies, and armies at the service of the American-British campaign to occupy Iraq. Hundreds of thousands of troops, hundreds of airplanes, and their aircraft carriers pour into the region amidst American threats to attack Iran, Syria, and Lebanon; dividing Saudi Arabia; and preparing to seize Pakistan's nuclear weapons. Islamic governments have prostrated themselves at the threshold of the White House. Qatar has even welcomed the headquarters of the American military, which was transferred from Florida, and America managed the invasion of Iraq from her lands.

For the invasion of Iraq, American forces crossed into western Iraq from Jordan, while the Gulf states gave the war complete support. Kuwait went so far as to designate 60 percent of its northern region as an American military zone for training and logistical services for the American and British armies! Over one hundred and forty thousand American troops along with forty-five thousand British troops crossed into Iraq from there.

Frightened, Syrian president Bashar al-Asad flew to London and other European capitals to assure his throne against convulsions from the earthquake of the war in Iraq. Iran, like every other government in the Islamic world, acquiesced as well and began to hunt the Arab mujahideen and Taliban, whom they surrendered to the Americans.

America invaded Iraq and entered Baghdad, with the support of Europe and an international mandate from the [UN] Security Council! Then it appointed an Iraqi collaborator government and forcefully imposed recognition of it on the Arab states and the Arab League!

In this way the Arab system announced its bankruptcy, with every leader panting accordingly, and rushing behind the [George] Bush administration! The common factor among this group is their race to combat terrorism to satisfy America and the master of the White House. Here we stand at the end of 2004, watching as Arab and Islamic intelligence services work side by side with American CIA and FBI officers, combating the terrorism of Islam and Muslims, from Syria to Egypt to Morocco to Algeria to Tunisia to Sudan to the Arabian Peninsula.

What a pity that the *ulama* of the Muslims has remained silent and cowering. Even from the pulpits of Friday prayer at the al-Haram mosque in Mecca the Sultan's hypocritical *ulama* condemn jihad and the mujahideen, defend the rulers, and call for protecting the blood of the unbelieving invaders! The television stations transmit the sermons of their imams in which they call for combating terrorism and demand that terrorists be hunted and their financial springs be dried up. They call to God that the terrorists be discovered and that Muslims be rescued from their evils.

The *ulama* on satellite television screens compete in a marathon contest of hypocrisy and treachery, until one of the most famous Muslim *ulama*, Ayid al-Qarni, emerged to shout on MBC, commenting on the September events, "Has the religion commanded us to kill people? Has it commanded us to destroy buildings? Why should we not focus instead on the missionary call to Islam? Why not call the members of the American Congress to Islam? In just a few years they will all enter Islam!"

I wonder if this poor man knows that 85 percent of the members of Congress are Jews or are married to Jews! And most of the remaining 15 percent are Crusaders and followers of the evangelical church, who believe that their Messiah will emerge only after a grand massacre that uproots the planet of Muslims! A mujahideen from Algeria told me that he wore a military uniform and prayed with the Saudi forces allayed on the borders of Iraq under the leadership of [U.S. general Norman] Schwarzkopf during Desert Storm. So how could the likes of this one know what the condition of the Congress is?

As for he who deservedly takes the nickname "The Devil of the Ulama," he is the vulgar degenerate hypocrite Sheikh Abd al-Muhsin al-Abaykan [adviser to the Saudi Justice Ministry], who shamelessly appeared on a series of programs on the Saudi satellite channel and on MBC, the Saudi-financed Lebanese channel, where he went so far as to support the collaborator government of [Ayad] Alawi [Iraqi prime minister], saying, "He is the legitimate ruler of Iraq, and allegiance to him is required." And when the host asked him, "but America is the one who appointed him and imposed him!" he said, "Even if unbelievers were appointed as rulers over Muslim lands, they are a legitimate imam toward whom allegiance is necessary." I don't really know through what religion such fatwas can arise, fatwas no religion would accept, even the Zoroastrians and the cow worshippers! All peoples and religions reject a ruler appointed by the enemy and consider him illegitimate.

As for this misguiding misfit, when the host asked him about the legitimacy of American forces in Iraq resisting their attackers, he said, contemplatively, "They are defending themselves against those who are attacking them in Iraq, and do not strike those who do not strike them!"

Others have joined this misguided chorus:

- Sheikh Tantawi of al-Azhar claimed that France's prohibition against the headscarf is an internal matter, and is not for Muslims to interfere with!

- The grand mufti in Pakistan, Sheikh Rafiya Othmani, said in a sermon at the closing ceremony of al-Bukhari, "Those who kill while defending themselves in the regions of Waziristan against army raids, they are not martyrs!" And the grand mufti added that jihad can only be authorized through a command by the ruler Musharraf, and that the Americans and their likes in Afghanistan are protected peoples and are off limits to assault.

- The sheikh of the awakening, Safa al-Hawali, has called on the mujahideen to surrender and repent to the pharaohs of their countries. To repent from jihad against the Americans in the land of the two holy sites!

May God rebuke them all and make them rest in the cracks of hell!

It is ironic that while writing this book, the sounds of gunfire and music and celebration broke out outside. I wasn't expecting that Jerusalem would be liberated so suddenly! Or that India had withdrawn from Kashmir! So, I paused to find out about the noise and learned Muslims were celebrating the Christian new year. The clock struck precisely midnight and the mad cows were unleashed! Without a doubt it was a night of parties and dancing, wine and debauchery for millions of Muslims! There is also no doubt that their governments and media apparatuses provided all forms of corruption and the revelers required.

In short, this Muslim reality points to our desolation, loss, defeat, and ruin. If not for what God and Mohammed promised, which is absolutely true, then hope would be lost. I really have no idea what else must happen to the *ummah* before it mobilizes for jihad. What more is needed than Jerusalem's distress call? What more is needed than the al-Aqsa intifada? What more is needed than Afghanistan? What more is needed than the news from Chechnya and what it has suffered? Bosnia, Kosovo, and what they have endured? What more is needed than the news media's stories concerning the tribulations of Muslims in every place?

What will shake the *ummah* and move its feelings more than the roar of the September 11 attacks and the image of the hawks of Islam and its martyrs tearing down the symbol of American haughtiness and might? What more than the image of fifteen youthful Chechen widows, in the prime of their lives, strapping explosives to their bodies and waging jihad in the heart of Moscow? What more is needed than the scenes of the numerous American and British military on Muslim lands and their pronounced plan to destroy Iraq and occupy its land and people. What more? What more?

The souls of the people have died, and the Islamic street is apathetic, but for a few demonstrations here and a few distressed cries there. But the discontent is enormous, the air is thick, and the revolutionary climate is burning, bringing with it tidings of the arrival of jihadist fervor, thanks first to God, and then thanks to the American tyrants, the wicked malice of the Jews, the greed of the crusader campaigns.

As for the condition of the jihadists, God has been helpful and has had mercy on the martyrs and settled them in his paradise. And God has made patient the prisoners and has been able to deliver them from the prisons of Guantanamo and its more vile branches in the prisons of Muslim rulers. And God has preserved the scattered and has lightened their circumstances and has reaffirmed the purposeful on their course and helped them keep the standard fluttering despite their injuries—and to pass it on proudly to the next generation.

The jihadist movement in its entirety, its organizations, leaders, symbols, and ranks, indeed, all of its supporters, is today passing through the most severe trial the modern jihadist movement has faced since its launch forty years ago. This is because of the unjust campaign America is conducting against it. Earlier, many jihadist organizations suffered severe and wide-ranging catastrophes and injuries, such as what occurred to the mujahideen in Syria, Tunisia, Libya, Algeria, Egypt, and other places. But the trial of the current global war against terrorism, as they call it, is distinct in its scope, thrust, and extent of our losses.

America had inaugurated it and had mobilized its allies from the NATO countries and other unbelieving nations, as well as the apostate powers represented by the Arab rulers and their apparatuses of repression. This campaign reached its apex after the events of September 11, when America destroyed the Islamic emirate of Afghanistan, which constituted the last refuge for the elite jihadist groups and their cadres. Hundreds of the movement's cadres were killed in the battle to defend the emirate. Then America followed up on this by imprisoning six hundred mujahideen from various Arab countries in Pakistan and transferred them to its own prisons. Similarly, it was able to detain, through cooperation with its allies among the unbelievers and apostates in the Muslim lands, hundreds of others and registered on the terrorist list other jihadist groups, so as to expel their members from every country in the world. Then, what remained of the jihadist membership, particularly its symbols, leaders, and foremost cadres entered a state of dispersion and flight, as a result of the greatest global security campaign history has ever witnessed.

This is our condition, and the condition of our brother mujahideen. But, despite all of the disasters that befell the jihadists in every place, God continues to call on us to rain down on America and its allies. We ask God that he grant us conditions that realize these events. Our apostate enemies say, "We have sympathy for America and none for you." We say to them, "God is our master as he is yours" and "our dead are in paradise, while yours are in hell, and there is no comparison."

CHAPTER 3
The Sharia Rulings for This Situation

We believe that sharia rulings have determined jihad to be an individual duty incumbent upon all Muslims in a situation such as exists today. Likewise, reason and logic point to the fact that armed jihad is the solution for putting an end to the crises of the current situation. The sharia evidence for this is clearer than the eye of the sun. This is the reality: general resistance to this foreign infidel occupation, to the apostate power cooperating with him and bearing down on the chests of Muslims, is a duty necessitated by the Islamic sharia, and it is a reality that good sense demands.

Among the sharia's most important rulings concerning the situation of Muslims today are:

- The lands of Islam are today in a state of direct or indirect occupation at the hands of the enemy. Waging jihad against the occupation is an individual duty of all Muslims.
- The governments of Muslim countries are apostate infidel governments, as they have replaced the sharia and its rulings with other than what God revealed, and because of their clientage to infidels. Fighting a Muslim ruler who has apostatized against Islam or has become an infidel is an individual duty of all Muslims.
- Islamic sharia rulings uniformly state that those who cooperate with the infidels and their helpers are guilty of unbelief and apostasy and oblige that they be fought.

Jihad against the infidels is of two kinds:
- Voluntary jihad (jihad against the infidels in their own lands), because the infidels are not concentrating so as to fight Muslims. In this instance, fighting is a collective duty incumbent upon only some Muslims. The minimal collective duty of this sort is to "plug the breaches with believers to terrorize the enemies of God, . . . " and so forth.
- Defensive jihad (driving the infidels out of our lands) is an individual duty incumbent upon all Muslims, indeed, the highest of individual duties. It is applied in the following circumstances:
  — If the infidels have entered a Muslim land;
  — If the ranks have met and the armies have engaged;
  — If the imam calls individuals or a nation to arms and requires them to mobilize;
  — If the infidels imprison a group of Muslims.

Sheikh 'Abdallah 'Azzam discussed the first situation, when the infidels descend on a Muslim land by saying, "Those who preceded us in interpreting the Qur'an absolutely agree that in this situation jihad is duty of all Muslims in the land the infidels are assaulting, and also upon those who are near them, so that the son goes out to fight without his father's permission and the wife without her husband's permission and the debtor without the creditor's permission. And if the people of this land are insufficiently numerous, or indolent, or shirking battle, then the individual duty expands in circles, from most proximate to the next most proximate. And if these are insufficiently numerous, then the obligation falls on those who come after them, and those after them in turn, until the individual duty has diffused throughout the whole earth."[1]

Many ask if there is a limit to combat. God has answered this: "The punishment of those who wage war against God and His messenger is execution, or crucifixion, or the cutting off of hands and feet from opposite sides, or exile from the land. That is their disgrace in this world and a heavy punishment is theirs in the Hereafter." This is the judgment against those who fight Muslim society, corrupt the earth, and violate the possessions and honor of the Muslim people.

This is some of the evidence and justifications for general Muslim mobilization. If the unbelievers enter the land of Muslims, then repulsing the unbelieving enemy is the highest obligation after belief.

I say, if we contemplated the situation of Muslims today, we would find that jihad has become obligatory of them from all four corners of the earth. This is driven by the penetration of the enemy into the majority of Muslim lands. There is not a single Muslim land that is not occupied at the hands of various sorts of unbelieving Jews, Crusaders, and others, including the Chinese. The people in these countries, their neighbors, their neighbors' neighbors, and everyone beyond them have become either incapable, lazy, or remiss. Therefore, the individual obligation for jihad has spread to all Islamic people.

As for the remaining Arab and Muslim lands, the heartlands of dar al-Islam, these are indirectly occupied by the Crusaders and the Jews through the stewardship of apostate rulers who have placed their armies at the service of the infidels. They are led by America, its mistress Israel, and their Crusader allies who filled these countries with land, sea, and air bases and who occupied Muslim lands with this modern method, by concentrating their forces in centralized bases, as opposed to distributing them broadly. They were content for the apostates to distribute their armies of hypocrites, ignoramuses, scoundrels, and wretches who perform the occupier's role by proxy, as the Crusaders mobilize their forces from their bases at times of need.

Through this vile method, through gathering its troops in centralized bases and relying on the apostate forces for day-to-day services, the new occupiers avert provoking Muslims to jihad and allow the apostate rulers to claim independence and the *ulama* of the Sultans to distract the people from jihad and call them to obey the apostate holders of authority! The outcome is one—the lands are occupied, the riches are plundered, and the infidels impose all kinds of humiliation on the believers at the hands of their apostate helpers. God's sharia is inactive, and the word of the infidels reigns, while the righteous are the inmates of the prisons and torture chambers.

If we turned to the third condition—the imam's call to arms—then, there is no single legitimate imam for Muslims anywhere on earth. All they have today are those who fight against God, slandering and sowing corruption on the earth. There is today no lawful imam who can call Muslims to arms for jihad. There are, however, imams of unbelief and apostasy, calling the despised to arms against the believers. So then, has jihad collapsed because of the absence of a lawful imam? If so, who will repulse the assailant?

There is not a Muslim country on earth that has not seen orthodox proselytizers calling people to God, whether hardworking *ulama*, sincere missionaries, or faithful commanders of jihad. They called the people to jihad and they called them to arms. Even if these leaders and commanders of jihad are absent from some countries, Islam pays no heed to the borders the Crusaders drew up between our countries and the nationalities, citizenship regimes, and passports they invented. The Islamic *ummah* is one and will remain one. The commanders of jihad have called all Muslims to jihad and to arms. Muslims everywhere are obliged to respond and mobilize and to repulse the attacker.

If we turned to the fourth condition for the compulsory obligation of jihad—the enemy has imprisoned a group of Muslims—what can be said?

- The number of Muslim youths abducted from different countries around the world and taken to the shameful American prison Guantanamo has, according to the American sources themselves, today exceeded seven hundred prisoners.
- An even greater number of Muslim youths are imprisoned in Western Europe (Britain, France, Spain, Germany, Belgium, Italy).
- In Russia there are thousands and a small number like them in Kashmir, the Philippines, Eritrea and African countries, Central Asian countries, and the countries of Turkestan.
- As regards the prisons of the tyrants of the Arab and Muslim countries, the numbers published by human rights organizations indicate that they approach tens of thousands at times in one country alone! There is no doubt that the number of imprisoned Muslim youths in these countries exceeds one hundred thousand!
- There is barely a country that is innocent of torture, rape, murder, and violating the honor of men and women. So has jihad become necessary.

Regardless of race or color, language, wealth or any other consideration, the sharia has classified people under two categories: believers and nonbelievers (infidels). It determined, as is apparent in the texts of the Book and the Sunna, that the people of faith are all brothers and constitute one *ummah* (nation). It also determined that nonbelievers, regardless of their sects, race, or language are one *ummah*. With such clarity, it was then decided that mankind and demons on this Earth are divided into two *ummah*, the *ummah* of faith and the *ummah* of infidelity.

God Almighty has very clearly ordered the believers to support each other and keep away from nonbelievers; this is the basis for the principles of loyalty and disavowal. This is not a marginal issue in faith, but rather a crucial one, for upon it a man's kinship to either *ummah* is founded. For there are two populations, and only two permitted: a Muslim supporting a Muslim, and an infidel supporting an infidel. God has commanded that we adopt this principle, and he told that if we do not protect each other, *"There will be great tumult and oppression on earth, and great mischief."*

- A Muslim protecting another Muslim is deemed good by God and is a victory and success.
- A Muslim protecting an unbeliever is the same as protecting the devil and becoming a member of the devil's party, and he deserves an eternity in hell as punishment.
- The protection of a Muslim given to unbelievers renders him one of them and foils his good deeds and leads him to apostasy.
- God has emphasized that the Jews and Christians are among the unbelievers and the verses of the Qur'an have very candidly designated them among the unbelievers, whose protection is forbidden.[2]
- Obedience to those who despise God's sharia, even in very few matters, is a path to apostasy. Appointing unbelievers as consultants, advisers, and aides and placing Muslims under their wishes and commands is a manifestation of protection to the unbelievers and forbidden by God.
- It is forbidden to give advice to unbelievers that may empower them and make them victorious over the Muslims. However, more dangerous and clear apostasy is fighting on their side, under their flag, and serving their interest.
- Sacrificing one's soul for the sake of the unbelievers is a faithlessness that casts one out of the Muslim community.

The breaking of these laws today narrates the condition of the leaders in Muslim countries like [Perez] Musharraf and his Pakistani government in their alliance with the United States. They [Pakistan] believe that the United States will triumph over the Muslims, and they are securing their position on its side. They will regret their actions, and their punishment will be in the hands of the believers when God's victory prevails.

As we have mentioned, Qur'anic verses, Hadiths, and the writings of scholars are all in agreement with these interpretations. These truths are the fundamentals of Islam and the basis of our doctrine. They are briefly and clearly summarized in the text of the Qur'an addressing every Muslim: "And he amongst you that turn to them (for friendship) is one of them . . . if any do that, [they] shall have no relation left with Allah." This is very clear. Whoever takes the unbelievers as friends is then an unbeliever, and an apostate like them, and shall have no relation with God.

The duty of all Muslims is to declare war on a leader when he departs from Islam. As we have mentioned earlier, all of the calamities suffered by the Muslims and the disasters that have befallen them relate to the absence of the law of God from their life and result from the faithlessness of their leaders and their loyalty to the unbelievers. Truthfully, examining the apostasy and faithlessness of the leaders and their "Islamism," in this current state of affairs, becomes a critical and serious matter, because it is the gateway for finding a solution for the problems of the Muslims today. The Islamism of a leader or his faithlessness is completely tied to the laws by which he rules, meaning:

• If the sharia prevails, then the ruler is Muslim.
• If the ruler is Muslim, then the requirement is for him to rule according to sharia.
• If he does not rule through sharia, then he is an unbeliever.

God has sent down that if the ruler is an unbeliever, then he cannot rule. This is simple to understand:

Muslim ruler = rule according to what God sent down.
Ruling by other than what God sent down = an infidel ruler.

Ruling by God's sharia, supporting the believers, and being an enemy to the infidels are the requirements of being a Muslim ruler. It is necessary to listen and obey everything the ruler orders, as long as it is not an offense against sharia. Muslims must respect the ruler's pacts and agreements, and fighting by his side is an obligation when Muslims are called on for jihad in the name of God against the infidels and apostates. It is necessary to be patient with the ruler and obey him, even if he takes your money, or whips your back, or if he strays from the right path and is oppressive in his rule, as long as his infidelity is not proven.

Scholars are all agreed, though, that leadership is not granted to an infidel, and if infidelity suddenly befalls the ruler, he should be removed from power. If infidelity befalls him, he no longer rules his state and he loses the right to obedience, and it becomes an obligation on all Muslims to rebel and remove him from power, and if possible they should appoint a fair imam (ruler) to replace him.

Leadership is not granted to an infidel, or a tyrant, or an immoral person. God will not permit unbelievers to have power, dominance, or command over the believers. Scholars have forbidden the sale of Muslim slaves to unbelievers; they have also forbidden unbelievers from being appointed to positions where Muslim are under their control. From this point of view, a Muslim female is forbidden from marrying an unbeliever, because the husband manages the household; therefore the wife will be under the control of an unbeliever. However, the opposite is permissible—a Muslim male may marry an unbeliever. In short, according to the unanimous consent of scholars, it has been determined that a ruler who has become an infidel and an apostate must be removed from power.

The condition of faithlessness among our leaders is very apparent as seen from the two most important perspectives on apostasy:

1. Ruling without the guidance of God, and replacing the rulings of God with the rulings of humans, and ruling not according with what God has revealed;
2. Loyalty to the unbelievers, including the Jews, Christians, and others, and fighting the Muslims on their side and serving their interests.

This is in addition to the forms of faithlessness that our leaders have embraced in words and actions, which provide all the motive required for the Muslim community to fight and kill them.

Chapter 3. The Sharia Rulings for This Situation

1. This section was followed by a long list of Islamic scholars, dating back centuries, stating the same point in different words.
2. The Almighty said: "O you who believe! Take not the Jews and the Christians for your friends and protectors." (Al-Ma'idah 51). And the Almighty said: "Take not for friends and protectors those who take your religion for a mockery or sport, whether among those who received the Scripture before you, or among those who reject Faith." (Al-Ma'idah 57).

CHAPTER 4
The Resistance Begins

Editor's Note: At the end of the previous chapter, Abu Musab al-Suri went into a long historical recital of Western and Arab history since the Islamic invasion the Middle East to the present. Large portions of this historical narrative are inaccurate, but the distortions do illuminate how al-Suri and kindred spirits view our supposedly common history. However, it does little to shine a light on the current struggle and was therefore reluctantly discarded.

W ho, then, confronted the Christian Crusades from 1990 to 2001? The truth is that the Christian Crusaders made their move only after they had eliminated all possible obstacles from their way. They had destroyed nearly all legitimate authority and had eliminated the elements that could build a resistance front among the Arab and Muslim people.

These new Crusaders also had all opportunities for success in battle. During the first, and even the Second Crusades [the Second Crusade, as used by al-Suri, refers to the colonial period from the seventeenth to the nineteenth centuries] there was some type of equilibrium in the confrontations on the ground between the enemies' soldiers and the forces of the mujahideen. This was even the case with the armies of the Second Christian Crusades, which the forces of the mujahideen confronted numerous times. However, the technological advancement of the American military has made it far superior to any others. When this fact is added to our true leaders being eliminated, we see that the battlefield has become semidesolate and that the confrontation is completely unbalanced.

As to the core of the resistance to the Third Christian Crusades and its apostate consorts during the period of 1990 to September 2001, I can list the most important resistance elements as I remember them:

- The armed jihadist movement in Algeria (1991–95), which was extinguished within the following two years because of a highly sophisticated and successful intelligence mission carried out between the Algerian Intelligence Services and their French counterparts. The latter were able to sidetrack and destroy the jihadist movement after isolating it from its public, which had veered off the path of righteousness.
- The armed jihadist confrontations that took place in Libya against the Mu'ammar al-Qadafi regime from 1993 to 1995, the most prominent of which was an attempt made by the al-Jama'ah al-Islamiyyah al-Muqatilah in Libya. The regime was able to contain the military activities of this group, and its work became mainly missionary and secretive in nature and was also practiced actively outside the country.
- The movement to establish sharia in Northwest Pakistan in 1996, which the Pakistani government was able to eliminate because of the cowardliness of the Muslim populous and the failure of the revival movements in Pakistan from coming to its aid.
- The movement of the army of Aden in Yemen, which was led by the martyr Abu-al-Hasan al-Muhadir. This movement was extinguished immediately in its infancy stage in 1998.
- The jihadist movement in the al-Nabatiyyah Mountains in the north of Lebanon. This movement was led by the martyr Abu-'A'ishah, and it was extinguished in its infancy stage in 1999.
- The Taliban movement, which began in 1994, established its emirate in 1996, and then saw its emirate overthrown in 2001. The Taliban movement had numerous followers among the Arab, Pakistani, and Central Asian jihadist groups. This movement was the most important jihadist phenomenon in this past century.
- The armed Palestinian intifada, which began in 2000 and is still ongoing. It is among the most important chapters in the jihadist confrontation and resistance against the Third Christian Crusades.
- A number of limited jihadist as well as individual attempts or operations carried out by mujahideen everywhere in the world against different forms of the Christian presence in the Muslim and Arab world. This has been carried out in different countries in the past century . . . such as the humble resistance operations in Saudi Arabia that targeted

the Americans. The most important of these operations would have to be those that occurred in Riyadh and in al-Khubar.

- The resistance and self-defense operations that were carried out all over the world by the jihadist movement as the mujahideen were being hunted down everywhere in the aftermath of the events of September 11. They also had to deal with the sordid acts of the Pakistani government, which was cracking down on those who fled to safety and were seeking a haven on its land.

- The jihadist movements that were dispersed in Central Asia against the socialist governments supported by the Soviet Union, including Tajikistan (1993–2001) and Uzbekistan (1997–2001).

- The Muslim's jihad in East Turkistan (1996–2001) against the Chinese government.

- The resistance that was carried out against the Christian forces on different battlefields during this period; such as what occurred in Bosnia from 1994 through 1996, as well as the events that occurred in Chechnya during the same period of time, and to this day.

- The heroic confrontation carried out by the mujahideen in Somalia, as well as those of the ancient and still ongoing jihadist movements in the Philippines, in Kashmir, in Eritrea, in Burma, in Indonesia, and in numerous other movements on different fronts, where Muslims have been or are now fighting against the imperialistic Christians and other infidels.

- Some operations carried out by al Qaida against the American presence in the region, the most important of which were the bombing of the American embassies in Nairobi and in Dar al-Salam, the attack on the USS *Cole* in Aden, and the last operations—the suicide missions carried out in the attacks on New York and Washington on September 11, 2001, which opened a whole new chapter in the confrontation between Christians and Muslims and changed the face of history and the fundamentals of the struggle.

A calculated look at the struggle between Muslims and the Third Christian Crusade since 1990 until the invasion of Iraq in 2003, reveals the equation:

The Jewish nation (headed by Israel)
plus   The Christian nation (headed by America, the U.K.,
         Russia, and NATO)
plus   The sects of the apostate rulers in the Islamic world
plus   The hypocritical forces, especially the Sultan's scholars,
         and all of the corrupt leaders of the revival movements
         in our countries against the armed jihadist movement's
         organizations and individuals
Equals The defeat of the resistance jihadist resistance movement
         and the paralysis of the Islamic revival movement

Here are my equations for the struggles we faced against other Crusades
The First Christian Crusade has the following equation:

The Christian nation
versus   The Muslim nation
Equals   The Muslim nation's victory

The Second Christian Crusade—the imperialistic phase—is as follows:

The Christian nation
plus   The Jewish nation
versus   The Muslim nation
Equals   The Muslim nation's victory.

The Second Christian Crusade—the independence phase—is as follows:

The Christian nation
plus   The Jewish nation
plus   The sects of the apostate governments
versus   The Islamic revival
Equals   The defeat of the Islamic revival.

It is necessary to understand these amazing historical equations and to
learn from them the reasons for the defeat and the elements that lead to a
victory, so as to have it repeated again.

The first element of truth from these equations is that we were victorious in the first and second equation and we were defeated in the third

one and completely destroyed in the fourth [the fight against the Third Crusade]. It is very clear that the Muslim nation was victorious when it confronted its enemy militarily despite the tremendous difference in numbers and equipment.

The equations also demonstrate that we were defeated when only a portion of the Muslim nation got involved in the battle against the enemy, while the rest just stood watching on the sideline. We were completely destroyed when the majority of this portion withdrew from the battle, and some even went on to betray the nation and to join the enemy.

Therefore, the first lesson we must learn from these equations is that we must return the Muslim nation to the battlefield so that the battle becomes once again a battle of a nation and not just that of a few, as it has become these days. The first thing required in this matter is that these "few" must convince the rest that those who stand by the enemy become the enemy. They must be convinced that confronting the enemy is at the core of jihad and it is not something off the path of righteousness.

The Muslim nation once stirred when it was provided with a religious authoritative source as a role model to follow, whereas neither the Islamic revival nor jihadist groups could form an authoritative source that could convince the nation to move along with them. Therefore, any group that wishes to create a resistance front must first form an authoritative source that will be able to gather the whole Muslim nation around it.

We were able to defeat the enemy in military confrontations on the battleground, but he defeated us when he planned his conquest in a modern intellectual manner. In doing so, he dismantled the foundation of the notion of resistance in the nation. We must, therefore, rebuild this foundation, and we must launch the resistance. The Jews did get involved in the Second Christian Crusades, but only as an aid to colonialism. However, they were a leading and inciting force to the Third Christian Crusades, and we must confront them as such. We must give the destruction of their front, Israel, and their instrument, America, the importance that is appropriate to their roles and the danger that they pose in the next phase.

The third and fourth equations show that the apostates technically settled the victory in the enemy's favor by cheating the nation with a fake adherence to the Muslim faith and a fake show of nationalism. Therefore, it is an obligation of those who are heading the jihad and resistance movements, as well as their media, and their calculating and intelligent leadership to reemphasize the role of the prime instigator of those apostates—that is the Christians—and to incite the resistance to go up against them. This will bring the nation back into the battle and will convince it of taking up arms against the apostates who should be considered as followers of the Christians and, thus, part of the true and principal enemy; the apostates are nothing more than a screen for the true enemy.

The last equation emphasizes America's role as a leading force and means we must give the confrontation with America priority over any other entity. It also points to the internal contradictions in the Christian alliances and its three axes (America-Great Britain/West Europe/Russia), and to the importance of working to dismantle this alliance and to isolate the American Zionist axis as much as possible.

Looking back, we see that all the European nations stood behind and supported their armed forces and their kings during the First and the Second Crusades. However, with the spread of peace movements in many segments of the European community, as well as the increased knowledge about Islam in Europe, millions of people stand in opposition of these Crusades, even in Great Britain! Conversely, the majority of those American Zionists stood in support of their reckless, Christian president, [George] Bush, and of his armed forces. That is a matter that we must pay attention to when we lay out the plans for the next resistance movement.

Final remark: This is the most important one, and it constitutes an essential cornerstone in understanding the nature of our current struggle. It also must be a principal beam in the jihadist creed for the resistance in this era. It is as follows:

We must face down and eliminate the hypocrites amongst
the Sultan's scholars and the corrupt amongst the leaders
of the Islamic revival, who see it as their role to defeat the
Muslim nation and its jihadist youths by supporting the enemy.

My heart is saddened and my soul devastated whenever the religious programs and the Friday sermons continue to be aired over the satellite stations from Mecca, from the Prophet Muhammad's mosque, and from the biggest mosques in every capital of the Arab and Muslim nations to witness the important role that is provided by the official religious organization in their service to the goals of the United States.

Programs about fighting terrorism became equivalent with those about fighting crime, gangs, and drugs. One cannot help feeling resentful over the fact that we must always defend ourselves or be looked upon as law-breaking individuals who should be punished because we dare to resist the United States, its crusades, and its invasions or stand up to our ungodly leaders in our own countries, those who actually offer assistance to the infidels' campaigns.

I have discovered five major evils of the present scholars of the Sultan:

- Supporting apostate leaders who rule the Arab and Muslim nations without applying God's Law and without using the Qur'an as a resource for consultation. These leaders are devoted to the infidels and to God's enemies.

- Supporting governing by the law of the Christian American occupier in the Muslim nations; the claim that this is necessary and authorized because of necessity permits them to take such a role. They also permit good relations with the Jews and they give religious legalization to the invasion of Palestine with the claim that all of the events had occurred because of political, military, and economic treaties and agreements between the infidels and the religious legal leaders. These included: [Yasir] Arafat and his authorities responsible for the Oslo and Madrid Conventions as well as the Road Map to Peace.

- Forbidding resistance against the Christians and the Jews, by describing it as terrorism to Muslims; in doing so, they remove the religious legality of jihad.

- Declaring that the mujahideen and the forces of resistance are sources of destruction on this earth, and, consequently, authorizing their imprisonment, their torture, and the crackdown on them by those legally in charge. They allowed hundreds of thousands of these soldiers, their apparatuses, their airplanes, and their destructive smart bombs to make the mujahideen their target; these trusted men were not to be questioned in their judgment or decisions. So how could they ever worry about terrorists getting to them!

- The disaster that was the worst among all of these and the ultimate cause in the destruction of even the roots of Islam and the resistance in the Muslim nation is the actions of the hypocrite scholars, those scholars of the Pentagon, those corrupt leaders of the Islamic revival as far as destroying the faith of the Muslims by calling for a reform in Islam, a middle ground, an open-minded Islam, a modern-day Islam, a cultural dialogue, a wisdom in the call . . . and numerous other fake slogans through which the Americanization of Islam is accomplished today. Satellite stations and other such media systems have taken it upon themselves to spread such calls, the way a cancer spreads uncontrolled in the body of the nation; opposing it entails a risk of being accused of the crime terrorism, the least punishment for which is the death penalty.

CHAPTER 5
The Islamic Awakening

A SUMMARY OF THE COURSE OF THE ISLAMIC AWAKENING (1930–2001)

B riefly stated, the Islamic resurgence movement has become inadequate and depleted. It has failed to realize its objectives and has reached utter despondency. It can no longer influence events. Most dramatically, it has been rendered utterly hopeless, and the only hope of resurgence is for them to conduct a review of the movement's approaches, purposes, objectives, and mode of operation in accordance with Islamic sharia through a committed Muslim establishment and in consideration of the new actualities on the ground and against the background of contemporary American Crusade expeditions, launched in a post–September 11, 2001, world and in the aftermath of invading and occupying Iraq.

Though I belong to the jihad and contribute to its publications, the arguments that I had advanced are naturally brief and are proportionate to my interaction. However, I would like to take the liberty of offering to Islamists an admonition, based on the revelations of the Qur'an, the teachings of the Prophet, and the practices of the Muslim *ummah*.

> They are to forsake any association with the rulers, to dissociate themselves from the Three Branches of their regimes—the Executive, Legislative, and the Judiciary—that operate in a manner inconsistent with the laws of Allah almighty. Any linkage with either of these branches is unlawful, and is never sanctioned by the sharia laws. Any association is inherently wrong according to the injunctions of Allah, and is only justified by vague, unreliable political causes and apologies.

My special recommendation to the adherents of political movements is to pursue a professional career in the areas of public information, politics, and civil domains, bearing in mind that their focus would be resisting the colonial forces and the dissociation with the wicked and sinister triangulation of power (the ruler, the masses, and their stooges) who voluntarily or involuntarily are in opposition to the advancement and development of the *ummah*.

As much as it may be hurtful and brutal, yet I would like to draw the attention to a merciless truth: the pillars of the post–September 11 world have declared there shall be no noninterventionism or pacifism when it is time for a showdown. This means that we are bound to resist them; wage a military campaign of armed struggle or jihad, a dogfight; or engage them verbally and sentimentally, which is the minimal form of resistance against them.

The Achievements of the Jihadist Movement over Forty Years

During the past forty years, jihadists made great achievements and victories all over the Arab and Islamic world, although they could not reach their stated goals, which could be summarized as follows:
1. Ideological and Curricular: The jihad, through its scholars and media, was able to stand as an exceptional model within the modern Islamic awakening movement. The scholars and media were able to shape its curricula through books and lectures. In addition, the blood of the martyrs added life to that curriculum by providing an example to those seeking to please God.
2. The Accomplishments of the Call for Islam and the Community: During the past four decades, the jihadists acquired a vast following within the nation in general and the awakening movement in particular. The offerings of the martyrs [suicide bombers] is an example and guide to all those seeking God.
3. Military Accomplishments: This is the most noticeable achievement of jihadists, because they were able to gain with their blood and suffering notable military achievements. Some experiences presented an example of ongoing long-term revolutions similar to those that took place in Syria, Algeria, and Tajikistan. They were categorically able to decapitate multiple heads of infidelity and enemy leaders. The mujahideen were able to hang many of the tyrants and God's enemies, among them presidents, ministers, and major and small supporters. And the soldiers of God were able to pay back the aggressors with what they

deserve in many countries. Also, the jihadists were able to play an important role resisting the crusaders' attacks on Muslims on many occasions. Some of these important roles were played in the open arenas of confrontation with foreign enemies from the Philippines, Indonesia, Kashmir, Eritrea, Somalia, and in the present confrontation in Iraq.

In addition, they offered their participation in jihad against the Russian atheists in Chechnya in an ongoing battle. Likewise, they steadfastly fought in Bosnia against the Serb and Croat Crusaders, who were supported by various global Crusades' powers, defeating their genocidal project that targeted Muslims in that region. But their greatest success was in Afghanistan, where they were able to overthrow a bloody communist regime and remove a great power [the Soviet Union]. As a result, the nucleus of the Islamic abode was reborn through the establishment of the Islamic monarchy in Afghanistan with the erection of an emir for the believers. This monarchy provided an example of ruling with the sharia by shielding the believers and allowing them to live their lives in accordance with the rules of God and their religion against the will of the new world order.

Then the mujahideen gave the greatest example of success by opening the twenty-first century, the so-called American Century, with a confrontation inside the beating heart of America.

This long road of confrontations spanned more than forty years, with thousands of battles and challenges. The heroes of these battles proved to the enemies of God that, despite the state of deterioration the majority of Muslims live in, the miracle of the prophet of Islam is alive. However, those days are gone and many great stories have been forgotten.

4. Political Accomplishments: Despite the fact that the jihadists failed to achieve their goal of overthrowing the ignorant systems to establish the Islamic system on their ruin, they accomplished many political achievements, the most important of which are:
   - Threatening the ignorant systems by exposing their falsity and removing their legitimacy.
   - Exposing the normalization projects with the Jews and the West, especially those Westernizing projects, and the use of Crusaders' methods.

- Also the jihadists were able to confront the awakening movement's divergences from its curricula, practices, and propaganda.
- With the help of God, they were able to prove to the invaders that the nation, despite its collapse, is not easy to seize.

Political achievements can only be reached through jihad. There is no doubt we will be successful, but it will not be a product of Internet chats, electronic clubs, or political battle. Seriousness cannot be a product of frivolity, and righteousness would not be borne out of vagrancy or sinning.

The Course of the Jihad and Its Experiences (1960–2001)

We must begin this section with a definition of what a jihadi is. To start, I would say that a jihadi is one who exerts efforts to make Allah's word higher than anything else. This implies fighting for Allah's sake and sacrificing oneself and property for the victory of Allah's religion and the defense of Muslims (their religion, blood, honor, properties, and their land). Whoever does this job, to see Allah's face and to keep Allah's word higher than anything else, is a mujahid. And if a team or a group agreed and gathered for this job, then they are mujahideen.

This chapter, however, is designed for a special kind of mujahideen. This special group is defined and separated from the others by carrying a weapon. This is the individual or group that fights Islam's enemy under the banner of "There is no god but Allah and Muhammad is Allah's messenger." By definition, these mujahideen put aside limited methods and techniques and replace them with fighting.

This definition puts aside the issue of methods and techniques and limited targets and surpasses it. I also said that the jihadi stream is a period and phenomena that emerged from the Islamic revival (awakening) during the last century. Specifically, the jihad movement comprises organizations, groups, assemblies, scholars, intellectuals, and individuals who adopt the ideology of "armed jihad" against the existing regimes in the Arab lands and the Islamic world. They also adopt the armed methods against the colonialist forces that attacked our Muslim lands.

We must also bear in mind the important separation between mujahideen and those organizations that carry weapons against the different enemies of the Islamic nation. These groups do not perform jihad for the sake of Allah and do not do the "jihad task" as a religious duty. Rather, they fight for nationalistic, liberationist, or political objectives against dictator regimes. These principles are part of a secular ideology and may be good, but they are not rewarded in heaven. Also, carrying weapons for reasons of manhood, protection, heroism, or showing off is not worship of Allah and will not be recompensed. It is of no use in the other life, and if he gets killed, it is not a martyrdom.

Classifying the Components of the Jihadi Phenomenon

1. The Jihadists—These are groups of individuals that have adopted the ideology of taking on the jihad against the apostate tyrant regimes. The basis of their emergence and their goals generally define them as covert organizations, with goals and targets limited to a specific country or nation and a pyramid organizational structure. The Individuals making up these groups are linked with their leader through a pledge of allegiance.
2. The Mujahideen Groups—These are organizations and groups that specialize in jihad against the invaders of Muslim countries, especially the Jews or the occupying Crusaders, like the Americans or Westerners generally; or the godless, like those in Russia or China; or the idol worshippers as in Chechnya, Bosnia, India, Kashmir, Southeast Asia. Most of the time these organizations assume the shape of a national liberation movement, but with an Islamic, jihad form, as we said before. Their goal is to free that country and then turn it into an Islamic-ruled country.
3. The Mujahideen Individuals That Strive to Stop Evil through the Use of Arms or to Push away Oppression—This is jihad carried on by individuals not part of a specific group or led by an emir. Their operations are meant to expel evil and are carried out as an act of self-denial based on concepts and religious convictions meant to eliminate infidels and their leaders or to destroy establishments that serve alcohol or purvey prostitution or any other corrupt practice that is contrary to Islamic laws. Sometimes these targets are infidel religious and holy places where they practice their rituals, or the target is to remove any kind of appearance that is considered to be against religion.

The Foundation of the Contemporary Jihadist Current and Its Development Intellectually and as a Movement (1960–2001)

At the end of the colonial period, a number of opinions existed on the best direction for Islamists to go. Some said that the solution was educational reform and political seclusion. Others thought that the solution lay in legal avenues provided they stay within what these governments would allow. However, a third group (which we are talking about in this section) realized that corruption is widespread and there was no other way but to carry arms, especially after Arab governments and their brutal agencies proved their effectiveness by assassinating key movement leaders or throwing them in prison for many years. Here, the idea of the modern jihad started to take shape—during the late 1950s and beginning of the 1960s.

The Muslim Brotherhood movement gave birth to jihadi ideas and spread them throughout the Islamic population. Its leadership participated in Egypt and Syria during the Palestine war of 1947–48, and afterward Hassan Al-Banna formed his own special secret military apparatus for the group's jihad activities. After the death of Hassan Al-Banna in 1949, the members of the military apparatus led the "Secret Resistance" in Egypt during the 1950s. The apparatus participated in supporting 'Abd-al-Nasser's movement by toppling King Faruq. But this "doomed man" ['Abd-al-Nasser] had prepared with the enemy a program that was designed to finish off the Islamic movement. Nasser's main target was the Muslim Brotherhood movement, and he jailed its leadership and thousands of its members in 1954. In 1956 he widened this campaign and hanged some Brotherhood members, including the best of their thinkers and leaders.

As for Syria, which is another important nest for the Muslim Brotherhood movement, military coups destroyed the national independence regimes that fell one after another since 1946. This continued until 1963, when the Arab Baa'th Social Party came to power. Its priority was to eliminate the Islamic revival like the Brotherhood and others and to combat Islam and all its components . . . Egypt and Syria thereby created the jihad ideology and its operational theories.

The pioneer of the modern era for the jihad ideology is, without a doubt, Mr. Teacher and martyr, Sayyid Qutub. He started his life as a poet, writer, researcher, and critic. He lived through the growing phases of the ideology and the turbulent times of Egypt's modern history during the 1940s, 1950s, and 1960s, when he contacted and stayed close to the Muslim Brotherhood.

A field trip to America had a great effect on him, and there he discovered the modern Crusaders' campaign against the Arab and Islamic world, He used what Allah had given him—a sharp pencil and sensitive spirit—and the prison atmosphere that 'Abd-al-Nasser put him in—to write his wonderful ideas that truly are the basis for the modern jihad ideology.

His book *Signs on the Road* was a small book yet his most important. It contains the summary of the jihad ideology and his revolutionary ideas regarding jihad theories and overthrowing governments. His extensive library also included other books like *The Merits of Islamic Conceptions* and *This Religion* and *Jahiliya of the Twentieth Century*. In total, they provide a complete program for the modern jihadi movement ideology.

The ideology of the Qutub was a qualitative transformation of the Islamic revival ideology path, in general, and for the Muslim Brotherhood, in particular. However, the traditional leadership of the Brotherhood in Egypt stood against Qutub and his theories in governance, loyalty, and exoneration. The Brotherhood's leadership drew away from Qutub to prevent a clash with the authorities. At this junction, the Muslim Brotherhood movement and the modern Islamic revival split into two distinct and conflicting schools.

Sayyid Qutub still tried to put his ideology to use, and he attempted to form the first secret jihadi organization to carry out his ideas. A bunch of young mujahideen, most of whom were members of the Muslim Brotherhood, made up this first organization. However, their plans were discovered and foiled, and Qutub was consequently executed. However, what he dreamed in prison was achieved.

I do not believe there is any language spoken by Muslims today that Qutub's many books have not been translated into. Today, the crusaders and their leader, America, realize he was a giant and are feeling the consequences of his ideas. They attack him and the mujahideen who follow him with the so-called war on terrorism. Even as this is written, they combat him and try to distort his image by using their media and educational programs in our countries in particular.

Islamic ideology was also spread as a by-product of the Saudi government's attempts to strengthen its rule. To do so, they gathered hundreds of thousands of foreign students from different Arab and Islamic countries and gave them scholarships to Saudi universities that specialized in religious teaching. From those centers, hundreds of thousands of students and Muslim youths graduated and returned to their countries carrying those ideologies. Currently, the Saudi government is trying to change these programs in response to American pressure to change the Islamic educational structure as part of America's ongoing ideological war. Before America began its pressure, Saudi Arabia was a regular refuge for exiles, especially the Brotherhood's leaders chased from Egypt. Also many of the Brotherhood and sheikhs escaped from Syria and its Baa'thist government's oppression.

As the jihad ideology spread, there were many jihadi attacks on the current regimes in the Arab and Islamic world. The important ones are listed below:

- The Moroccan Youth Movement in the Far West (Marrakech). Led by Sheikh 'Abd-al-Karim Muti' against the government of the mortal King Hassan II (1963).
- The attempt of the martyred Sheikh Sayyid Qutub and the jihad organization against the regime of 'Abd-al-Nasser in Egypt (1965).
- The movement of Sheikh Marwan Hadid against the Ba'ath regime in Syria (1965).
- The jihadi movements against the communist regimes in Afghanistan before the Soviet occupation (1965–75).
- The experiment of the Front Organization (Ekingilar) in Turkey during the civil war there (1972).
- The Movement of the Islamic State led by the martyr Sheikh Mustafa Bui'li, blessed be his soul, in Algeria (1973–76).
- Jihad Islamic revolution in Syria under the leadership of the leading disciples of the fighter Sheikh Marwan Hadid (1975–82).
- The movement of the jihad organization and the Islamic Group in Egypt against Anwar Sadat and then against his successor Hosni Mubarak (1981–97).
- Jihadi attempt against the regime of al-Qadafi in Libya (1986).
- Some limited jihad attempts and the coup attempt organized by the military under the (Trend) party in Tunisia (1986).
- Tests of various jihad groups in Algeria (from 1991).
- Jihad confrontations against the communist regime in Tajikistan (from 1992).
- Limited jihad attempts in the Land of the Two Holy Places (Saudi Arabia) (from 1994).

- Jihad clashes in Libya (1994–96) and the experience of the Islamic militant group.
- The armed uprising (Nafath Shara'ah movement) for Northwest Pakistan (1996).
- Attempts to form groups of jihad in Morocco (from 1996).
- Jihad attempts against the regime of [Islam] Karimov, the American communist, in Uzbekistan. And forming the Islamic Movement of Uzbekistan (1998).
- The jihad experience of the Aden-Abin Islamic Army in Yemen (from 1999).

Also in the same period, many jihad movements were initiated against various occupiers and foreign aggressors in Muslim countries. The most important of those movements include:

- Jihad and resistance movements against Indian occupation in Kashmir and the Indian state of Assam.
- Jihad movements against the Hindus in Burma and Al-Arkan.
- The jihadi liberation movements in the Philippines, such as the Moro Liberation Front and the Abu Sayyaf group.
- The groups that initiated jihad in Eritrea against the Ethiopian occupation.
- Ethiopian occupation jihadi groups in the Horn of Africa (the Ogaden and Afar).
- Islamic party in eastern Turkistan, which initiated jihad against the Chinese occupation of Turkistan.
- Al-Tawhid group, which was formed by the Mujahideen Al-Sunna, during the civil war in Lebanon in confronting the Christian Coalition and the Al-Nasiriyah sectarians supported by the Syrian regime (1975–82).
- Jihad against the Soviet occupation of Afghanistan (1979–92).
- Islamic Resistance Movement (Hamas) in order to resist the Israeli occupation in Palestine (from 1987).
- Islamic jihad movement, to confront the Israeli occupation of Palestine (from 1989).
- Kurdish Islamic groups confronting Saddam Hussein's regime in Iraq. Then against the secular Kurdish parties aggressions in Iraqi's Kurdistan (from 1990).

- The jihad experience in the Serbian aggression against Bosnia (1994–96).
- The jihad experience against the Russian occupation of Chechnya and the Caucasus (from 1995).
- Jihad confrontations against Christian aggression in Indonesia (from 1998).
- Afghani jihad against the Russians (1984–1992).

The Afghan Resistance

The armies of the obsolete Soviet Union occupied Afghanistan publicly in 1979 after having done that indirectly through a number of communist military coups since 1965. The entry of the invaders made the common Afghan people join in jihad and resist. As I have indicated earlier in the course of my research, nobody expected this poor "backward" people to resist such a giant invasion. It seemed as if America had recognized the annexation of this area to Russian colonialism as they did with Central Asia and the Caucasus, and so forth. But the valiant resistance of the Afghan people between 1979 and 1982 was eventually noticed by the American administration, and the U.S. Congress decided to adopt the issue of the Afghan jihad as an arena where America could possibly take revenge against the Russians for their aid in Vietnam.

America sponsored a global alliance to confront the Russians and the Warsaw Pact in Afghanistan, and it dragged behind her the NATO alliance and all its Western European allies as well as its great economic allies such as Canada, Australia, and Japan to construct a political, media, and economic alliance supporting her in this war. A fiscal policy was initiated to provide a share of the financial aid that ran into the millions of dollars for each country, and everyone contributed.

But the most important aspect of the alliance created by the U.S. support for the Afghan jihad was from the Arab and Islamic world. The most important role was that of Saudi Arabia, Pakistan, Egypt, and the Gulf Cooperation Council. Saudi Arabia and the Gulf countries contributed the bulk of the financial support for the war, whether official or not by encouraging and allowing for a flood of public contributions to reach the Afghani mujahideen. Saudi Arabia's religious virtue also played a big role in the jihad. They have control over the holy shrines; their religious institutions play a prominent media/propaganda role.

Pakistan also played a key role, because its border with Afghanistan extended for more than 2,200 kilometers and included many major crossings that assured the passage of supplies and various forms of other support to the Afghan jihad. The Pakistani military intelligence (ISI) played a crucial role in this regard. It was led by General Hamid Gul, who played a key role in establishing jihad parties and supervising the formation and distribution of financial aid and arms among them. I personally witnessed the provision of services (logistics), and various types of support to the field, that even extended to a limited participation of the Pakistani army in the fighting, especially the use of heavy weapons during border battles of Jalalabad in 1989.

As for Egypt, it has been one of the most prominent participants. It had an agreement with the Americans to repay part of its debts in the form of arms sent to Afghanistan through Pakistan. And I also witnessed this; it was commonplace for us to have opened some boxes of ammunition and weapons that had the insignia of the Egyptian army.

The third ally, which was introduced by America, or rather, allowed to enter the line of supporters of the Afghan jihad, was the Islamic revival. Emotions raged in the ranks of the revival's leaders. Muslim brothers were being subjected to genocide and brutal occupation from the invading atheists. This is why America gave the green light to Arab rulers and the governments of the Arab and Islamic world to ignite the front of the Islamic movement.

And the Arab and Muslim countries responded to Mr. America, because they wished to polish their reputation by helping other Muslims. Of course, many of these rulers hoped that the Islamic cadres they sent forth would find martyrdom thousands of miles away and therefore not come home to plague them. But the American green light triggered Friday sermons, lectures, conferences, festivals, publications, literature, newspapers, every means of expression and propaganda in the revival arena, in order to promote and advocate the Afghan jihad and call. So, the call and revival of Islam was heard everywhere.

Here I would like to point out two problems, or, if you want to say, two great lies imposed by the Western media, particularly the Americans, and their media information offices in the Arab and Islamic world. . . . These must be clarified to the people in general and Muslims and jihadists in particular. They are:

1. The supposed role of America in the victory of jihad in Afghanistan, and
2. The truth of the uncertain relations between the Afghan Arabs and America during the Afghan jihad.

I want to remind the reader that my testimony comes directly from what I have witnessed in the field and my close proximity to events during this period of time among the jihadis.

The Supposed Role of America in the Victory of Jihad in Afghanistan

The American media is controlled by Jews and Christian Zionists and has sought various means to portray the victory of the Afghan jihad as purely the success of American policy and CIA programs in Afghanistan. They have presented this lie through various means of propaganda, starting with films like *Rambo*, which showed his invasion of Afghanistan, where he shot down aircraft, destroyed strongholds, and liberated hostages. Rambo rode horses, led armored vehicles, and flew a Russian helicopter! And, though injured repeatedly, did not die! He was able to impress his audience with his muscles and give out guidance to the Afghan people with his half-paralyzed lip. And in the end, he brought the message that, without America, the war would not be won.

The American media also focused their lies on the role of Stinger missiles and how they brought victory in the Afghan jihad. There is no end to stories about how they turned the tide of the battle when the Russian planes began falling from the sky! This lie has been published by various media and advertising, documentary films, books, the press, and intelligence officer memoirs, and so forth. Note that the Americans only sent a limited number of Stinger missiles ten years after the Soviet Union entered Afghanistan and just before their retreat. In fact, they were not even used in the last decisive battles, and only a limited number of aircraft were ever brought down by Stingers.

I don't know on what facts people believe these lies. The Afghan people sacrificed more that two million martyrs, and five million refugees, out of a population of not more than sixteen million people. Their determination is what won the war. For instance, the Stingers had no role in the destruction of more than fifty thousand of the Russian armored military vehicles and the killing of more than thirty thousand Russian soldiers on the ground, along with over one hundred and fifty thousand communist Afghan militia.

The Truth about Relations between the Afghan Arabs and America during the Afghan Jihad

The global media present this lie as it were a fact:

> American intelligence (CIA) created the "Afghan Arabs" and their leaders such as Sheikh Osama bin Laden, and Sheikh 'Abdallah 'Azzam, for the destruction of the Soviet Union. This creation then turned against them and some of them destroyed their Towers in New York and Washington, while most returned to their home countries to attack and kill American nationals, and to fight the rulers of the Arab and Muslim world. Thus, the phenomenon of armed jihad in the Arab world is a product of the Afghan jihad, and therefore is a CIA creation, which has gotten out of control.

This is an extremely dangerous lie and demeans the reputation of jihad and jihadists. The truth is that the Arabic jihad in Afghanistan is the outgrowth of previous Arab jihads in other areas of the Islamic world. The modern jihadi is the outcome of the Islamic revival of the 1930s and directly descends from it in the early 1960s. Many of the jihad, the most momentous jihad experiences, occurred between the early 1960s and early 1980s, predating the Afghan jihad by twenty years. Sheikh 'Abdallah 'Azzam, for instance, is the symbol of the mujahideen in Palestine, and the Jordanian regime exiled him from Amman for his jihadi theories and his opposition to the regime. And Sheikh Osama bin Laden grew up in the Islamic revival and supported more than one movement for jihad in the Arab lands. For example, he contributed to the jihad in Syria in the early 1980s before heading to Afghanistan.

Also, many of the cadres, trainers, and top leaders who carried the task of establishing camps and the establishment of the infrastructure of the Arab jihad in Afghanistan belonged to Arab organizations and jihadi cadres in Egypt, Palestine, Syria, Lebanon, and Yemen and other places. They were the nucleus of the Arabs flocking to Afghanistan to join the mujahideen, a force that grew to approximately forty thousand Arab mujahideen during the early 1990s.

As for Americans helping to train Arabs or helping structure training programs, these are mere lies and fabrications. I have personally worked in the area of military training and was in contact with leaders of the Arab jihad in Afghanistan. I can personally attest that the notion of American helping in training is unfounded.

As far as the allegation of a CIA connection, perpetrated by the media, and that the mujahideen were brought to destroy the Soviet Union, this is false. For instance, Sheikh 'Abdallah 'Azzam was among these mujahideen, and he was not in league with the CIA. I knew him and often went to see him. I even worked with him for a short time. However, the bulk of my work was with Sheikh Osama bin Laden. The goals of Sheikh 'Abdallah were brief, and he often talked about them in his tapes and lectures:

1. The Establishment of an Islamic State in Afghanistan—Starting from there, he planned expanding to the liberation to Palestine and Jerusalem. He used to talk about going to liberate Moscow and Beijing and Jerusalem from Afghanistan. This was his hope and his thinking.
2. The Militarization of Young Muslims—This was the second goal of Sheikh 'Abdallah, and he summarized it as follows: I want to have at least forty mujahideen from each Arab country, half of them to become martyrs and the other half to return to their country to carry the call of jihad.

His second goal occurred to a degree he never imagined. More than forty thousand young Arab-Muslim non-Afghans came to Afghanistan. Over half of them were trained militarily and over half of these participated in fighting. There were (in eight years) approximately one thousand martyrs. Most of the rest returned home to continue jihad from there. Just by looking at the tapes, books, speeches, and heritage of the martyr Sheikh 'Abdallah 'Azzam—Abu Muhammad—you can see the enormous size of the hatred that the sheikh harbored for America and its collaborators. Why would he not hate them? He is one of their victims in Palestine, Jordan, and then Pakistan, where he was ordered to be killed on an American order in the era of Benazir Bhutto and her interior minister, Nasrullah Babaar.

About Sheikh Osama bin Laden

Bin Laden has faced strong accusations and there were many writers and books filled with slanders. They said that there is a close relationship between the Bin Laden family and [George] Bush Senior in the petroleum industry; particularly with one of Osama bin Laden's brothers. Moreover, it was said that bin Laden was working closely with Saudi intelligence in

Peshawar and that he was preparing and organizing the Arabic jihad in Afghanistan at the behest and under the supervision of Saudi intelligence.

There were many allegations and lies in the media connecting bin Laden with Saudi intelligence as well as American intelligence. Some of the accusations went so far as to declare bin Laden an official agent of the CIA. They claim that he only turned against them when the Americans invaded Saudi Arabia and settled there after what they called the war and liberation of Kuwait. Some of them went even further and considered him still to be an agent when New York was struck. They claim it was done for the benefit of the Jews and that U.S. intelligence had prior information about the attack and chose not to prevent it in order to use the incident as a pretext to attack the Arab and Muslim countries and to destroy Afghanistan as well as invade Iraq!

They presented such evidence as that the Americans could not find Osama bin Laden and this was done intentionally! Many continue to go on with this unreasonable fiction. The reality and truth is simpler and does not need all these complications.

Sheikh Osama bin Laden made his way to Afghanistan after the Russian invasion to offer financial support to the Afghans. A trustworthy man told me in 1986 that bin Laden decided to settle in Afghanistan and to fight in the Afghan jihad. There was a sheikh called 'Abdullah 'Azzam who had established a service agency in 1984. Osama bin Laden worked with the sheikh for a period of time. Subsequently, he separated from him and created his own organization, which he called al Qaida in the beginning of 1988. He broke with the sheikh because of the increasing number of Arab mujahideen who came from Saudi Arabia and Yemen who had a very close relationship with Osama bin Laden.

His move from Saudi Arabia to Afghanistan was public knowledge and legal. There was no opposition to the move from the Saudi government, because at that time there was agreement between the Saudi government and the U.S. government on matters concerning the Afghan jihad. This state of affairs continued until 1990.

When the Kuwait war broke out, Sheikh Osama reestablished al Qaida for jihadist goals both inside and outside Afghanistan. His views were shared by the other mujahideen organizations, which wanted to use Afghanistan as a training ground for members of al Qaida. This was being done by other groups as well, and like others, he worked toward a general goal, which was the creation of an Islamic state after Afghanistan's liberation. I myself worked intermittently in the field of military training in different al Qaida camps between 1988 and 1991. I also worked as a lecturer in the field of Islamic jurisprudence and politics. I also taught guerilla tactics.

Through my work, I was involved with the founders and senior members in the Arab-Afghan jihad and know that at that time al Qaida had no interest in operations outside of Afghan territory. Sheikh Osama's only outside project was directed at Yemen. In addition to that, Osama supported and funded other jihadist organizations and groups in many places. To the best of my knowledge and because I was close to Sheikh bin Laden at the time, I believe that what I have said is the truth.

In 1991 I left Afghanistan and returned to my residence in Spain, cutting off my relationship with them. I did not have any contact with them again until 1996, when we all gathered at the invitation of the Taliban in Afghanistan. Sheikh Osama had by now traveled, with most of the senior members, to Sudan. There was no indication that they went there for jihad.

The field of Arab jihad in Afghanistan during the days of the Soviet jihad was complicated because of the enormous role of Saudi intelligence and different agencies in military and other aid. Many of their officials and representatives had a direct relationship with the Arab Service, which was headed by Sheikh Abdullah Azzam and Sheikh Osama bin Laden. Sheikh Azzam and Sheikh Osama, along with the others, considered the relationship with the Saudis as useful work for the Afghan jihad. The mujahideen hid no secrets from Saudi or Pakistani intelligence. However, there were other jihadist groups that did not work with Saudi or Pakistani intelligence because they did not trust them. I was one of them. This was the case even though I was close to Sheikh bin Laden during that time.

It was said that the Americans had been training and supporting the Arab mujahideen from al Qaida. This is a blatant lie. The Arab jihad has been guided by the Salafist ideology and did not deal with certain individuals in the Saudi government when they came to offer their help or open up camps, such as the military consul [Abu Mazin] at the Saudi embassy. If the mujahideen refused to deal with officials from the Saudi government, then how can it be said that they cooperated with foreigners and Americans.

I recognize that the media and various books that dealt with Sheikh al-mujahideen Osama bin Laden did not give him credit for that period and afterwards. They did not recognize or explain the timing of his ideological shift as well as the changes in his methods. Because they ignored this shift in his ideology and methods, bin Laden and al Qaida adopted a position against the United States of America.

There were two important factors that caused this situation and I will mention them in order of importance:

1. Sheikh Osama had basically built al Qaida on the basis of the struggles of the Egyptian organization called Al-jihad al-masri ("the Egyptian jihad"), as well as on the training activities of other jihadists in various other places. Most of the mujahideen were not originally members of al Qaida. They came together for the sake of cooperation and mutual benefit. They committed themselves to their ideology, and I was one of them. We were, in fact, so committed to our ideology that during training in our camps, we would fire shots at the portrait of King Fahd and other high princes in the Saudi family.

   Through their books, conversations, lectures, behavior, and so forth, the young al Qaida members made a profound impact on Sheikh Osama when he arrived in Afghanistan. Many young men from Saudi Arabia arrived in Afghanistan for jihad at the time. They had similar thoughts and feelings as Sheikh Osama and called their ideology the Saudi Islamic Awakening (Al-Sahwa). This Islamic awakening is a blend of the Muslim Brotherhood ideas and the official Wahabi school. I was very close to Sheikh Osama at this time, and he discussed this subject with me many times. Despite what many others thought, Sheikh Osama and the other Saudi mujahideen did not consider the Saudi government illegitimate. King Fahd and the Al-Saud family are Muslims and legitimate under Islamic law. This is the case even though they are corrupt and decadent. They are respected by the official senior *ulema* (religious scholars). When the *ulema* issued a fatwa (religious decree), the mujahideen, including Osama, would respect it. There was no similarity in thought between us (the foreign jihadist) and the brothers in Afghanistan. The only thing we shared in common was our religion and our dedication to the Afghan jihad. There were differences in opinion as well as in operation. Moreover, there were differences in jihadist thought and disagreements over political objectives. These differences amongst us were very sharp and clear. Sheikh Osama reflected on jihadist ideology and came to adopt it and soon became one of the most symbolic figures in jihadist ideology.

2. The position of the Saudi government and its administration as well as its official *ulema* during the Kuwait war and the presence of American

troops on Saudi soil. What followed these events were major changes that revealed the magnitude of the disaster and the role of the great infidel that governed the Arab Peninsula. The religious establishment told lies about the state of affairs. Sheikh Osama, using his keen mind, recognized the reality of the situation. He understood the goals of the Americans in the region. His stay in Sudan (1992–96) gave him time to reflect on the situation. During this period, he shifted his view of the Saudi government from peaceful opposition through the media to more serious and stern opposition. He accused the government and the religious establishment of being liars.

When the Sudanese government expelled Sheikh Osama and he returned to Afghanistan in 1996, there was a group around him that was inspired by an ideology that consisted of an international opposition against the U.S. government and its allies. Sheikh Osama was affected by the jihadist wave, concluding that if he wanted to get rid of corrupt regimes in the Arab and Islamic world, including the Saudi regime, he would have to face America.

Sheikh Osama determined that if a strike was made at the American presence, the Saudis would be forced to defend their American allies. Once this happened the Saudis would lose their legitimacy in the eyes of the people. When they lost their legitimacy, the religious establishment would have to defend the Saudi government. And when that happened, the religious establishment would also lose its legitimacy. Sheikh Osama chose this second strategy, and I think he was very accurate in that choice, because it indicates that he understood the whole situation in Saudi Arabia and its religious, social, and political makeup.

Following the collapse of the Soviet Union, Sheikh Osama witnessed the downfall of the dictatorial states in the Warsaw Pact, such as the East German government, Romania, Poland, and others. He became convinced that if the United States collapsed, all of the corrupt regimes in the Arab and Muslim world would also collapse. For these reasons, he concentrated his efforts on the jihad against America. When people visited him, he would tell them that the mujahideen must fight against the head of the snake, as he called America.

I came to Afghanistan in 1996 after bin Laden had been there for four to five months to conduct an interview with him for a BBC documentary concerning opposition to the Saudi government. Later, in May 1997, I interviewed him for CNN concerning Islamic studies. I sat with him [Osama] many times and came to share his beliefs. Because of this, I returned to Afghanistan to reside there permanently during the Taliban period.

Throughout my four-year stay, I had many chances to visit Osama. I also visited many other friends who were working with him. When I was in his presence, I would tell his Arab and Persian guests what his beliefs were. I spoke about his views to the senior members of Al-Sahwa (awakening) and the young mujahideen. I think that the ideas Osama selected to launch the jihad against the Americans are the key to solving the problems in the Arab Peninsula and the whole region. Notwithstanding my opinion of the details of the operation and the organizational framework needed to carry out this operation, his ideas are basically correct.

As he laid out the reasons for jihad, Sheikh Osama became more and more committed to the struggle against America. Consequently, he established the tactics for this struggle. The media and various commentators have stated that Osama worked with the Americans during the Russian jihad and then turned against them. Such statements are false. The media attacks him because they are his enemies and despise him. These lies are built on spite and ignorance. The truth, in short, was that at the time Osama and the other Muslims had similar goals to the Americans. Their mutual goal was to drive the Russians out of Afghanistan. When the war ended, everyone became aware that the next enemy would be the remaining superpower. This superpower would establish a new global order and would invade Bilad al-Haramain [The Land of the Two Holy Places, that is, Saudi Arabia]. It will prepare a new Crusader campaign to invade the Middle East. Bin Laden upheld his duty and declared jihad against this superpower, as did his network.

Other independent Islamic groups also declared jihad against the superpower. I was one of them. To make my point clear, I will offer a possible scenario: If the French or other Europeans, such as the Russians, or even China, were to help us in our jihad against America, which is a possibility, there will be shared interests and goals between us. However, if we overcome America, then it is likely that France, Russia, or China will, in their turn, invade our land. If this takes place, we will direct our jihad against them. However, if we find that they are cooperative and wish to be good neighbors, they will see that our religion has a peaceful side to it. Alas, I do not think this will be the case, because in all likelihood they will conspire against us at the appropriate time and circumstances.

The Influence of the Afghan Jihad on the Current Jihadist Movement

During this period of religious growth, which took place during the period of 1986–92, Peshawar became the center of contact and interaction between various groups and different ideas, such as different political and reformist movements as well as jihadist trends. Many of these ideas, including non-Islamic beliefs, were adopted by the Islamic awakening. Moreover, the city was crowded with hundreds of Arab and Islamic charity groups and agencies, even foreign agencies. Furthermore, hundreds of influential Islamic figures, such as noted *ulema*, sheikhs, poets, writers, political leaders, and so forth, came to Peshawar for various reasons.

I want to discuss the effects of the interaction in Peshawar on the contemporary jihadist movement. In the early days, a group of no more than ten people went to Pakistan to help the Afghan mujahideen after the Soviet Union declared its intention to invade Afghanistan. So, from 1979 to 1982 there were only these ten, and only three or four of these individuals entered Afghanistan to participate in the jihad. However, during that period, a number of individuals traveled to Afghanistan to provide financial assistance to the Afghan mujahideen and then departed.

The history of the Arab jihad in Afghanistan did not really begin to unfold until in 1984, when Sheikh 'Abdullah 'Azzam devoted his entire time to the Afghan jihad. I heard from some people that he was working to support the Afghan jihad in Amman, Jordan. But, the authorities in Jordan harassed him and he was forced to flee to Islamabad. There he worked as a professor of sharia at the Islamic University. He did many important things there such as the following:

- He established a "service bureau" to distribute aid to the mujahideen and Afghan refugees.
- He established a magazine called *Al-Jihad*, which served as his publicity forum for the Afghan jihad.
- He established a camp called Al-Sada near the Afghan border, located inside tribal areas in Pakistani territory, to train the Arab youths who were coming in small numbers since 1984.
- He traveled to many places to publicize the Afghan jihad and urged the youths to travel to those camps. While touring, he declared that jihad was a duty for Muslims.

I heard from some of Sheikh 'Abdullah 'Azzam's tapes that the number of youths in Al-Sada camp in 1984 amounted to twelve mujahideen. There were a total of twenty-five mujahideen by 1985. In mid 1986, this number rose to slightly fewer than two hundred mujahideen. These mujahideen were from various nationalities, most being from Saudi Arabia, Egypt, and Palestine.

At the end of 1985 or beginning of 1986, Sheikh Osama bin Laden arrived in Afghanistan to participate in the jihad. In previous visits, bin Laden would come to offer financial support and then leave. But this time, he came to personally fight in the jihad. Sheikh Osama bin Laden, with the cooperation of some senior members of the Egyptian jihad who had arrived earlier, established a military base on a route that led to a densely forested and mountainous region. This military base was located in a region called Jaje.

However, the Russians attacked this military base during Ramadan in 1986, and our young mujahideen, who were with Sheikh Osama and Sheikh 'Abdullah 'Azzam, fought a month-long fierce battle against the Russians. They were able to gain a major victory over the Russians and were even able to kill some of the Russian commanders. This battle, which was a victory for the Arab mujahideen, was widely publicized by Sheikh 'Abdullah 'Azzam through his media network.

Osama bin Laden went on a publicity campaign in Saudi Arabia, and as a result of this campaign, Arab mujahideen came to Afghanistan in large numbers. By 1987 their numbers had risen to a few thousand, most being from Saudi Arabia and Yemen. From 1989 to 1990, the number of mujahideen climbed to more than forty thousand Arab and Muslim fighters from various countries. Following the assassination of Sadat in 1981 and throughout the Mubarak period, the pressure on Egyptian Islamicists was so great that many senior members and their followers fled to Peshawar.

When the jihadist uprising, which took place in Syria from 1975 to 1982, was completely destroyed, many of the jihadists fled to all parts of the globe. Some of them ended up in Afghanistan. My friends and I settled in Peshawar and I was lucky to be there. Some jihadists from Palestine, who were students and friends of Sheikh 'Abdullah 'Azzam, followed him there. There was a military jihadist movement in Libya that was crushed by the Libyan government. The surviving senior members fled to Peshawar. The civil war in Lebanon had ended and the Sunni Muslim groups in the north of Lebanon had been attacked by Syrian intelligence.

Subsequently, some of them fled to the region. There were even some Islamists from Iraqi Kurdistan.

These individuals, who came from all over the Islamic world, formed a jihadist movement in Afghanistan. In time, this movement expanded. The ideologies of the Egyptian Jihad and the Islamic Group had a profound influence on the other jihadist groups, even though there was factional strife between them. There were students of the sharia, Salafists, and Sururis from Saudi Arabia. In addition, there were other groups from different places. These various jihadist groups espoused the notion of a righteous Islamic government. They argued for wa'la [wa'la means "loyalty"; by that they mean loyalty to their religious leader]. They also called for the implementation of jihadist ideology throughout the Arabic- and Persian-speaking regions.

The Syrian jihad, as well as the author's book concerning Arab history, had profound effects on the Afghan jihad. Furthermore, the school of Al-Sahwa made a deep impact on the Afghan jihad. This impact was felt deeply in the medical, educational, and humanitarian professions. The experiments in jihadist ideology were expanded and internalized by classic Salafists, Muslim Brothers, and official as well as unofficial Saudi Islamic agencies and other similar organizations.

The refugee tents and training camps of Pakistan and Afghanistan became centers of dialogue and discussion between the various Islamic schools of thought, and the environment was permeated by the notion of jihad. These people considered jihad the correct way in life, and the ideology of jihad came to have a strong influence on the Arab mujahideen. Thousands of young men who came from all over the Islamic world were inspired by this jihadist ideology, which coalesced into a complete and all-embracing school of thought. It was called the Arab Afghan school of thought.

As the jihadist experiment ripened, new jihadist organizations were formed in many countries like Libya, Algeria, Tunisia, Morocco, Jordan, Iraq, and Lebanon. This also took place in other Islamic countries like the Philippines, Indonesia, Turkey, and others. In short, it can be said that a new generation of jihadists was born with unique views and attitudes. This generation was born in the Arab jihad in Afghanistan. They called this jihadist generation the "Afghan Arabs." They had clear attitudes and correct beliefs about jihad. They were motivated by their commitment, belief, and confidence in Allah to crush the great power. They were no longer afraid of this power or the power of the governments in our countries, because they had been triumphant over the Soviet Union. It is correct to say that anyone who participated in this battle has achieved an Arab victory against the great power of the time. Through this victory, the Arabs were elevated to a state of greatness after years of humiliation.

The Jihadist Movement and the Stage of Dispersion and Asylum (1991–96)

When the Afghan jihadists were at the doors of Kabul and other main cities had fallen to them, the Americans and Westerners hatched two plans for Afghanistan. The first plan involved Afghans and the second one was directed at Arabs. The Afghan plan involved using the government of Pakistan to achieve it. The plan was to prevent the establishment of an Islamic state in Afghanistan that would be ruled under Islamic law (sharia). To achieve this goal, the Americans wanted to foment a civil war among the different factions to exhaust their armaments as well as to get rid of thousands of jihadists.

From 1992 to 1996, they were largely successful in this endeavor. Consequently, the jihadists fled and went into hiding during this period. When the mujahideen returned to their respective countries, their governments did not treat them like heroes even though they had worked with Arab governments and the Americans toward a common goal. Rather, many were arrested, interrogated, tortured, and accused of many crimes.

These events made the mujahideen aware of the fact that the Arab governments were not ruling according to Islamic law, and they began to view these governments as traitors. For the reasons stated above, they created secret organizations to fight against these corrupt regimes with the goal of overthrowing them and establishing Islamic states. As a result, they were confronted by the intelligence and security services and were eventually destroyed or dispersed. Many of these jihadists could not stay in their countries. Consequently, they spread all over the globe prior to the war on terrorism. Those who could not return went to the following countries:

- Western Europe—Many of them went to Western Europe as political refugees, the most important countries being Britain and the Scandinavian states, followed by other Western countries as well as some Eastern European countries, Australia, and Canada. Most of these refugees were senior members in Arab Afghan organizations.
- Sudan—Bashir and his supporters had taken control of the government and established a regime which was Islamic. From 1991 to 1995, their

policy was to open Sudan to jihadist organizations. As a result, many jihadist groups, such as the organization of Al-Jihad, the Islamic Group in Egypt, Sheikh Osama and al Qaida, the Libyan Armed Islamic Group, and others came to Sudan.

- Other Countries That Did Not Pose a Security Threat—There were states that did not pose a security threat to the jihadists from the various Arab countries. This was prior to a security agreement between Arab and various other countries concerning terrorism and related issues. The countries that did not pose a threat included Yemen, Turkey, Philippines, Indonesia, and Thailand, as well as countries in Latin America and even some African countries. Many Arab Afghans went to these countries.

- Bosnia and Chechnya—When the Afghan jihad was terminated, a new jihadist front formed in Bosnia (1993–95). During these two years, Muslims were being massacred by Croats and Serbs. When Muslims heard of these massacres, thousands of young mujahideen from the Arab and Islamic world went to Bosnia. Some Arab Afghan mujahideen, led by the martyred commander Khattab, also went to Bosnia. In the last quarter of the twentieth century, Khattab undertook an honorable jihad in many places as well as Bosnia.

The years 1992–95 were largely uneventful for these political refugees. However, they were able to spread their jihadist ideas in the abovementioned countries. But already in 1990 the United States had launched a war on terrorism that escalated over the years, reaching a high point in December 2001. This war had been mild until the year 1995. But after 1995, the United States set up a program that was aimed at destroying terrorism. This program involved the expulsion of jihadists who had been residing in the aforementioned countries, where governments unleashed their security services against the jihadists.

Many of the jihadists had been publishing jihadist ideas in different countries, especially in Scandinavia and Britain, where conditions were favorable for the preaching and publishing of these views. When the Americans launched their program against terrorists, it became more difficult to carry out jihadist work. However, they were able to publish many books, lectures, speeches, and so forth. They visited many mosques and preached their views to the congregation with the aim of creating an Islamic awakening. As a result, there was a flowering of jihadist and Islamic ideas, more so than in Arab and Islamic countries.

Countries in the Arab and Islamic world criticized Western countries for allowing the jihadists to spread these views, which they associated with terrorist groups. Subsequently, there were a number of conferences in Western countries that discussed the ideas and views expressed by these Muslim refugees. They concluded that the ideas and views expressed by these people were those of militant Islamic terrorists.

Consequently, from 1995 to 2000, many governments in the West and elsewhere attacked and shut down the operations of these groups. While I was in Britain (1994–97), I witnessed a unique jihadist experiment. I was able to write for many jihadist magazines, such as *Al-Fajr* magazine, which was run by the Armed Islamic Group of Libya. I was also able to publish for a magazine called *Al-Mujhadoon*, which was run the by the Jihad Group of Egypt, as well *Al-Ansar*, which was owned by the Armed Islamic Group of Algeria. I was able to write for *Al-Ansar* while it was still a jihadist-oriented magazine. Moreover, I was able to attend many lectures, meetings, and so forth in London. Many of these lectures and meetings were published or recorded and sent to different parts of the world. This was done to spread the Islamic awakening.

This was the state of affairs when we were struck by a security-intelligence "tornado," which led to the deportation and imprisonment of many jihadists all over the world. At the same time, Sudan and Yemen were pressured until they expelled many extremists. Similarly, Turkey, Syria, and Jordan arrested and repatriated many Islamists, while hundreds of jihadists were harassed and arrested in Europe. Many of them were arrested and imprisoned without any judicial procedure. They suffered the same fate as their brothers in the Arab and Islamic world and the third world. The jihadists entered a new, problematic phase. They were in need of a refuge that would allow them to regroup and continue their work. By the will of Allah, this refuge was to be Afghanistan.

The Arab Afghans under the Rule of the Taliban (1996–2001)

I want to write about the contemporary Islamic jihadist awakening, because I am one of the few left alive who can write about this historical experience. My goal is to transmit these views to the next generation, especially to those who undertake jihad.

Our era is one of injustice and lack of righteousness. I feel that I have a historical responsibility to write this book. For the sake of brevity, I will discuss the contemporary jihadist situation without going into too much detail. I will make my argument through the following points:

- The Taliban movement had its beginnings in the province of Kandahar, which is in the southeast of Afghanistan. The movement appeared in late 1993. Subsequently, they were able to take control of central, southern, and eastern Afghanistan. Following the capture of Kabul in 1996, they proclaimed Afghanistan an Islamic emirate and Mullah Muhammad Omar was chosen to be the leader of the Afghan government.

- When the Americans launched their program to combat terrorism in the early 1990s, which reached a high point in 1995, the senior members of different jihadist groups decided to return to Afghanistan because of the favorable conditions prevailing in the country at the time. Consequently, many individuals and groups returned to Afghanistan in 1996.

- The Taliban welcomed the returning jihadists, including Sheikh Osama and the members of al Qaida. Moreover, they welcomed many of the older Arab jihadists. As a result, many jihadists from all over the world flocked to Afghanistan.

- The sharia was the only law in 94 percent of Afghan territory. The Taliban proclaimed that Afghanistan was the only "dar al-Islam" (house of Islam) on earth. As a result, many Muslims from all over the Islamic world immigrated to Afghanistan. By 2000 the Taliban had established many camps, tents, and shelters for these Arab Muslim immigrants in the main cities of Afghanistan, especially in Kabul, Kandahar, and the eastern cities, such as Khost and Jalalabad.

- Many moved to Afghanistan in spite of the economic and political sanctions imposed on the country. Moreover, the international media was constantly attacking the Taliban government. From 1996 to 2001, thousands of people came in and out of Afghanistan.

- From among these thousands of people, 350 families as well as 1,400 mujahideen and Arab immigrants from different nationalities, and hundreds of Central Asian men who left their families behind, decided to stay in Afghanistan for different reasons. Most of the Central Asian men, who came mainly from Uzbekistan and Tajikistan, belonged to various local Islamic movements. They fled from the last corrupt communist regimes in the world. Others fled from Chinese-controlled eastern Turkistan. Many of the older commanders in the Arab jihadist organizations became hopeful about reviving the jihad in their respective countries with the hope of overthrowing these corrupt governments and establishing Islamic states.

- Many new groups, coming from different Arab countries, came to Afghanistan to organize for jihad. They tried to adopt the tactics of the other jihadist groups.

- Most of the immigrants who entered Afghanistan were there for jihad, even though they did not belong to any jihadist organizations. These jihadists could be broken down into the following groups based on their numerical strength:

  — Trainers. This group of people came for a short period for the purposes of training. They usually only stayed for the duration of the training period, which could take from a few months to a year.

  — Immigrants. This group of people either arrived as single individuals or with families. They came to reside in the dar al-Islam permanently under the rule of the Taliban. They came to rebuild Afghanistan as well as to fight in the jihad. They had no jihadist goals outside of Afghanistan or against their respective governments. This group of people had no enemies either inside or outside the country.

  — Jihadist organizations. These organizations came from various Arab and Islamic countries. They had well-defined jihadist goals against their respective countries. They came to Afghanistan to rebuild their organizations as they had existed in their respective countries. To that end, these organizations tended to be "ethnically based, secretive and hierarchically structured."

  — Sheikh Osama bin Laden and al Qaida and their followers. Al Qaida's plan was to organize a jihad against the United States of America. They wanted to use Afghanistan as their base of operations. In this struggle, their protectors would be the new government of Afghanistan, which was the Taliban and their emir, Mullah Muhammad Omar.

  — The Central Asian organizations and groups. These people had different aims and goals. Some of them wanted to reside permanently in Afghanistan and support the dar al-Islam as they carried out jihad. Others wanted to undertake jihad in their native countries. There were two large groups in the latter category, those being the Uzbek

Mujhadoon and the East Turkistan Mujhadoon. East Turkistan was occupied by China. There were other jihadist groups as well.
— The Pakistani Mujahadoon. This group consisted of individuals who had been students at religious schools (madrassas) in Pakistan. Their ideology was very similar to that of the Taliban. Moreover, there were other jihadist organizations that had fought in Kashmir. Some mujahideen were not affiliated with any of these groups. Because Afghanistan and Pakistan shared a border, the number of these mujahideen was much larger than any of the aforementioned groups.

This was a period of jihadist growth and expansion. Sheikh Osama bin Laden launched many media campaigns against America and its wars to subvert Islam. He called on Muslims to liberate the lands of Al-Haramain from the American and Western occupation. Moreover, he urged Muslims to fight against America because it was supporting Israel and Zionism in Palestine. He also called for the liberation of Al-Aqsa mosque.

These campaigns were well coordinated and directed and the American media responded with a huge media campaign of its own against bin Laden. There was a heated struggle between the American media and the jihadist media. Both media campaigns were broadcast to millions of viewers through American, Arab, and international satellite TV. Al-Jazeera TV broadcast this struggle to hundreds of millions of Muslim viewers throughout the world. As a result, jihadist ideas became global and well known to the Muslim viewers. Despite American attempts to link the jihadist movement with Osama bin Laden and al Qaida, it had no effect on the various jihadist organizations or their goals. They remained ethnically based, secretive, and hierarchically structured organizations. They also remained independent organizations with no ties to bin Laden.

Following the September 11 attacks, the United States officially blamed the attacks on these independent organizations and bin Laden. There were also at this time many upheavals in the Arab and Islamic world. One of the most important of these upheavals was the Palestinian intifada (2000), which began with stones and developed into armed attacks and suicide operations. The situation in the Arab world steadily deteriorated because of the destructive sanctions imposed on Iraq since 1991, and the United States, along with governments in the Arab and Islamic world, undertaking an international war on terrorism.

As a result, Osama bin Laden became a symbolic figure for the Arab jihadists in Afghanistan. Bin Laden and the other jihadists also became the biggest subject of discussion in the international and Arab media. This helped bin Laden become a major influence on the Islamic awakening movement and other jihadist organizations.

By the year 2000, the Arab jihadist groups had become more entrenched in Afghanistan. There were fourteen major jihadist organizations in the country that were officially recognized by the Taliban government. They were well entrenched in the security services as well as in the Ministry of Defense and Interior. These jihadist organizations coordinated their activities very closely with the Taliban government. However, the Pakistani groups had their own unique arrangements, which differed from other organizations'. These fourteen organizations included the following:

The Non-Arab Groups

1. The Uzbek Mujahadoon. In terms of numbers, this group was larger than the others. Their goal was to fight a jihad against the Uzbek government and topple the regime of Karimov, the American-backed communist. This jihad would only take place after the Taliban consolidated its hold over Afghanistan. The Uzbeks would be trained and organized by the Taliban. The Uzbek emir, Muhammad Tahir Jahn, recognized Mullah Muhammad Omar as the official imam. The military commander of the Uzbeks, Jumah Bey, also recognized Mullah Omar as the official imam. There were roughly five million Uzbeks in Afghanistan. Most of them had fled to Afghanistan during the era of Russian imperialism as well as during the reigns of Vladimir Lenin and Josef Stalin. The Uzbek jihadists were well organized and educated. Moreover, they were well financed by the Uzbek diaspora.
2. The immigrants from Chinese-controlled eastern Turkistan. This was a small group that had secretly fled the Chinese-controlled region. Their situation in eastern Turkistan was very difficult because of Chinese immigration into their homeland, which was encouraged by the government and which resulted in a change in the ethnic makeup of the region. The Muslims were turned into a minority in eastern Turkistan, which the Chinese called "Xinjiang," which means the new land in Mandarin. Mao Zedong had instituted a cruel communist program against the Muslims of eastern Turkistan. The jihadists of

eastern Turkistan went back to their homeland and recruited mujahideen who were brought back to Afghanistan and trained in military tactics that were to be used against the Chinese government. Their emir was the martyr Abu Muhammad Al-Turkistani. He was an active and pious mujhad, who was killed by Pakistani forces in November of 2003. This group recognized Mullah Omar as the official imam. However, facing strong American pressure, the Taliban ordered the East Turkistan group to cease its attacks against China, because the Taliban wanted friendly relations with China as a way to counter the American threat.

3. The Turkish mujahideen. This was a small group composed of Kurds and Turks. This group worked in a very secretive fashion. Their program consisted mainly of training. I do not know if they had any program for jihad in their country.

Arab Groups

1. The organization of al Qaida under the leadership of Sheikh Osama bin Laden. Their program is well known. As I mentioned above, Sheikh Osama recognized Mullah Omar as the official imam.

2. The armed Islamic group of Libya. Their emir was Abu Abdallah Al-Sadq. Their goal was to wage a jihad against the al-Qadafi government in Libya. Moreover, they wanted to aid and support any jihadist issues around the world. Finally, they supported the Taliban government.

3. The Islamic jihadist group in Morocco. Their program consisted of training Libyan jihadists. Their goal was to overthrow the Moroccan government. The emir of this group was Abu Abdullah Al-Sheriff.

4. The jihadist group of Egypt. This group had dispersed and lost many of its members. Their goal was to rebuild their organization and recruit new members. Moreover, they wanted to declare jihad against the Egyptian regime. Their emir was Sheikh and Doctor Ayman Al-Zawhiri.

5. The Islamic group of Egypt. In terms of numbers, this group was very small. They did not carry out any significant jihadist activities. They had rejected the idea of jihad against the Egyptian government. Most of them resided in Iran. Before the fall of the Taliban, some of them had immigrated to Afghanistan.

6. The gathering of Algerian mujahideen. Their goal was to recruit Algerians and train them for a jihad against the Algerian government. This government had committed numerous atrocities against them.

7. The gathering of Tunisian mujahideen. Their goal was to recruit young Tunisians and train them for a jihad against the Tunisian government. They had a number of training camps. Some of them had participated in the Bosnian jihad.

8. The gathering of Jordanian and Palestinian mujahideen. The program of this group consisted of recruitment and training for a jihad in Jordan and Palestine. Their emir was Abu Musab Al-Zarqawi.

9. The Khaldan Camp is a general training camp. This is the oldest Arab camp. It goes back to the days of Sheikh 'Abdullah 'Azaam and his Services Bureau. The emir of this camp is Sheikh Al-Mujhad, known by the name Ibn Al-Sheikh Salah Al-Libi, and his supporter, Abu Zubayda. The goal of the camp was to train and support jihad in any part of the world. The camp was established in 1989. Roughly twenty thousand individuals have been trained in this camp over the years.

10. The Al-Sheikh Abu Khbab Al-Masri Camp is a general training camp. This camp specialized in the use of explosives and chemical weapons.

11. The Foreigner Groups Camp. I established this camp for my group. This group was linked to the Taliban and had a general training camp. There was a center for lectures and studying. I established the camp in 2000. The camp was set up to provide training and education in various fields, such as political thought/ideology, sharia, and military training. This camp was established because the Arab Afghans lacked an adequate facility. Moreover, the camp served as a propagation center for the ideas of the international Islamic resistance movement. This group was tied to the Islamic Emirate of Afghanistan and contributed to the defense of the government. We coordinated our activities with Mullah Omar.

I outlined our goals to Mullah Muhammad Omar. On the 15th of Muharram, 2001, I recognized Mullah Omar as the official imam. Consequently, my group was tied to him and we carried out our work through the Ministry of Defense.

Sheikh Osama and al Qaida attacked two American embassies in Nairobi and Dar-es-Salam. Subsequently, they carried out a suicide operation against the American destroyer USS *Cole*, which was docked in the port of Aden. These attacks occurred during the period from 1997 to 2000. As a result of these attacks, the United States intensified its war against the Taliban and Afghanistan. Sheikh Osama responded to the American threat with a large media campaign that urged Muslims to fight the Americans. The United States then threatened to declare a war against international terrorism, especially against Sheikh Osama, and imposed economic sanctions on Afghanistan and blocked any media broadcast coming from the country.

On September 11, 2001, the United States was attacked by a group of al Qaida members who carried out an historic suicide attack against the Twin Towers in New York and the Pentagon. Even though al Qaida did not take responsibility for the attack, it was no secret who the Americans blamed for the attack. Consequently, the United States decided to invade Afghanistan and topple the Taliban government and put a new puppet regime in its place. Furthermore, the United States wanted to completely annihilate the Taliban and the Arab jihadist groups in the country.

I was in Afghanistan and witnessed the unfolding of these historic events. I do not wish to stray from the subject but, God willing, I will write a book about these events. I will, however, speak briefly in this chapter of the impact of September 11 on the jihadist movement.

I believe that the September 11 incident put a dramatic end to the jihadist movement. The jihadist stage has come to an end, thereby terminating a period that began in the 1960s. The jihadist movement has now entered a difficult stage. From 2001 to 2004, many senior members of different jihadist groups have disappeared as a result of the American campaign against terrorism.

Two years after September 11, the United States invaded Iraq. This invasion introduced a new historical era for the jihadist movement. There was an Islamic awakening not only in the Arab and Islamic world, but also across the entire globe.

The September 11 Attack and Its Consequences

By any scale, the September 11 attack was a devastating blow to the enemy. I hope this will be the beginning of the end for the hegemonic, barbaric state called the United States of America. This country personifies the contemporary barbaric Western civilization. America inherited all of the evil, imperialistic traditions of Europe and Russia. On the basis of this imperialist inheritance, they established a contemporary Zionist-Crusader regime.

Although al Qaida was the dominant organization from among the various Arab Afghan groups in Afghanistan, the Arab Afghan mujahideen were also part of the general jihadist movement. This jihadist movement was composed of mujahideen from all over the Islamic world, and many of these members were jihad-oriented *ulema*, philosophers, writers, and so forth, who only wanted to liberate Islam from corruption through the establishment of an Islamic state. The Americans associated all of these disparate jihadist groups with al Qaida. This was an unrealistic view of the true situation, but by taking this action, the United States was able to brand all these groups as terrorist organizations. This was a cunning pretext, which allowed the United States to declare a war against international terrorism.

When the two towers and the wall of the Pentagon collapsed on the heads of several American generals, there was a corresponding collapse on the Islamic side. There were major losses on the Islamic side, including losses for the Islamic awakening. The jihadist movement and its constituent organizations sustained the heaviest blow. Many of the senior members, as well as others, faced harsh and difficult times. Every Muslim in every part of the world was affected negatively as a result of this war on terrorism. Many jihadist organizations and their members, in fact, did not support the September 11 attack because they felt that it would elicit a terrible response that would harm Muslims across the globe.

Moreover, many Muslims felt that they would be defeated in the war on terrorism. Consequently, many Muslims supported America's war on terrorism in the Islamic world. Furthermore, many Islamic charity groups and aid organizations were shut down following the announcement of the war on terrorism. September 11 also led to the fall of the one and only Islamic emirate in the world that supported jihadist organizations. In this light many of the criticisms coming from the Islamic world seem to be reasonable.

To clarify, if you follow American politics and read the books that are written by American intellectuals and foreign policy analysts, and study the ideas of [Richard] Nixon, [Henry] Kissinger, and [Samuel] Huntington, you will realize that their political goals for the twenty-first century involve world domination, especially hegemony over the third world, the Islamic world, and the Middle East. This program would have been implanted even if the September 11 attacks had never taken place. In his book *Victory without War* Nixon declared that the twenty-first century would be an American century. Moreover, he argued that America should work to undermine and unravel the Soviet Union. Nixon also wanted to hinder the development of China by encouraging ethnic strife. Furthermore, Nixon argued for a "slowing down" of the process of integration and union in Europe as well as a delay in the technological/industrial advancement of East Asia. Finally, he stated that Islam was a reviving force that had to be crushed before it constituted a real threat to the West.

During the Carter administration in the 1970s, the United States created a rapid response force that would be employed to invade the oil-rich countries. In addition, there were political forces that were built on the extremist Crusader ideology. These political forces were inspired by the Bible and the Torah. Their philosophy merged the Zionist outlook with fundamentalist Christianity. Their support of Israel and the Jews was motivated by religion, and they pledged to support Israel until the battle of "har-majdun" in Northern Palestine [The Day of Judgment for Jews]. This battle would also be the signal the second coming of Christ.

There were other evil philosophies, such as the notion of a struggle between civilizations and the eventual dominance of the white race over the earth. The media openly discussed these evil ideas, including neoconservatism and its role in the Bush administration. Western media also addressed and discussed the role of Christian Zionism in the Bush administration.

Following the fall of the Soviet Union, the United States turned its attention toward the Islamic world. The West held many security conferences on what they called Islamic militancy. [Ronald] Reagan, [Margaret] Thatcher, and [Mikhail] Gorbachev held an important meeting in which they declared Islam an enemy of Western civilization. Subsequently, they decided to incorporate the former Warsaw Pact states into NATO, which would spearhead the Crusader wars against Islam. There is ample evidence for the above-mentioned arrangement. However, I will not deal with it here because it is a well-known fact among Arabs and Muslims.

The United States, Israel, and Western Europe were plotting against us even before September 11. The United States would have used any pretext to attack the Muslim world, even if the September 11 attacks had never occurred. This happened in the past when they used the Iraqi invasion of Kuwait as an excuse to place troops in the Arabian Peninsula. Similarly, they fabricated many excuses to invade Iraq in 2003. Moreover, they will use Iraq as a springboard to invade Syria and the Arabian Peninsula. The evidence indicates that the September 11 attack is not the cause behind the American aggression against the Arab and Muslim world. Rather, the 9/11 attack merely accelerated the inevitable American aggression against the Islamic world.

Through the international media and the frequent speeches of politicians, it is well known that the American aggression is motivated by the desire to control the oil of Central Asia. The United States needs a system whereby the oil can be transported from Afghanistan to the Arabian Peninsula. This setup will allow the United States to besiege China as well as to surround Iran from the east. By toppling the Taliban, the United States will prevent the return of any Islamic regime in the country. Moreover, the attack on Afghanistan will serve as a warning to any Islamists attempting to establish an Islamic government in any other place in the world. The U.S. attack on Afghanistan was not motivated by revenge against Sheikh Osama bin Laden and the Arab Afghans or the Central Asian mujahideen. Rather, the Americans attacked Afghanistan because it was ruled according to Islamic law.

The other reason for the aggression had to do with Taliban opposition to the American international order. Moreover, the attack was motivated by American interests in the region. This attack created a situation for the Islamic awakening and jihadist forces that must be confronted immediately. Muslims must know that this attack was carried out by the United States against Islam. It was organized and carried out with the cooperation and support of Jews and European powers, including Russia. When the Soviet Union disintegrated, the Berlin Wall came down and the former Warsaw Pact states joined NATO. The United States and its allies assigned the Arab and Muslim states a role in the war against terrorism. This role was assigned to them prior to September 11.

The war on terrorism is driven by economic and geopolitical interests. The war has deep religious and historical roots. I will not discuss the 9/11 attack, because it has been extensively covered in the media. However, I will mention the impact of 9/11 on the jihadist groups and organizations in Afghanistan.

The Effect of 9/11 on the Jihadist Movement in Afghanistan

The Americans began their aggression by launching a series of air strikes that lasted from October 10 to November 11. For the ground offensive, the Americans relied on the Northern Alliance, which engaged in combat on three fronts. From the north, they advanced toward Kabul. From the southeast on the Pakistan border, they moved toward Kandahar. Lastly, from the northeast, they advanced toward Jalalabad.

The Northern Alliance are a bunch of thieves and criminals. Some of the tribes in the Northern Alliance support the American program, and the Americans helped them capture the cities one by one. The Taliban were besieged and subsequently surrendered to the Americans and their allies. One week after the fall of Kabul, they declared that the Taliban had been defeated and [Hamid] Karzai assumed power. The Americans' ground forces gained control of Afghanistan and began implementing their ugly and dirty program by spending millions of dollars.

Subsequently, the Americans, under the leadership of Bush, declared a war against international terrorism. Pakistan aided the United States in the killing and imprisonment of the mujahideen who were inside its territory. In addition to America's main allies, the governments in the Arab and Islamic world participated in the war against terrorism. This state of affairs led to the complete destruction of the jihadist movement. The Arab mujahideen and immigrants faced the worst genocide in their history. This was the fate that Allah had in store for them. From 2001 to the writing of this text (September 2004), their losses included the following:

- The martyrdom of about four hundred Arab mujahideen during the defense of Afghanistan. They faced serious losses on all fronts, and many of them were killed in the intensive bombing campaign. Some of them fled to Pakistan. The government of Pakistan captured one hundred and fifty mujahideen because of tribal treachery.
- In 2002 some of the mujahideen fled Tora Bora and were captured by Pakistani forces. Subsequently, they were handed over to the Americans.
- These prisoners were transferred to the Guantanamo Bay detention facility. This detention camp has a very bad reputation.
- From 2002 to September 2004, nearly one hundred mujahideen were martyred in different battles with the Pakistani army, especially in the border regions and on different travel routes.
- Some Arab Afghans had fled with their families to Pakistan. The Pakistani government captured some six hundred mujahideen from the latter group and handed them over to the American government.

Some were sent to Guantanamo, while others were imprisoned in Afghanistan.

- Iran captured more than four hundred Arab mujahideen and handed them over to their respective countries. Iran admitted this action openly. There are still some one hundred prisoners in Iran at the moment. The Iranians are negotiating with the U.S. government concerning the fate of these prisoners.

From among nineteen hundred Arab Mujahideen in Afghanistan, roughly sixteen hundred have been captured or killed. In all, nearly 75 percent of all Arab Afghans have either been captured or killed. This was accomplished through cooperation with the intelligence services of Europe and the Islamic world. Many friends or relatives of jihadists were also arrested and imprisoned, even though they had no connection with jihadist organizations or groups. The mujahideen of central Asia, especially the Uzbeks, also suffered tremendously in this war. Many of them were either killed or captured. Roughly five hundred Uzbek mujahideen were martyred, not counting those who were captured. Many were killed in Waziristan by Pakistani forces, which were supported by the American military.

Many of the East Turkistan mujahideen faced a similar fate to their Uzbek brothers. The emir of the East Turkistan group was martyred along with some of his supporters. His name was Hasan Abu Muhammad Al-Turkistani. He was pursued and killed by the Pakistani army (may Allah strike them down).

In mid 2003, Defense Secretary [Donald] Rumsfeld declared that the American military had killed or captured more than three thousand terrorists. I believe this figure is accurate. Roughly half of them were killed in Afghanistan, Pakistan, and Iran. According to official British statistics, nearly three terrorists and their supporters had been arrested and detained. Over a dozen other jihadists have been captured throughout Europe. Among Arab countries, Yemen carried out a huge campaign against jihadists and Arab Afghans as well as their supporters. The government killed or captured hundreds of them. Saudi Arabia also carried out a campaign against jihadist groups, which were accused of having ties to al Qaida. The Saudi government captured 220 mujahideen. They imprisoned and interrogated thousands of mujahideen. The reason behind the Saudi and Yemeni campaigns had to do with the fact that the largest group of Arab mujahideen had come from these two Arab states. The last major campaign took place in November 2003 in Morocco. The government of Morocco arrested hundreds of mujahideen and their supporters. Subsequently, many were executed, while others were imprisoned for life. Still others received long prison sentences.

Throughout the globe, many mujahideen and their supporters were accused of committing terrorist acts. The war on terrorism stretched from the horn of Africa to the Philippines, Indonesia, and Southeast Asia. The American counterattack clearly was waged across the entire globe.

This unprecedented disaster came about for three main reasons:

1. The figure of three to four thousand jihadists killed or captured is, in fact, a low estimate. The real numbers are much larger than that. The majority of the mujahideen living in Afghanistan were killed or captured. This was also the case for the mujahideen who were residing in the Arab and Islamic world as well as in the West. The jihadist movement was uprooted and decimated.

2. The strike on the Arab mujahideen in Central Asia, Afghanistan, and Pakistan killed off most of the senior members of the jihadist organizations and the first generation of Arab Afghans. By 2000 only about one hundred and fifty of these mujahideen had survived the onslaught. The flower of the jihadist movement was killed or captured. Only a fraction of the mujahideen survived or were not captured.

3. The American attack decimated the senior leadership of those jihadist organizations, who represented the third generation of mujahideen— those that had arrived in Afghanistan during the second phase of Arab Afghan immigration (1996–2001). Praise be to Allah that a number of them survived and spread across the globe.

The jihadist movement, which arose in the 1960s and thrived in the 1970s and 1980s, had great potential during the Taliban period in Afghanistan. Unfortunately, following the events of September 2001, the jihadist movement was utterly destroyed, bringing this period to an end. By the will of Allah, a new jihadist movement has arisen to confront the Zionist-Crusader campaigns. (Through my writings, I am participating in this new jihadist movement.) This period is marked by a U.S.-led war against terrorism. America has carried out a direct military invasion of Afghanistan, Iraq, and the Middle East. As a result, we have seen the emergence of new battlefields that will give us the opportunity to confront the Americans.

CHAPTER 6

Armed Jihadist Experiences in the Late Twentieth Century

U nfortunately, what has happened until now regarding Islamic work in general and jihadist work in particular can be summed up in terms of a lack of authors and a lack of literary works. Therefore, the majority of the experiences of the jihadist movement, or of any movement for that matter, has fallen into oblivion without being recorded by those responsible for them. I refer not only to those who participated in the jihad itself but also to those who witnessed it. As far as I know, there have been many experiences about which nothing has been written, or if something was written, nothing was published. This has cost the Islamic nation many valuable lessons and interesting stories of the first and second generation of the jihadist movement from its birth until the end of twentieth century and the beginning of the twenty-first century.

Conversely, some enemies, media sharks, or those who might be described as the Don Quixote(s) of the Islamic revival (the "fat cats" who have dodged jihad to sit in their air-conditioned houses) have trespassed against the jihad experiences by writing about them instead of allowing the mujahideen to do it themselves. I have tried to be the exception to this rule, because I am one of the few who has actually been personally involved in the movement. I also have been in close contact with many who have participated in other experiences, which I will summarize in this segment.

To reap the full benefit from this segment, I will summarize the most important jihadist experiences that occurred in the second half of this past century. It will be based on what I was told directly by the people involved in these experiences and those whom I got to know well during my involvement with the jihadist movement. I hope it will encourage some of those still among us to write about their own experiences. I will recount these jihadist experiences in chronological order.

The Experience of the Moroccan al-Shabiba (Youths) Movement

This jihadist movement was established by Sheikh 'Abd al-Karim Muti'. He tried to establish an armed jihadist organization to revolt against King Hassan II of Morocco. Many members of the organization's cells were arrested and jailed. Those who were able to escape these misfortunes emigrated to other countries, and the movement died out. I had a chance to read some of the writings of Sheikh 'Abd al-Karim Muti' and found that they contained a generally mature and distinguished jihadist ideology. I also found a book recounting the history of that experience. However, I unfortunately had to leave it behind in my library when I had to leave London quickly in 1997. I also had an opportunity to meet one of the elder members of that organization while I was residing in London (1994–97). He told me about some of the historical and important chapters of their experience, but I do not recall the details right now.

The Experience of the Egyptian Jihad Organization (1965–2000)

The martyr Sayyid Qutub put into action his thoughts and mission. He established an organization made up of a select group of young jihadist men in Egypt, the majority of whom were members of the Muslim Brotherhood. Qutub wrote what became a famous historical document that he titled *Why They Executed Me*. The document, which was later published, states that some of the jihadist youths formed a few covert cells whose ultimate goal was confrontation with the regime of President 'Abd-al-Nasser, because of the monstrous attacks carried out by the Egyptian judicial and security apparatuses against the Muslim Brotherhood members both in 1954 and in 1965.

These attacks resulted in the execution of many of the Brotherhood and the imprisonment of tens of thousands of them in the most infamous prisons. Qutub stated in his document that these men asked him to be the emir of their organization and that he had accepted the role of a guide and a godfather to them. He stated that he had prepared a few military plans with them and that he had been arrested with them as a result of this effort. Sayyid Qutub was sentenced to death and was executed along with several of those men.

In several of Dr. Ayman Al-Zawhiri's recordings and meetings, I heard the doctor say that some of the students and young contemporaries who were touched and influenced by Qutub's teachings had continued to secretly spread his call and his mission. Those covert efforts later transformed into the initial cells of the Egyptian Jihad Organization. Some of the leaders and cadres of this group were arrested as a result of the assassination of President Anwar Sadat in 1981. Some of them are still in jail to this day!

It seems that many jihadist attempts took place in Egypt after this most famous one that is known as the events of the military parade. There was a weak and failed coup attempt, led by the martyr Salih Sirriyah, that resulted in a number of jihadist cadres being tried and executed. Nevertheless, beginning around the mid-1970s, the jihadist organization was active again and became well defined during the era of President Anwar al-Sadat. Then, in 1986 a number of its leaders (namely Dr. Ayman al-Zawahiri) and its cadres left for Afghanistan.

I believe the jihadist experiences in Egypt were among the most mature in the Arab and Islamic world on an intellectual and procedural basis. They also were the most productive and the most memorable. Furthermore, they were among the most important experiences as regards organization and dynamics. Unfortunately, I found out from Dr. Ayman al- Zawahiri that not a single person took the time to document the history of these experiences, which include stories of the torture and interrogation methods used by Egypt's security and investigative services.

When I was in Kabul in early 2001, Dr. al-Zawahiri sent me a rough draft of a book on this topic. I reviewed it and found it to be good but very limited with respect to the duration and value of those jihadist experiences. I discussed this point with him and encouraged him to expand on the topic, because he was the best living witness to these events and had an obligation to record this history. Unfortunately, he had to decline the offer, because, during that time, he was constantly occupied with military operations in Afghanistan.

After their arrival in Afghanistan, Dr. Ayman al-Zawahiri and a number of the jihad organization's cadres tried to establish a unique jihadist experience that would stand out among the existing jihadist experiences of the day. This was done during the Arab Afghan periods of 1991–96 and

1996–2001. I will summarize the following points as best as I can recall
from having been there since the beginning and from having lived with
their leaders:

- In 1986 Dr. Ayman al-Zawahiri arrived in Peshawar, along with a
  squadron of cadres from Egypt's Jihad Organization. He had just been
  released from jail after serving three years for organizing jihad in Egypt
  and for his role in the assassination of President Sadat. The doctor and
  his group had a very prominent presence and played a significant role
  among the Arab Afghans during the period from 1986 to 1991.
- There was cooperation on many levels between them and with Sheikh
  Osama bin Laden, who was planning to establish his own organization. The organization, which was known as al Qaida, was officially
  established in 1988. Its cadres and trainers exerted great effort, and the
  most relevant of them were the jihad organization cadres. The most
  significant among them, in turn, was the martyr Abu 'Ubaydah al-
  Banjashiri. He died while leading an operation (the sinking of a ship
  in Lake Victoria) for al Qaida in Kenya at the time when the latter
  was established in Sudan (1992–96). There also was the martyr Abu
  Hafas al-Masri, aka Muhammad 'Atif, who received his martyrdom
  in the battles that occurred when the principality was overthrown in
  November of 2001. He died as a result of American bombing of his
  headquarters. He was the military leader for al Qaida in Kandahar. The
  jihad organization benefited greatly from these cooperative efforts,
  which afforded them financial support and helped establish independent training camps in Afghanistan as well as directing and following
  up on movement activities in Egypt.
- The essence of the strategic goal of Egypt's Jihad Organization was to
  launch a military coup led by soldiers who were members of the organization and who were embedded in the Egyptian army since the time
  of President Sadat. The organization's cells continued their work until
  they were annihilated by the overwhelming onslaught of arrests. Their
  general plan, as I gathered from Dr. al-Zawahiri in numerous meetings
  with him, was to initiate a coup using cells readied during that period.
- Following the assassination of President Sadat, and because of the
  intermixing of members of the al-Jama'ah al-Isalmiyyah Organization
  (who carried out the operation) and members of the jihad organization
  (who also were involved in the operation), a number of military cadres
  of the jihad organizations were arrested, the most prominent among

these being the martyr Major 'Isam al-Qamari. Nevertheless, this
security blow did not stop them from continuing their covert work
within army cells or within the civilian arena.

- Al-Jama'ah al-Islamiyyah Organization adopted the strategy of the open
call and the people's revolution because it was influenced by the methods
of the Iranian revolution. This led to the implementation of an annihilation policy against them by the Egyptian Ministry of Interior, especially during the era of its criminal minister Zaki Badr. Consequently,
the al-Jama'ah al-Islamiyyah Organization decided to retaliate against
the provocations of the state and the policy of "striking daggers in the
heart," as Zaki Badr called it, by assassinating the leaders of the regime
in response to the state's killing of the leaders of al-Jama'ah. The jihad
organization, which shares leadership with the al-Jama'ah organization, decided to establish a presence in Peshawar, Pakistan, and in the
bordering states of Afghanistan during the period of the Afghani jihad.
It decided to be involved in this confrontation, sidestepping the covert
planning required for a military coup, in the belief that this tactical
plan could run concurrently with that strategic plan.

- The arrest of one of the civilian operatives of the covert jihad organization led to the arrest of one of the military members of the organization, which, in turn, led the authorities to the majority of the military
cadres of the organization. Thus began the collapse of the internal
organization in Egypt around late 1989 or early 1990, I believe.

- The organization's misfortune intensified because of two security hits
that led to the arrest of about nine hundred covert civilian members
followed by about six hundred more. These men composed the organization's youth foundation inside Egypt. It was a foundation that had
been highly organized during the Afghani jihad period.

- Following the success of the coup that put Hassan al-Turabi and
Omar Al Basheer in power, the leadership of the jihad organization
moved to Sudan accompanied by Sheikh Osama bin Laden and a select
group of his leaders and his cadres. After that, the jihad organization
began to work in very favorable conditions along the southern border
of Egypt with Sudan. That was accomplished with the support of the
new Sudanese government and its intelligence services. Al-Jama'ah
al-Islamiyyah followed suit, and the organization set up a training
camp as well as a number of bases in al-Khurtum, thus starting to
reorganize itself with the help and financial support of Sheikh Osama

(a fact that was later known and much publicized). The goal then was to overthrow the regime of President Hosni Mubarak and to establish an Islamic regime in Egypt that would reshape the strategic balance among all the enemies in the Middle East.

- However, after having stood by the Sudanese government and helping it refurbish its army and build its economy, the army turned on the mujahideen (including bin Laden). Their betrayals began by turning against the Libyan brothers among the mujahideen, followed by the Egyptians, and so forth.
- This last blow destroyed the organization's plan against Egypt. The Sudanese government forced Sheikh Osama bin Laden to stop funding the work program in Egypt and exerted so much pressure that it finally expelled them all.
- Following a long nomadic period that lasted from 1996 to 1998, Dr. Ayman al-Zawahiri, along with his remaining cadres, joined up with Sheikh Osama bin Laden in Afghanistan to reside in the shadows of the Taliban. Others of the remaining cadres and cells were left waiting in different parts of the world.
- The jihad organization and al Qaida attempted once again to cooperate in funding and training. However, by then, Sheikh Osama bin Laden was convinced that there must be a unified objective of confronting America, whereas the jihad organization remained, like all its counterparts, fixated on regional goals, covert methods, and an ideological and jihadist curriculum.
- Around the end of 1997, Dr. Ayman al-Zawahiri signed a bulletin issued by Sheikh Osama bin Laden entitled *The Global Front for the Liberation of the Sacred Sites*. Al-Jama'ah al-Islamiyyah, however, stayed away from this issue. Very soon, the jihad organization began to pay the price for its involvement in this matter by facing global American security offensives against the jihad movement. The latter's cadres and members, who were scattered in different parts of the world, began to fall. A number of them were kidnapped from different countries and turned over to the Egyptian government. This happened in Thailand, Albania, Azerbaijan, the United Arab Emirates, and so forth. Others were arrested and jailed in countries where they happened to be living. Such was the case of those who were living in Great Britain at the time.

- Despite this new world order, which was suffocating any and all regional covert jihadist attempts, Dr. Ayman al-Zawahiri continued (with whoever was left of the cadres) on his journey with his unique determination and patience.
- The organization started its own training camp, gathering what was left of its cadres, and attempted to move on with its mission. However, the events that were taking place around them, especially the wave of arrests that hit members of the organization in countries abroad, convinced Sheikh Dr. Ayman al-Zawahiri of the opportunities available for jihad and for work in Afghanistan with Sheikh Osama bin Laden in his war against America. I witnessed the changes in his plans personally, and I had lengthy conversations with him in which we discussed the long-term effects of these developments and how they should be dealt with shortly before the events of September 11.
- Around the middle of 2001, Dr. al-Zawahiri pledged his allegiance to Sheikh Osama bin Laden and officially joined the jihad organization to al Qaida. This led to the division of the remaining small group of cadres who were with him in Afghanistan. They split into two groups: the first followed him on his new path, and the second insisted on staying with its traditional jihadist course of eventually establishing an Islamic regime in Egypt by overthrowing the current government and its president, Hosni Mubarak. This group was led by Brother Abu-al-Samah, aka Salah Shahatah; he was a lawyer who had been a member for a long time in the cadres of the organization and was among the eldest of the Arab Afghans.
- The events of September 11 did not give either group the opportunity to implement their plans. Soon, all the surviving Arab Afghans were united in a common battle of self-defense, survival, and the defense of the Islamic principality (which was eventually overthrown). The majority of the cadres were martyred in these battles. Dr. al-Zawahiri lost his wife, his only son, and his infant daughter during the monstrous American-led air strikes. And so, he joined Sheikh bin Laden to settle in mobile hiding places and to continue on their path of jihad and instigation. As for the squadron that went with Tharwat Shahatah on their own jihad path, it was reported in the media that they were arrested and jailed in Iran.

- That is the summary of the jihad organization's movements undertaken by Dr. al-Zawahiri outside of Egypt. I do not know if there were any seedlings for this movement's plan that will continue to grow.

As for the ideological identity of the Egyptian jihad, we have seen from this review that its existence as an active organization was over. It was begun in 1960 and it ended around September 2001. However, the important thing to remember is that the ideological school of thought of the jihad organization remains the most prominent, the most important, and the most memorable of the last century. It was born in the writings of Sayyid Qutub, which included the foundations of the modern-day jihadist ideologies.

On a personal level, I have come to know the jihad group's experience from an up close and personal level because of my strong ties of friendship with the Brotherhood who came to Afghanistan and with their leaders. Furthermore, there was among us cooperation and a working relationship, starting with Dr. al-Zawahiri and continuing with most of the others. I saw in them the ultimate example of a patient and ideological mujahideen. I am indebted to them all intellectually, and I wish to thank Sheikh Dr. 'Abd al-Qadir Ibn 'Abd al-'Aziz aka Sayyid Imam al-Sharif, the mufti for the jihad group, who was also their scholar and their emir in the Afghanistan era. His acquaintanceship, his books, and his conversations have left a great impact on me intellectually.

Another great influence and important role model for me was Dr. al-Zawahiri, who is an exemplary mujahid, a great thinker and writer, and an excellent role model. There were many others, of course, the majority of whom have passed away.

The Jihadist Experience in Syria (1965–83)

The jihadist experience in Syria was started by Sheikh Marwan Hadid, God rest his soul, who was raised by the Muslim Brotherhood. While studying agricultural engineering in Egypt, he was influenced by the teachings of Sayyid Qutub and returned to Syria full of enthusiasm at a time when the secular nationalist, socialist Ba'ath party had taken over the regime. Hadid took to the mosques in the city of Hamah, preaching against committing evil, and calling people to the path of righteousness and to the establishment of the sharia. He was arrested several times.

In 1965 the government forces attacked him and his followers while they were in one of the mosques. The armed confrontation led to the death of several of them and the arrest of the sheikh and several of his students. They all received the death penalty. However, under pressure from the scholars of the time, headed by Sheikh Muhammad al-Hamid, the Syrian president at the time [Amin al-Hafidh] set them free.

Sheikh Marwan knew he was about to face an unavoidable and great confrontation with the regime and that it was coming soon. He also was warned of a secular Ansarie plan, which was about to be implemented. However, when he was unable to convince the Muslim Brotherhood group to join him to prepare for the confrontation, he did so on his own, accompanied by his students. They were able to prepare militarily by joining the Islamic faction of the Palestinian Liberation Organization. Thus, he was able to prepare the first jihadist group of his jihad organization.

In 1970 Hafiz al-Assad and his Ansarie, Alawite group within the Syrian army carried out a peaceful coup that was referred to then as the Reformist Movement. It was thus that the Ansarie sect leaped from the depths of the community to the forefront, taking the reins of the regime and ruling the Muslims in Syria, just as Sheikh Marwan, God rest his soul, had feared.

Thus, Sheikh Marwan Hadid returned to the fight along with the leaders of both divisions of the organization of the Muslim Brotherhood (who had split off during that period), with the purpose of uniting them against the regime. One faction, which was state organized, was presided over by Sheikh 'Abd al-Fattah Abu-Ghadah, and his vice president, 'Adnan Sa'id al-Din. The other division was led by 'Isam al-'Attar. Despite the great differences between the two factions, they agreed not to join with Sheikh Marwan and, instead, chose to continue with their peaceful missionary path.

When Sheikh Marwan Hadid became convinced that the organization of the Muslim Brotherhood was not going to go along with him in his mission of confronting the regime, he formed his own organization, which he called the Fighting Youths for God's Faction. He established three principal centers for it: Hamah, Aleppo, and the third in Damascus, where he moved secretly to begin preparations for the confrontation with the Ansaries.

The Muslim Brotherhood organization expelled Sheikh Marwan from their organization along with a group of those who were influenced by his jihadist and revolutionary thoughts. They attempted to break his will. But, he continued to recruit supporters, the majority of whom were youths from the Brotherhood. That is when he uttered his famous quote, "If the Brothers throw me out the door, I will get in from the window, and I will drag them to jihad," and that is precisely what happened!

In 1970 Sheikh Marwan was arrested after an armed altercation with the security services in his hideout in Damascus. He remained in jail until 1975, during which time he lost half his weight from the torture he endured. It was said that he was then executed by lethal injection. There was no grave for him, and his family was not allowed to have a funeral for him.

The leadership of the Fighting Youths organization was handed down to the sheikh's students and was taken over by the martyr 'Abd al-Sattar al-Za'im, God rest his soul. The organization decided to undertake a covert plan of confrontation by assassinating the major Ansarie leaders of the state, a feat they accomplished in the period between 1975 and 1979. The regime was unable to identify them until the end of that period and then only with the help of the Jordanian security services.

The youths' organization declared jihad on the Syrian regime in the summer of 1979. It also changed its name to the Youths Fighting for the Muslim Brotherhood. Thus began the guerilla warfare in Syria. The principal division of the Muslim Brotherhood, that which was state organized, disassociated itself from that confrontation and requested the establishment of investigative committees to prove that it had nothing to do with these events. Conversely, 'Isam al-'Attar adopted the confrontation, claimed it as his own, even publicizing his bank account numbers to collect donations for the jihad movement, of course—from Germany!

The al-Assad regime, which became uneasy as a result of the military attacks by the mujahideen youths, decided to confront and eliminate all of the Muslim Brotherhood factions, including all factions of the Islamic revival. As a matter of fact, it included all the religious sects in the country! The confrontation took on a warlike aspect between the Sunnis, who were the Muslims in Syria, and the Ansarie, who were the minority in Syria, also known as the Alawite sect (so named by the French during the occupation).

As the Muslim Brotherhood organization saw the success of the mujahideen increasing, they suffered the wrath of attacks by the regime against them. As with all religious factions, because of the mujahideen's actions, the Muslim Brotherhood organization announced its withdrawal from war in 1979, just a few months after it began. They attempted to co-opt the leadership of the confrontation and take over. Their policy played a principal role, although not the only one, in bringing down the armed jihad against the regime in Syria.

As a result of the policy of the Muslim Brotherhood, and also because of the security blows of the government that had itself succeeded in regaining power, the Fighting Youths crumbled, and the majority of their cadres ended up in jail or dead. The survivors fled to neighboring countries such as Iraq and Jordan (whose governments were at that time in opposition to the Syrian government), which had opened their borders to Syrian protesters of all political factions.

Under the leadership of 'Adnan Sa'id al-Din in 1980, the Muslim Brotherhood organization gained control of the jihadist revolution in Syria and recruited whoever was left from the youths, the organization of 'Isam al-'Attar, as well as a large segment of the scholars' groups in Syria.

The Muslim Brotherhood organization led the jihadist revolution in Syria to its military and political demise in 1980 during a bloody confrontation that took place in 1982 in the city of Hamah. This massacre destroyed the military apparatuses of both sides, and the Muslims suffered the loss of over fifty thousand men during a period of a few months of mass annihilations carried out by an Arab government in the twentieth century.

This is how the Syrian jihadist experience ended. It was the longest and most important confrontation in the jihadist movement against any apostate government in the Arab and Islamic world.

God gave me the opportunity to witness that period, because I had joined the Fighting Youths organization in the beginning of 1980, and then after leaving Syria at the end of that year, I joined the Syrian branch of the Muslim Brotherhood organization, which had established itself in Jordan, where I worked with them in their military. Then, during the events of the Hamah intifadah in 1982, I was a member of the military leadership of the Muslim Brotherhood organization that was established in Iraq, where I was part of the military apparatus cadres. I was also a part of the higher political leadership of the Syrian Muslim Brotherhood. All of this gave me an insider's look at the events taking place and at the reasons that led to our defeat. It is the history of all of this and the lessons taken from it that I recorded in a previously written book.

The Experience of the Islamic State Movement in Algeria (1973–76)

The Islamic State Movement was an armed jihad movement in Algeria that was established and led by the martyr Mustafa Abu-Bi'li. He was among the mujahideen who had participated in the Algerian liberation revolution in 1954. After Algeria gained its independence in 1963, he realized that the secularists, the communists, and the socialists had reaped the reward of the Algerian people's jihad, which had lasted more then a century. Therefore, he launched the aforementioned jihad movement to regain the revolution and to establish the sharia as the law of Algeria.

He carried out his movement during the time of the President al-Shadhili Ibn Jadid in 1973. I have listened to a recording of his in which he addressed the president, ordering him, warning him, and promising him jihad if sharia was not established as the law of Algeria. I also heard some other audio recordings of his in which he discussed his jihadist principles and in which he sent warnings to the Sultan's scholars.

His movement did not last long; as he was ambushed by the Algerian intelligence services during a meeting he had with some arms dealers. He was martyred in 1976, as were some of his aides. Others who were with him were arrested, tried, and jailed. Some of his students attempted to revive the jihad, attacking the government after the military coup against the democratic regime in 1991. They attempted to play a role in uniting al-Jama'ah al-Islamiyyah in 1993 before it was divided and taken over by the Takfiriyyin [Islamists who pass judgment, declaring that an individual or group previously considered Muslims are, in fact, nonbelievers. It is the practice of passing an excommunication judgment against a Muslim or a group of Muslims].

The Experience of al-Jama'ah al-Islamiyyah in Egypt (1975–2001)

I will summarize the essence of my experience with the al-Jama'ah al-Islamiyyah in Egypt according to information I obtained through studying its history and through my contacts with its leaders and the people who established it. Al-Jama'ah al-Islamiyyah was established and became active in several Egyptian universities in 1975, as a result of President Sadat's economic open-door policy and as a result of him allowing the activities of all Islamic groups, in his attempt to curb any left-wing political movements that had been growing in that era. Al-Jama'ah al-Islamiyyah was rooted in the Brotherhood ideological curriculum as well as that of previous Salafist systems. It made the implementation of sharia in Egypt its goal. The group gained popularity among the people, because their leadership adopted the open call to righteousness and preaching against committing bad deeds. Cells of al-Jama'ah began to spread throughout the mosques in Egypt. Their starting place was actually in the region of Upper Egypt, to which the majority of the organization's leadership belonged, and then its movement expanded on to the universities on the coast in the north of Egypt. Al-Jama'ah al-Islamiyyah took Sheikh 'Umar 'Abd al-Rahman as their emir because he was known for his strong stands, such as when he passed a fatwa forbidding Muslims for praying over President 'Abd-al-Nasser when he died, as well as many other positions he took during the presidency of Sadat.

In response to President Sadat's treacherous visit to Israel and his declaration of the agreement of Camp David, as well as the peace agreement with the Jews, al-Jama'ah al-Islamiyyah issued some of the most important jihadist ideological works: One of its leaders, the martyr 'Abd al-Salam Faraj, published one of the most important jihadist research works of modern times (*The Missing Religious Obligation*). The importance of this work was in the fact that it contained the most important fatwas of modern-day jihad against the established governments in the Arab and Muslim countries, including Egypt. He issued a fatwa against them calling for jihad against them, their soldiers, as well as their security apparatuses. He reasoned that they should be put to the test of the fatwas of Ibn Taymiyyah in which the latter speaks of fighting the Tatars and any Muslims who help them (whether they do it willingly or out of ignorance). That literary work was among the most important starting points for the modern-day jihadist, Salafist schools of thought.

Al-Jama'ah al-Islamiyyah was successful in heroically assassinating the treacherous president, Anwar al-Sadat, in the famous operation during the annual military parade in 1981. He had gone out to the people, standing on his platform in full military uniform, but God struck him dead along with some of his aides. The operation was led by the heroic martyr Khalid al-Islambuli. He was a hero to al-Jama'ah al-Islamiyyah, to Egypt, and to the entire modern-day jihadist movement. The operation itself was only one part of a coup against the Egyptian government; it was the only part that was successful.

When President Hosni Mubarak came to power after his assassinated predecessor, Anwar al-Sadat, al-Jama'ah al-Islamiyyah got into a war of attrition with the Egyptian government, which had orchestrated a plan to annihilate it by arresting and assassinating its cadres and its leaders. The government began this war by assassinating one of al-Jama'ah's most prominent missionaries, the martyr 'Ala' Muhyi al-Din. The government continued on this path, especially during the era of the interior minister, Zaki Badr, who was a criminal of ill repute. Therefore, the leadership of al-Jama'ah al-Islamiyyah decided to get into a war of attrition with the government, which had begun a wave of arrests from within the Jam'ah's ranks.

The leadership of al-Jama'ah al-Islamiyyah in Egypt found a perfect field of opportunity in the Afghani jihad against the Russians. It was a perfect place for it to train its cadres, to expand, and to organize itself. It had a prominent presence in Peshawar, Pakistan, as well as in the training camps and the Arab fronts in Afghanistan. Among its most prominent leaders in Afghanistan was Sheikh 'Umar 'Abd al-Rahman, Sheikh Rifa'i Taha, and Brother Tal'at Fu'ad Qasam, God give them all their freedom. There was also Brother Muhammad al-Islambuli, the brother of the martyr Khalid, who assassinated the pharaoh of Egypt; there was also Brother Mustafa Hamzah and many others. Al-Jama'ah al-Islamiyyah in Egypt gave a squadron of its best men and cadres as martyrs in the battle for Islam through the Arab jihad in Afghanistan.

As a result of the security tempests that swept through Afghanistan and Pakistan, instigated by America, the majority of the leaders and the founders of al-Jama'ah al-Islamiyyah of Egypt moved to Sudan pursuant to an invitation from the rescue government, which opened its doors to all Arabs. The government promised to make way for them to work across the country's northern border with Egypt, and indeed, al-Jama'ah field work began from there. Soon after arriving, though, misfortunes happened to the jihad Jama'ah, and they were asked to leave under armed threat by the Sudanese security forces when the backstabbing Sudanese decided to change their policies and to bend to America. The leaders of al-Jama'ah al-Islamiyyah were dispersed in different countries, and the majority of them headed to Yemen.

With the extensive crackdown on them, the most prominent among them headed to Iran, while some hid under the cover of political asylum in Europe. Among the most prominent of those who went to Iran were Rifa'i Taha, Sheikh Mustafa Hamzah, Sheikh Muhammad Shawqi al-Islambuli,

Until his capture in Pakistan in 2006, Syrian Mustafa Setmariam Nasar, also known as Abu Musab al-Suri, was al Qaida's foremost strategic thinker. His book, *The Call to Global Islamic Resistance*, has been called the *Mein Kampf* of the jihad movement. *(©Handout/epa/Corbis)*

Abu Musab al-Suri established terrorist training camps in Afghanistan and sleeper cells in Europe that provided logistical support for terrorist activities. Al-Suri is believed to have been one of the chief planners behind the July 2004 Madrid train bombings (top), which killed more than 170 and wounded 500 rush-hour commuters, and the July 2005 London bombings (bottom), in which 40 died and 350 were wounded. (*Top photo*: AP/Paul White; *bottom photo*: AP/Sergio Dionisio)

Before he left Spain, al-Suri managed to establish several sleeper cells, one of which was instrumental in assisting in the logistical support for the strikes on the World Trade Center and the Pentagon. It is believed a close associate of al-Suri traveled from al-Suri's training camp in Afghanistan to Spain and met with Mohammed Atta, the leader of the 9/11 operation, just a few weeks before the attacks, which claimed the lives of 2,993 (including the 19 terrorists) and injured more than 6,290. (*Top photo*: U.S. Navy/Photographer's Mate 2nd Class Bob Houlihan; *bottom photo*: U.S. Navy/Chief Photographer's Mate Eric J. Tilford)

American and local anti-Taliban forces raided a deserted al Qaida training camp (*top*) near Garmawak, west of Kandahar, Afghanistan, in January 2002, discovering training literature and even graded tests (*bottom*) measuring students' ability to make bombs, use antiaircraft weapons, and target the best spots on the body for a kill shot. Al-Suri opened his own training camp for budding jihadists in Afghanistan, lectured at other al Qaida camps, and assisted in experiments with chemical weapons. *(Both photos: AP/John Moore)*

and others. Among the most prominent of those who headed to Europe were Abu-Talal aka Tal'at Fu'ad Qasam, who settled in Denmark, and Osama Rushdi, the advisory council member of al-Jama'ah.

Al-Jama'ah al-Islamiyyah of Egypt was on good terms with the [Ayatollah Rudollah] Khomeini government of Iran, because it had a different stand toward the Iranian government than any other jihadist movement did: it had praised the Iranian Islamic revolution, and its ideologies, and some of al-Jama'ah's leaders, including Sheikh 'Umar 'Abd al-Rahman had attended some of the summits organized by the Iranian government. This gave al-Jama'ah a safe haven from the crackdown they were experiencing everywhere else.

While the majority, if not all, of the prominent leaders and the cadres of the jihadist movement began a mass exodus to Afghanistan during the period between 1996 and 2001, the prominent leaders of al-Jama'ah al-Islamiyyah, for their part, preferred to remain in Iran and chose a totally different direction than the general one of the Afghani jihad. Some of the most prominent features of their stance were:

- The failure to publicly support the Taliban and their fight against the Northern Alliance. They did not support the leaders of the Afghani jihad nor did they even make attempts to go anywhere near Afghanistan.
- Al-Jama'ah cleared itself completely through its media sources and its Web site from bin Laden's activities in his war against the Americans. This was in clear contrast to what the Jihad Jama'ah did, led by Dr. Ayman al-Zawahiri. When al Qaida alluded to al-Jama'ah's cooperation with it, the latter issued a bulletin denying such a claim.
- Al-Jama'ah adopted the principle of stopping all calls for armed confrontations with any government. It also declared an initiative to stop the violence on their part against the government in Egypt. This is a stance that deserves great consideration because it removes al-Jama'ah from the jihadist movement entirely and it had consequences that overstep the boundaries of what is considered al-Jama'ah's business alone.

Al-Jama'ah al-Islamiyyah of Egypt had ideological principles that distinguished it from any other organization in the jihadist movement. These principles were later reversed, a fact that removed al-Jama'ah from its path. Among the most important of these differences were:

- It adopted what could be considered a middle-ground between the ideologies of the general Islamic revival and those of the jihadist movement concerning leadership matters. They were convinced that rulers who ruled by any other law than sharia were apostate. They felt this way about Egypt's government and considered its president and its regime to be apostates. Consequently, they legitimized the fight against that government's enemies as self-defense.

- Al-Jam'ah adopted the principles of an advisory council as well as that of a group leadership. They elected Sheikh 'Umar 'Abd al-Rahman as their emir, considering him as a legal figure and a symbol for al-Jama'ah.
- They overcame religious legal problems in the concerns of the religiously approved principality. This started a big and extended debate between them and the Jihad Jama'ah of Egypt as well as other segments of the jihadist movement, beginning in the early nineties in Afghanistan. The debate was over the legitimacy of the leadership of an incarcerated emir, as was the case of Sheikh 'Umar 'Abd al-Rahman in America. They considered the leadership of their commanders who were incarcerated in Egyptian jails to still be valid and that, therefore, they could be involved in any advisory council decision. I am not here to argue this principle, only to record the history of the events so as to report the impact of these ideologies on the path of al-Jama'ah since the middle of the 1990s.

Besides these stated problems, I find hardly any principal systematic differences between the curriculum of al-Jama'ah al-Islamiyyah of Egypt and that of the rest of the jihadist movement's other schools of thought, as far as their Salafist jihadist ideology and their opposition to the application of the democratic system (on the basis of its religious invalidity) in Islamic work. They accused any Muslims who followed the democratic system of making their own interpretation of religion.

However, these systematic issues got al-Jama'ah involved in practical problems as it had entered in a battle against the Egyptian government. This occurred when al-Jama'ah's military apparatus found itself faced with the juristical requirements of a war of attrition against the Egyptian regime. Conversely, they also realized that their leadership was composed of three principal branches:

1. The incarcerated commanders in Egypt, whom they agreed to name (the historical leaders).

2. The political commanders who were being hunted down all over the world.
3. The leaders of the military apparatus of al-Jama'ah, either inside or outside of Egypt, which was facing a bloody military confrontation with the regime of Hosni Mubarak.

These systematic issues, which carried long-term effects, quickly affected the path of al-Jama'ah starting from the middle of the 1990s and up until after the events of September 11. What made matters worse was the fact that the military branch, led by Brother Abu-Hazim aka Mustafa Hamzah, had planned to assassinate Hosni Mubarak, and the operation almost succeeded in accomplishing its goal during an African summit in Addis Ababa. Nevertheless, the operation failed, and some members of the group were arrested and confessed before they were executed. This operation caused great distress to the Sudanese government, which had organized the operation and had supplied logistical support to it.

The arrest of Sheikh 'Umar 'Abd al-Rahman in America: the sheikh had made the wrong decision by moving to America to reside there with the aim of spreading the call to righteousness and providing financial and media support to al-Jama'ah. He was falsely accused in the events of the first attacks on the World Trade Center in New York and was sentenced to two hundred years of jail time! No attempts for sentence reduction or defense were successful. The leadership of al-Jama'ah al-Islamiyyah quasi-officially declared that their practical emir was then Abu-Talal Tal'at Fu'ad Qasam, who had resided as a political refugee in Denmark. They also adopted the principle of confrontation along with others in al-Jama'ah who supported the military apparatus, led by Mustafa Hamzah.

The branch, which believed tenaciously in confrontation, got involved with another branch, opposite to it in its ideology, which called for truce negotiations with the Egyptian government. This was exemplified by the behavior of the incarcerated (historical) commanders as well as some of al-Jama'ah's leaders in Europe, the most prominent of whom was Brother Osama Rushdi, when that branch denounced the events of al-Uqsur in Egypt (the attack carried out by one of al-Jama'ah's active cells on tourists in Egypt, killing many people in the operation). The incarcerated, historical leaders as well as some leaders residing in Europe (mainly Osama Rushdi) were quick to denounce the attacks and the perpetrators on religious grounds. As a matter of fact, Osama Rushdie went so far as to publicly attack this operation and those who stood behind it among the political and military leaders of al-Jama'ah. He got into a literary confrontation with the biggest names among his professors, such as Sheikh Rifa'i Taha.

Furthermore, I remember that the historical leadership in the Egyptian prisons surprised the entire world by its proposed initiative to stop the violence in Egypt from its side, and by inviting the Egyptian government to reciprocate the move by stopping any confrontations. This initiative occurred when we were in Afghanistan during what became known as the Second Arab Afghani Term in the Taliban era. That was around the end of 1997. I personally, along with the most prominent leaders of al-Jama'ah al-Islamiyyah present in Afghanistan, followed up on the events of this initiative as they unfolded. Other prominent figures who were visiting us at that time from Iran and who eventually took up residence in Afghanistan around the middle of 2000 were also there following these events along with us. I can summarize the stages of that initiative in the following principal points:

- Some of the imprisoned leaders of al-Jama'ah al-Islamiyyah of Egypt proposed an initiative, presented through their lawyer, Muntasar al-Zayyat, in which they declared that they would stop all armed activities in Egypt. They invited the Egyptian government to reciprocate this move, and they received immediate support in this matter from branch leaders in Europe, especially Brother Osama Rushdie.
- Outside of Egypt, there was a commotion among members of the military and political leadership of al-Jama'ah al-Islamiyyah of Egypt. This was especially true among the principal figures in Iran and Afghanistan. There was disagreement over the stance toward the crackdown on the military field of operations in Egypt and the possibility of engaging in military activity. There was also disagreement over the situation of Sheikh 'Umar 'Abd al-Rahman, who was imprisoned in America. Nevertheless, all branches of the leadership of al-Jama'ah, even those in opposition to an overseas initiative, considered the unity of al-jama'ah to be the most important of all matters, including issues of principles and curriculum. However, some symbolic figures who represented al-Jama'ah showed signs of opposition to the initiative. Among the most prominent of those were Sheikh Rifa'i Taha, Brother Muhammad al-Islambuli, and Mustafa Hamzah. Nevertheless, they still all put on a front of unity following the meetings of their advisory councils. However, some members declared that they were putting their mem-

berships in al-Jama'ah's advisory council on hold because of their lack
of conviction in the matter.

- The Egyptian government repaid that initiative by turning it down
  and continuing in its security confrontations: the accomplished leader
  Sheikh Abu-Talal aka Tal'at Fu'ad Qasam was kidnapped in Croatia on
  his way to visit the leaders of al-Jama'ah in Bosnia. Furthermore, some
  of those individuals who were being hunted down and were in hiding
  in Cairo, disappeared from their apartments under mysterious circumstances. The Egyptian security apparatuses as well as the Egyptian
  media and the Ministry of Interior continued cracking down on al-
  Jama'ah and continued to oppose the proposed initiative until the end
  of 2003 when they began to show some partial cooperation.

- Al-Jama'ah al-Islamiyyah's unanimous decision to adopt the initiative gained support from both the internal and external leadership of
  the organization. The turning over of the leadership of al-Jama'ah to
  Brother Abu-Hazim aka Mustafa Hamzah, as they elected him emir,
  only added to the vexation of the government and made it more determined to continue on its path. The imprisoned historical leaders, as
  well as all those leaders living abroad who supported the initiative and
  who followed their philosophy, expanded their curricular stands to the
  point that they began to publish religious legal research and ideological studies that looked into what they referred to as the rejection of
  violence. They began to criticize the principles on which the jihadist
  confrontation against the apostate governments was based and about
  which they had previously filled the Islamic literature with literary
  works in its support.

- Al-Jama'ah al-Islamiyyah published certain books under the motto of
  "ideological reexaminations," through which it regressed ideologically
  and systematically until it reached the point of collapse. They began to
  discuss the sanctity of the infidels' blood and money and reached the
  point of declaring the assassinated President Sadat a martyr who had
  died unjustly, a victim of civil strife.

- Sadat's assassination was considered a great honor to the heroes of al-
  Jama'ah al-Islamiyyah and, in turn, to the entire Muslim nation. Now
  Sadat was being referred to by one of them as the martyr! I had the
  opportunity to review some of what was written in those books by
  reading excerpts from them that were published by the media. Without
  making any excuses for the imprisoned leadership or for that hunted

leadership that was, for all intents and purposes, ensnared in a circle of impotency, one can at this point say that al-Jama'ah al-Islamiyyah of Egypt had completely reversed its ideological identity.

- I will not broach the subject of the initiative from my point of view and that of all the mujahideens. I do remember, though, that we could have sat down all together under the protection of the Taliban, and we could have studied this matter and listened to all the excuses and reasons from those involved in it. However, this initiative was rejected in its entirety. Nevertheless, we maintain all respect and amicability to our brothers and their accomplishments.

- The Jihad Jama'ah of Egypt as well as the rest of the jihadist movement rejected the initiative and announced this fact publicly despite the limited access they had to the media during their stay with the Taliban, which was known for its technical seclusion from the rest of the world because of the embargo it was subjected to and because of its media policies that were different from those of the rest.

- The leadership members of al-Jama'ah al-Islamiyyah, who were residing overseas, were humiliated as a result of the initiative. However, all any one of them could do was to express his personal rejection of the situation while still keeping up the front of unity and solidarity with the historical membership members, which constitute the principle faction of the advisory council!

- When the events of September 11 occurred, those cadres of al-Jama'ah who had survived all the battles and were still living in Afghanistan finally left there. It may have been that al-Jama'ah's outspoken position on distancing itself from the Taliban and from bin Laden helped these cadres to be the least affected by all the waves of extreme hardships that destroyed al Qaida and the Arab Afghans as well as the majority of the jihadist movement.

- Toward the middle of 2003, the Egyptian government took the world by surprise when it showed partial cooperation with the initiative that had been started and proposed about six years before: it began to release batch after batch of al-Jama'ah al-Islamiyyah detainees. A few hundred of them were released, among whom was Sheikh Karam Zuhdi, who was one their historical leaders. Other leaders were also released. All those released from jail began to write books and curricular genealogical studies to compare any newly released eulogies to their old ideologies after they had obviously broken away from their previous beliefs. I heard from some media sources that these ex-prisoners were writing a book recounting their previous experiences and it was to be titled "The River of Memories." I did not get a chance to take a look at this book, but I did get to read excerpts published in the media about some of the fraudulent claims they were making. It appeared that this segment of al-Jama'ah had joined [Donald] Rumsfeld in his ideological war, and they had become a part of the American and the infidels' campaign in the fight against terrorism! Our brothers who had repented from the worship of God and the waging of jihad against His enemies did not miss the opportunity to put on record their criticism of the events of September 11 as well of their perpetrators.

- This last initiative from al-Jama'ah al-Islamiyyah was praised by every antiterrorism program that was filling the Arab media in those days. It became an example and a model to the scholars of Saudi Arabia and to others in the fight against all jihadist manifestations that were multiplying in Saudi Arabia and elsewhere, because of the reality of the latest American Christian Crusades.

- Around the beginning of 2004, the president of Egypt met with his counterpart of Iran during one of the international summits in Europe. Those who were watching this interpreted it as a key to the beginning of a new era between the two countries. Both presidents declared that they were determined to ameliorate relations that had gone astray since the days of the Khomeini revolution, when the shah went to Egypt to seek asylum.

- Immediately following that declaration, Iran went on to receive the leaders of al-Jama'ah al-Islamiyyah, and it even named one its main streets in Tehran after the martyr Khalid al-Islambuli. As Mohammad Khatimi returned to his country of Iran, the Iranian government agreed to the Egyptian government's repeated requests not to name the street after this martyr. Following these events, the media began to publish news of Iran's intention to hand over all of the Egyptian detainees, the Arab Afghans, and the members of al Qaida to the Egyptian government. It was then revealed that some of the Egyptian citizens residing in Iran had been indeed turned over to the Egyptian government, while others had escaped to Afghanistan. I do not know the extent of the truth of this last piece of information, nor whether these events affected the leadership of al-Jama'ah in Iran. I was not able to investigate any of this information.

The Jihadist Experience in Tunisia in the Early 1980s

The birth of the Islamic revival, as it is known today in Tunisia, dates back to the middle of the 1970s, when Sheikh Rashid al-Ghanushi and other Islamist companions of his established a movement that became known as the Islamic Current in Tunisia. Like others in the Islamic revival at the time, this movement was based on ideological principles that are very similar to those of the Muslim Brotherhood organization. Still, it did have special traits particular to Tunisia.

The Islamic Current in Tunisia included many different ideologies, some of which were missionary, some political, some education related, and others jihadist based. The latter were represented by Sheikh Dr. Salih Kirar. The Islamic Current in Tunisia got involved in numerous political altercations with the regime of the country's previous president, al-Habib Abu-Raqibah, and as a result, many of the Current's leaders were imprisoned, its newspapers stopped, and, on numerous occasions, its activity was threatened. Toward the end of its existence, it took on the fight with the government through the means of elections.

However, the Islamic Current's covert military apparatus, which was made up of a number of different ranking officers in the French army, had its own plan to prepare for a military coup they believed would place the Islamists in power. This plan represents the most important and the most serious jihadist attempt to overthrow the government in Tunisia. Even though this attempt cannot be considered one of the jihadist movement's experiences because of the ideological nature of the al-Ghanushi group, I would still like to give a brief overview of it, because the men who carried it out and who were involved in it had ideologies closer in nature to those of the jihadist movement then they were to the general political movement. This is what I came to find out later after I met some of these men personally.

- To the extent of my knowledge, there were a very few cells besides the Islamic Current that carried on the Salafist jihadist concept. They carried out a few simple, inexperienced operations that led to the martyrdom of some of them, the arrest of some others, and the escape out of Tunisia of the remaining. Among the latter was Sheikh 'Ali al-Azraq, who had issued a fatwa allowing them to instigate jihad against the regime. Shcikh al-Azraq was able to escape to Saudi Arabia following that failed plan, only to be extradited back to Tunisia by the Saudi government during the mid-1980s, where he was executed in one of Tunisia's prisons while repeating his allegiance to God and His Prophet. He was past seventy years of age. This is the story as it was relayed to me by one of the members, a Tunisian brother, involved in that experience.

- As for the coup that was planned by the Jama'ah of the Islamic Current (which later became known as the Resurgence Faction) and that was led by Sheikh Rashid al-Ghanushi, I was given a summary of it from some brothers who were themselves among those officers who had planned it and had overseen it. I can summarize it as follows. It was initiated based on the principles of a revolution and a coup that were full of courage and long-held political views. It represented the ideo-logical and emotional makeup of Sheikh Rashid al-Ghanushi. This is notwithstanding the curricular mix-up that was attributed to the movement of the Islamic Current and its top leaders since its start.

- The movement had an ambitious plan that focused on enabling cadres and the organizational entities to overthrow the governmental system and its leaders on all levels. Therefore, the movement had a plan that encompassed all aspects of politics, education, finance, media, and so forth. Among those apparatuses that were created for that goal was the military apparatus for the movement.

- The tactical planner for the military apparatus embedded a number of soldiers, who were volunteers in the Tunisian army, into the three military branches: the army, the air force, and the navy. Whenever possible, he also recruited anyone with Islamic tendencies into the army. Disregarding any marginal details, the Islamic Current was well planned and extremely covert in nature within a secular army that bans its members from any religious adherence and monitors even the slightest whispers of prayers or supplications to God from the faithful. This secular army considered such religious practices or tendencies to be a type of dubious behavior that could, at the very least, lead to dismissal from the army.

- Those young officers belonging to the apparatus stuck to a highly covert behavior in this matter, based on fatwas issued to them by the scholars of the organization. They made sure to keep any religious adherence on their part highly secretive, to the point where they would pray in secret. Should prayer times occur during a lesson or training session, these highly disciplined youths would sometimes even perform the prayer ritual only in their minds and hearts! They would fast only if they could do so without anyone noticing, and they even had to settle for allowing their women to only dress conservatively and not to wear the head veil so their secret would not be discovered! The organization continued on its plan for a military coup to overthrow the government for roughly ten years.

- A soldier friend of mine who was among those who oversaw the planning for this coup told me that this plan was a well-directed and ambitious one. The details of this plan, however, are (now) in the hands of the enemy. This allows us to mention some of these details so we may record this history. The movement was able to establish relations in neighboring countries and, thus, was able to put together a more fine-tuned plan. If my memory serves me correctly, I believe the date of execution for this plan was in 1986, after the Bourguiba regime had foiled the Islamic Current's chance of winning the elections by sabotaging the ballots in the first stages of the elections (to a point that surprised those who were supervising the election process); this was made especially obvious because of the Tunisian people's already-established reputation of lack of piousness and because of the already well-spread secularism in the country and the tendencies to follow and imitate the French mannerisms in their life. Nevertheless, there still appeared in Tunisia a sense of moral nobility, sympathy with the religion of Islam, and a trust in its political plan. These attributes were and still are present in all Arab and Muslim communities, without exception.

- According to those who were involved, a certain weakness and hesitation by a university professor from the civilian sector of the organization who was in contact with the command of the soldiers responsible for the coup led to the discovery of the coup attempt shortly before it was carried out. In turn, the interior minister at the time, who is now the president, Zayn al-'Abidin Ibn 'Ali, was quick to stage a peaceful coup with support from the American intelligence services and the security apparatuses' command, as well as from some of the organization's members who followed the politics route. As a result, President Habib Bourguiba was deposed because of old age and incompetency, and he was placed in an isolated palace, where he was allowed to live out his remaining days. In the meantime, most of those who were planning the coup were arrested, while others were able to escape.

- Because President Ibn Ali had arranged and carried out his coup in a hurry, he was always afraid of the depth of the roots of the Islamic coup attempt. Therefore, he was obligated to make a deal with Rashid al-Ghanushi and his commanding officers, in which he conceded to release the officers who were imprisoned until then in return for the organization's official recognition of the new regime and a promise to stop any attempts on the organization's part to overthrow the government.

- That is how the release of two hundred of the officers of the Islamic coup operation came to take place. They were given their choice of European countries to which they could apply for political asylum. The majority of the leadership of the civilian sector of the organization also left to Western countries. At the top of the list of those who left the country following this accord was Sheikh Rashid al-Ghanushi.

- Following this failure, the Resurgence Faction, as well as Sheikh Rashid himself, turned to the extreme opposite in their political spectrum to the point of adopting democratic ideals, or what was referred to as the "shunning of violence." Sheikh Rashid, however, established a London-based command center for his activities throughout Europe. He adopted an ideology and a path that is in conformity with Western ideals and accepted moderate Islamic views; however, this is not the appropriate place to discuss this particular issue. Sheikh Rashid published a book for this purpose, entitled *Political Freedoms in Islam*. This book desecrated many of Islam's principles, under the general call for the moderation of the curriculum he had created. He went so far as to negate and to eliminate certain religious teachings under the pretense of a claim for necessity of such actions!

- That is how the only serious modern-day attempt for the establishment of an Islamic government in Tunisia was annihilated.

- Sheikh Salih Kirar was arrested in France and was placed under house arrest about fifteen years ago, where he still remains to this day. The fear is that he would continue in his jihadist activities and ambitions, because he represented a very serious jihadist movement through the Jama'ah of the Islamic Current in Tunisia. God grant Sheikh Kirar his freedom.

- As for the jihadist movement itself and its cells in Tunisia, some of the Tunisian jihadist youths headed to Afghanistan toward the end of the 1980s and around the beginning of the 1990s. They attempted to establish a nucleus for the jihadist groups to gather around, just as the Libyan and Algerian youths of the Arab Afghan had tried to do, but all they ended up with were a series of failed attempts. The reason all these attempts failed is because of a lack of competent cadres among these young men, which could not take on the all the necessary responsibilities of such a mission.

- In 1992 the gathering of the Arab Afghans was over and some of the Tunisian mujahideen left to Sudan to attempt once more to establish such a mission; but that was all to no avail. Others among them went on to Europe to seek political asylum. Unfortunately, and despite having many faithful and good members among them, the reputation of the Tunisian brothers, among the mujahideen groups in general, became that of a scattered group with a less-then-perfect image. As for the Islamist soldiers in Europe, they were worn out by the severe crackdowns they were being subjected to and the sanctions they were facing from the Tunisian regime. They were also suffering from the recruitment attempts made by the Overseas Resurgence Faction, headed by Sheikh al-Ghanushi, which reached a level of financial and emotional restrictions by the latter on these soldiers. Eventually, some of these men had to give in and join the organization of al-Ghanushi because of their financial and emotional suffering. Others waited it out patiently, while keeping to themselves and with no power to do anything but to survive from day to day like many others of the mujahideen and the Islamist men in Europe around the end of the twentieth century.

- Around the beginning of the Taliban era, among those mujahideen who had gone to that Muslim principality were some Tunisian mujahideen who had had the honor of fighting in Bosnia in the jihad against the war of extermination that took place around the mid-1990s. Once again, they attempted to establish their own jihadist grouping, which at first seemed to be succeeding despite some obstacles, disorganization, and a viruslike extremism that had afflicted some of the Tunisian mujahideen. In the end, however, all these problems prevented this promising attempt from fully succeeding. Some of the more mature members among them were able to establish an independent camp of their own with an acceptable level of management through their cooperation with the cadres of other Jama'ahs. They offered great training services to the Arab groups that had gathered in that area during the Taliban era.

- However, as the brothers were busy establishing all of this, the turn of events in the world led them on a different course from the one they were on: the effects of the explosions that took place in Washington and New York on September 11 reached all the way to Afghanistan. As we have seen earlier, the American Crusaders arrived in December 2001. The Tunisian mujahideen situated themselves in a very particular location on the mountaintops of Tora Bora, in the mountains of Sulayman, west of Jalalabad. They stood by the other mujahideen brothers, because all Arabs were targeted in Afghanistan. The news came later of their heroic stands next to the rest of the mujahideen brothers in the battles of self-defense and in the battles to defend the Muslim principality.

- The Tunisian brothers had planned to take their jihad back to Tunisia, where they wanted to establish a jihadist organization that would bring them all together. They focused on keeping their communication with their brothers outside the country, making sure to provide all the requirements for such communication. They did not have much interest in the battle of the Taliban and the Muslim principality, and they were hesitant to get involved with the Taliban government or to consider it a religious legal leader in Afghanistan. This was because of some of the religious sources they rely on, as well as their focus on their own project. They were also not convinced of the attempts bin Laden and al Qaida were making, nor of the latter's military unidirectional penchant. Indeed, this was the case with the majority of the organizations and the Arab groups in Afghanistan. Nevertheless, despite all of these facts, when the American attacks occurred, every one of them got involved in that battle.

- That is how the Tunisian mujahideen performed their duty and stood as heroes in the jihad. Many of them were martyred and others were taken prisoners. Because they accounted for a very small number among the mujahideen to start with, very few of them, I believe, escaped the aftermath of the September events. I think that these Tunisians died while still hoping that God will eventually grant Tunisia another generation of mujahideen.

The Experience of the Fighting Islamic Group in Libya (1990–2001)

As far I as I know, there was a jihadist attempt by the first nuclear cells of the jihadist movement in Libya against the regime of Mu'ammar al-Qadhafi sometime around the middle of the 1980s. The discovery of those cells led to a crackdown on them and, eventually, to the exodus of its principal cadres to Afghanistan. This squadron of Libyan young men established itself on the Pakistani borders and in the various training camps spread out across Afghanistan. These men were diligently training their primary cadres in different areas, while they were attempting to reestablish their connections with the other Libyan brothers who had spread out in different countries.

They attempted to gather everyone back together for the purposes of training and preparing for a continuation of the jihad movement back in Libya. Among all the Arab mujahideen who were in that region at the time, these men were known for their time management skills and their perseverance in the military and behavioral training sessions they subjected themselves to. During the last three years of that period (1989–92), these men were able to establish themselves and were able to form the organization that was later known as the Fighting Jama'ah Islamiyyah in Libya. They were able to recruit the majority of the Libyan mujahideen who happened to be among the Arab Afghans.

The Libyan mujahideen participated competently alongside their brothers from other countries in the events of the Arab jihad in Afghanistan. Some cadres among them were very quick to distinguish themselves in the areas of training and on the front lines. Following these events, the men of the Fighting Jama'ah Islamiyyah broke away independently to their own guesthouses and camps, as did most other old and new Arab jihadist groups. They pledged allegiance to an emir from within their group for the purpose of organization. Thus began their leadership formation as a jihadist organization that started to take its place among the distinguished Arab jihadist organizations.

The Fighting Jama'ah Islamiyyah could be considered as an example of the jihadist Salafist groups, a fact that later became very obvious when they published their ideological curriculum in a book entitled *The Fighting Jama'ah Islamiyyah of Libya*. This was also made obvious to everyone through their monthly publication *al-Fajr* [The Dawn], as well as through a number of investigations they carried out that were published in the areas of ideology, politics, and sharia.

As the winds of unrest blew into Pakistan against the Arabs in a security crackdown directed by America, the Libyan brothers, unlike the majority of the Arab mujahideen who went back to their home countries, could not do the same. They were in the same situation as the mujahideen from Syria, Egypt, Tunisia, Iraq, and other countries where they were being hunted down by their governments. Therefore, like the majority of the mujahideen in their situation, the majority of the Fighting Jama'ah Islamiyyah of Libya headed to Sudan, which had opened its doors to all the mujahideen and Islamists when the regime of al-Bashir and his ally, al-Turabi, came to power in 1990. A very small number of these men, however, chose to head to Western and European countries to seek political asylum.

The period from 1991 to 1995, during which the Fighting Jam'ah Islamiyyah of Libya took up residence in Sudan, could be considered as an establishment period for them. They put together an ambitious plan to prepare their cadres in many different avenues, especially in that of religious-law (sharia) education. Many of them went to study in Saudi Arabia, whereas others headed to Mauritania. Indeed, by the time the Second Arab Afghan Term in Afghanistan came about (1996–2001), the Fighting Jama'ah Islamiyyah of Libya had already formed a number of the most distinguished cadres in the area of sharia; they were among the best of such cadres among all the Arab Afghans and within the jihadist movement entirely.

Some of the Libyan Arab Afghan cadres, those who had not joined the Fighting Jam'ah Islamiyyah of Libya, were working in the camps of the al Qaida organization. They had left to Sudan to continue their work with Sheikh Osama bin Laden in the areas of agriculture and finance that he had started in Sudan. However, the activities of the Fighting group and others among the Islamists and the mujahideen within Libya or located in Sudan, as their presence was very close geographically, was a matter that was very unnerving to the regime of Colonel al-Qadhafi. Therefore, he made an agreement for the exchange of criminals and laid out a plan with the (Muslim) al-Bashir regime to fight all the Islamist constituents. That is when the al-Bashir regime backstabbed the Arab Afghans; but it started with the Libyans. The Sudanese government asked the Fighting organization to leave Sudan, and it asked Osama bin Laden to ask all the Libyan constituents working for him to leave. The government's excuse was the pressure that it was facing from the Libyan government and its obligation to the agreements it had just made with said regime. There was nothing to be done to avoid this matter, and thus began the exodus of all the Libyans from Sudan, only to be scattered again throughout the region. Those who were working for the al Qaida organization joined the Fighting Jam'ah Islamiyyah of Libya, thus adding some very significant cadres to that group.

In 1993, when the jihad began in Algeria, the Fighting Jam'ah Islamiyyah of Libya rushed to be present in that battle because of the country's geographical proximity to Libya. Many of the organization's mujahideen were sent over to that region to participate with their brothers of the Armed Islamic Group [GIA] in the jihad against the Algerian regime. It was a very bitter experience; the influence of the ignorant and infidel elements led the Algerian intelligence services to the Armed Islamic Group, and they were able to break through its security and to control the leadership of the GIA. This led the organization onto a deviated and tainted path.

However, what is of concern to us here is that the criminal leadership of the Armed Islamic Group led by Abu-'Abd al-Rahman Amin since 1955 added to its list of crimes the murder of the majority of those foreign mujahideen who had come with the Fighting Jam'ah Islamiyyah of Libya! God help them, for they have veered off the path of righteousness in creating their own ideologies! What is certain is that they are definitely not following the true Salafist creed. Only a very few men were able to flee to regions where other organizations were situated, so that they may bear witness to the dangerous deviation that had taken place in Algeria! God help us all!!

In 1994 the Fighting Jam'ah Islamiyyah of Libya began its military activities in Libya through three different axes:

1. Guerilla warfare inside Libya against the different sectors of the government.
2. The establishment of some necessary elements in the region of the al-Jabal al-Akhdar in the East of Libya for the purpose of waging guerrilla warfare in the mountains and in the surrounding countryside.
3. The assassination attempt on Col. Mu'ammar al-Qadhafi. Unfortunately, the strategic elements in Libya prevented the success of this movement.

The facts were that the population of Libya is small, and the country has a large desert terrain throughout which the principal cities are scattered at wide intervals. The country is also situated on a narrow coastal border. Another factor involved was the inappropriate timing of the movement itself, as it occurred at the same time as Arab, regional, and global systematic coordination was beginning to take place to fight all jihadist groups. This made it impossible for any arrangements to take place between the direction of operation inside the country and that located outside of it.

This was also a factor in limiting the movements of the mujahideen into and out of Libya because of the dangers involved.

The tyrant's regime in Libya was quick to inflict great losses on the mujahideen, despite the varied and heroic operations carried out by these men against the security apparatuses, the army, and the governmental militia during that time. Thus, the cells of the Fighting Jam'ah Islamiyyah of Libya were annihilated in the al-Jabal al-Akhdar region and the leader, brother 'Abd al-Rahman Hattab, was martyred. Many of the men were also martyred in different cities, while others were arrested and imprisoned. The Fighting Jam'ah Islamiyyah of Libya was thus obligated to change its military plan, and it announced this in its bulletins, which it presented in a program named "Strategic Offense and Tactical Withdrawal." Its activities were then practically limited to the last axis of its plan, which was the assassination of al-Qadhafi. However, despite repeated attempts, even this last part of the plan failed, because this devious tyrant escaped with his life time and again. This is when the Fighting Jam'ah Islamiyyah of Libya had to stop its activities in Libya.

Since 1995 the so-called global war on terrorism has been escalating its crackdown on all the mujahideen everywhere. Many cadres of the jihadist movement have fallen prey to the systematic arrangement between each country's regime, that of the whole Arab region, and the whole world in general. Many of those cadres have suffered, because these oppressive security campaigns have focused on depriving the mujahideen of any safe haven or financial resources, while hunting down the principal jihadist elements of the movement to assassinate them or to extradite them back to their home country. The Fighting Jam'ah Islamiyyah of Libya had its share of misfortune because of all of these factors, as some of its cells were hunted down by the governments of Turkey, Syria, Jordan, Yemen, Sudan, and others. Some were arrested and turned back to the Libyan government, as was the case of those who were detained by the governments of Sudan, Syria, and Turkey. Those among them who were living abroad in Western countries were subjected to an immense crackdown and sanctionlike conditions, as was the fate of the rest of the mujahideen and the Islamists in general.

Despite the fact that many new and old Arab and jihadist organizations arrived in Afghanistan in 1996, it seemed that the leadership of the Fighting Jam'ah Islamiyyah of Libya hesitated to make the same move to this new haven. It appeared to be very wary of the idea of reuniting

the entire jihadist group in one location once again. I was among the first
to head to Afghanistan during that period. I was also among those who
encouraged them and everyone else to go to Afghanistan and to establish
a strong gathering so as to start over again. I believed that those who hesitated to do so were wrong in their decision. However, after the events of
September 11 occurred, and because of the aftermath of those events on
the jihadist movement, I am now inclined to believe that there might have
been some reasoning and sense to their hesitations. Nevertheless, everything moved on and they were still under constant threat even in those
countries they were hiding in. No one could have imagined the September
11 events or their aftermath. The success of the Taliban led to their control
of most of Afghanistan, and the Arab Afghans found great power in that
haven. Soon, all those who hesitated up until then were forced to head to
Afghanistan, especially after the security crackdowns they were facing
everywhere in the world. They were also tempted by what they saw the
other mujahideen enjoying through the power and the safety provided by
the Taliban. The prominent cadres among the leadership of the Fighting
Jam'ah Islamiyyah of Libya began to file into the Islamic principality in
Afghanistan along with other mujahideen like them.

The Fighting Jam'ah Islamiyyah of Libya hesitated to enter with its
cadres into the Taliban wars with the Northern Alliance forces because
they were afraid of getting involved in a war of attrition that was not in
their plans. Another possible reason for their hesitation might have been
that they were still not very convinced why they should get involved in
a Taliban war and their lack of understanding of the religious legality
of an emir of the faithful as an imam by sharia who must be followed.
However, after having studied the situation around the beginning of 1999,
they slowly began to get involved and to stand by the Taliban government.
They ended up playing a major role in supporting the Taliban in different
areas, especially in the fields of the military and the media.

During the Second Arab Afghan Term in Afghanistan, the Fighting
Jama'ah Islamiyyah of Libya proved itself to be among the best of the Arab
organizations as far as performance. They were one of the best among an
estimated fourteen organizations and independent military groups. They
had their own camp and more than one guesthouse, which they used as
the headquarters for their activities.

During a period in which the shadow of secularism was creeping over
the entire world, it started also infecting the thought process of the muja-

hideen, including those of the Fighting Jama'ah Islamiyyah of Libya, especially those elements among them who were not Libyan. Their interests began to shift to many different causes and areas even though their innate Libyan direction was always apparent and a constant attribute of their activities, their operational system, and their media productions.

Osama bin Laden and al Qaida were not successful in swaying the Fighting Jama'ah Islamiyyah of Libya to their goal of uniting the jihadi forces against America. Bin Laden was also unable to recruit them to his alliance, which he named the "Global Jihad Front against the Christians" and which throughout the entire five years ended up attracting only the Jihad Organization of Egypt led by Sheikh Dr. Ayman al-Zawahiri. It seems that the reasons for this were curricula issues, operational issues, as well as reasons pertaining to the direction and the strategic goal of the jihadist work of each organization. Thus, the Fighting Jama'ah Islamiyyah of Libya remained independent from the rest of the Arab Afghans in their plans and activities during their last days. When the events of September 11 occurred, the Fighting Jama'ah Islamiyyah of Libya, like other Arab jihadist groups, was busy with its own activities and movement plans. As a matter of fact, it might have been the most prominent among all of them as far as its activity and performance. The Americans carried out their attacks, by air and on land, with the help of the treacherous northerners, as well as that of the different factions that had deviated from the path of righteousness. All of this led all the Arab Afghans to enter into a battle of survival and self-defense for themselves, for the Islamic principality, and for the emir of the faithful and his regime that began to fall apart on many fronts.

The mujahideen of the Fighting Jama'ah Islamiyyah of Libya participated in that war, and they defended the borders of Kabul admirably. Another group from their organization took their posts in the South, in the regions of Kandahar and Hilmund. Many of them were martyred. Their leadership and the best of their cadres were always present at the forefront of the battles. Some of their leaders also played a very prominent role in certain battles that followed later in many different locations. Those who survived all the shelling and all these battles were then obligated to withdraw toward Pakistan. Since that time and up until this day, one of their leaders, Sheikh Abu-al-Layth, has taken over the command of the anti-American resistance groups at the borders of Pakistan and Afghanistan.

The fate of the Fighting Jama'ah Islamiyyah of Libya was similar to that of other jihadist groups ever since then: a number of its cadres were imprisoned as a result of the treachery of the Pakistani government, army, and security forces, God give them the reward they deserve for such acts! This treachery led to the death of some of these men and the arrest of others by the American forces, the leaders of the Christian Crusades.

Like their Arab and Arab Afghans counterparts in the jihadist movement, the losses endured by the Fighting Jama'ah Islamiyyah of Libya were great. Many were killed, many were imprisoned, and many became destitute. Those who managed to escape these afflictions, along with their counterparts from the jihadist movement in general, became like strangers in this new post–September 11 era, living in fear and in hiding throughout this world.

I developed very close friendships with the brothers from the Fighting Jama'ah Islamiyyah of Libya through our work together in many areas and on many occasions. The most important of these was the period during which I was living in London. During that time, I wrote a number of jihadist ideology–based articles that were published in their magazine, *al-Fajr*. Further, through mutual cooperation among us, we were able to uncover the Armed Islamic Group's deviations in Algeria, which began to occur around the end of 1995. That cooperative effort with them and with the Jihad Jama'ah of Egypt led to the condemnation of the Armed Islamic Group's activities in Algeria by the majority of the jihadist movement groups at the time.

I was also involved with them in another cooperative effort later on in the Second Arab Afghan Term during the days of the Taliban. We were again reunited in the fight against the aftermath of the events of September 11 before we left Afghanistan.

Indeed, I do believe that the Fighting Jama'ah Islamiyyah of Libya was a principal axis of the jihadist movement and distinguished itself from the rest through its presence and through its media productions. I also believe that the Fighting Jama'ah Islamiyyah of Libya's leaders, knowledge seekers, cadres, and all its various members, were among the most giving, the best mannered, and the most capable among all those involved in the jihadist movement.

The Contemporary Jihadist Experiences in Algeria since 1991

I had previously recounted an early jihadist experience that was led by the mujahid Sheikh Mustafa Abu-Ya'li in the early 1970s. The martyr

Sheikh Abu-Ya'li was one of the mujahideen who had fought against French colonialism in Algeria. Like thousands of other mujahideen like him, he dreamt of gaining independence from colonialism through jihad so that establishment of an Islamic government in Algeria might result. However, the French, who had mastered the art of freedom as well as they had the art of colonialism, made sure that those who took power after them in Algeria would be secular or socialist in nature. They made sure it would be someone who was raised on the principles and ideologies of the enemies of Islam. This was one of the reasons that led to the accumulation and buildup of oppression and tyranny that led our martyr, Mustafa Abu-Ya'li, to revolt against it. However, that movement was quickly crushed, its leader was martyred, and many of those associated with it were imprisoned for several years after that.

Toward the end of the 1980s, financial problems escalated in Algeria because of the vast corruption that had permeated all of the regime's elements and its command. That is when a revolution, known then as "The Bread Revolution," erupted, and the whole status quo of Algeria was at risk of being severely shaken. Therefore, al-Shadhili Ibn Jadid [Chadli Bendjedid], who was president at that time, tried to mediate the situation by declaring an economic open-door policy, by allowing the formation of different political factions, and by calling for free, democratic elections in 1989. Certain preachers of the Islamic revival, a movement that had been severely oppressed since the independence era in 1963, took advantage of this unforeseen act from the president. Sheikh 'Abbasi, Sheikh Madani, and others who responded to this call hurried to declare the establishment of the Islamic Salvation Front. The latter was a large grouping of all those who were seeking an Islamic political program. Millions of people, from various backgrounds and of different principles, got involved with this front, united in the cause of supporting an Islamic political program.

When the country's multiparty elections were over, the Islamic Salvation Front had beaten the strongest secular political faction, which was that of the government itself, the National Liberation Front [FLN]! The Islamic Salvation Front then took control of the majority of Algeria's cities, which helped them in their preparations for winning the parliamentary elections in 1990. Winning the first round of elections by a vast majority vote enabled the Islamic Salvation Front to win the second round of the elections and, thus, to establish a government and to be nominated for the presidency of the state.

Warning bells sounded all over the world, and the great Christian country [France] declared its readiness to intervene so as to prevent the Islamists from reaching their goal of taking over the government. Francois Mitterrand, the president of France at the time, announced that France was ready to intervene militarily to resolve the issue and to prevent the Islamists from taking control of the government. Therefore, the only solution then available to these forces was to carry out a coup that was supported by the West, especially by France.

Indeed, there was a coup, the leadership of the Islamic Salvation Front was arrested, and all demonstrations were squelched. The military regime that took over the government and annihilated the democracy with the treacherous West's support established the Sahara prisons, where they placed thousands of the Islamist detainees. That began the contemporary jihadist revolution in Algeria, which is considered to be one of the most important and worthy jihadist experiences for study.

Since the beginning of this experience in 1989, and until its end in 1996, I had direct contact and relations with some of its events. It was a bitter learning experience, the events of which I recorded in a book that I lost during our quick withdrawal from Kabul at the time of the American attacks on Afghanistan following the events of September 11. At this point, I can still present the most important of these experiences I lived through personally.

The Experiences of the Armed Islamic Group in Algeria (1991–2000)

There were hundreds of Algerian young men, maybe over two thousand of them, who had escaped to Afghanistan. They quickly proved themselves to be among the bravest and most persistent of the mujahideen, as was already known of them. Al-Qari Sa'id, as he was known, established himself as a prominent leader among the Algerian brothers. He began to establish what was later known as the "Algerian Afghans." I became friends with this man, and I lived with him for a while in Peshawar. This enabled me to have an idea about that experience, and he told me repeatedly about his ambitions to form a jihadist organization that would function in Algeria once the Afghani jihad was over. It was not a plan that he was in hurry to accomplish, but it was one that was being prepared for through the constant organization and preparation training. However, with the events of the elections, with what happened to the Islamic

Salvation Front, and with the military coup that took place in 1990, the Algerian brothers were forced to return to their country to confront the military tyrant government.

Al-Qari Sa'id went to Algeria to evaluate the situation and came back having made the decision to gradually move the men who were with him back to Algeria. Once he found some brothers in Peshawar to take over the mission, he returned to Algeria to continue with the intensive training for and organization of the repatriation project of the mujahideen.

Over 5.3 million people had voted for the Islamic project and had won the elections only to see their victory taken away from them and tens of thousands of them imprisoned. It was natural, of course, for them to react positively and excitedly to the calls of jihad against the military forces that, along with the support of the West (and especially France) had prevented them from reaping the rewards of their victory.

Many elements of the Arab Islamic revival permeated the Algerian Islamic revival arena at that time, and it is important to understand all of them so as to gain a better grasp of that complicated experience. Among the most important of these factors, as far as size and influence, were the following:

The Islamic Salvation Front. This front was made up of a mix of the revival school of thought, its leadership, and the independent Islamic missionary organizations. Furthermore, there were also many among the general Muslim communities who had believed in the Islamic political project, even without a specified curriculum; they were satisfied to just follow a general motto. The most important elements of this front were:

- The student body. This body was headed by Sheikh Muhammad al-Sa'id, and it was established by a group of Islamist students from the University of Algeria.
- The Islamic State Movement. This is what was left over by the movement of the martyr Mustafa Abu-Ya'li. They followed the Salafist creed, and they were led and represented in the Islamic Salvation Front by Sheikh Sa'id Makhlufi.
- A large segment of the followers of the Salafist group. They were headed and represented in the front by their second man in command, the famous preacher, Sheikh 'Ali Bilhaj.
- A number of the independent representatives of the Islamic Call.
- A large base of Muslim constituents who were sympathetic to the Islamic project.

The Muslim Brotherhood—the global organization section in Algeria. This group was headed by Mahfudh al-Nihnah, who named his faction the Movement of the Peaceful Community. Al-Nihnah refused to enter under the umbrella of the Islamic Salvation Group. He remained distant from this group throughout his entire life despite all the problems it faced, and he waged a harmful attack on the mujahideen.

The local Muslim Brotherhood-Islamic Revival Faction. This group was led by 'Abdallah Jaballah. Their ideology was composed of a mix of that of the Muslim Brotherhood's and that of the local Algerian Islamic revival's.

The Salafists. The ideology of a large segment of this group was based on that of al-Jami al-Madkhali, which takes its roots from Saudi Arabia's official scholars. A great number of them supported the Algerian government.

The Salafist extremist youths. I was told that some of them established a movement known as the Capital's Salafism in reference to Algeria. They called themselves the Group for the Preaching of Good and the Prohibition of the Forbidden, and their ideology varied from extremism, to excommunication, and, finally, to ignorance in matters of religion and the world.

A Branch of the Islamic National Movement. This branch was composed of the followers of Sheikh Mustafa Abu-Ya'li. It did not join the Islamic Salvation Front because of its democratic curriculum. They followed a jihadist, Salafist ideology.

The Algerian Arab Afghans. This is the name they eventually acquired after moving back and forth between Algeria and Afghanistan. They were among the most important elements of the Islamic arena in Algeria at the time along with a few marginal movements of little influence, such as the groups for preaching and the different Salafist movements.

A short while after the coup, a few tens of young men headed to the mountains, where they began their search for arms and began training for the confrontation with the government. Very soon afterward, their armed battles with the latter started.

The great preservation movement in Algiers, the capital, which was called for by the Islamic Salvation Front, led to the unexpected kidnapping of both leaders of the front, the two great sheikhs 'Abbas Madani and 'Ali Bilhaj, who had led a preservation movement that recruited thousands of protesters. This was a great shock to everyone, especially since there seemed to be no resistance to the act whatsoever! Some time later, while I was researching this issue, I heard that some members of the Islamic Salvation Front's advisory council had betrayed the two sheikhs and had not followed orders for the confrontation! I had kept a record in my now-missing documents of some details and names but, unfortunately, I do not have these anymore.

Thus, the Islamic Salvation Front ended up without a leader, and its principal elements went back to work in an unofficial status. Later on, Sheikh 'Abd al-Qadir Shabuti, Sheikh 'Abd al-Razzaq Rijam, Sheikh Muhammad Sa'id Makhlufi, and Sheikh Muhammad al-Sa'id all surfaced as the leaders of groups of the armed resistance against the government in the capital, in the mountains, and in other locations. A great armed, political unrest permeated the country, and there were many indications of a vicious civil war to come. Indeed, the civil war erupted with extreme consequences, and the mujahideen assassinated the new president, Abu-Diyaf [Boudiaf], thus bringing the armed clashes to their climax.

As I mentioned before, al-Qari Sa'id had gone to Algeria for a period of one month and, upon his return, he recounted to me the great efforts that were undertaken to gather the Arab Afghans along with those cells that were still left from the group of Mustafa Abu-Ya'li, with the intention to unite them with some of the cells whose ideology was Salafist jihadist and which were already present over there. He wanted to unite them all to form a single jihadist group. Al-Qari Sa'id returned after that and informed his deputy in Peshawar that he had indeed formed the group as planned and that it was named The Armed Islamic Group. That was around the end of 1990, or maybe early 1991.

A large segment of the advisory council of the Islamic Salvation Front broke away and established a new leadership, which got involved in negotiations and cooperation with the military government. Some others, like Muhammad al-Sa'id, rejected the truce negotiations and began a confrontation under the name of the Islamic Salvation Front. Soon after that, their group formed a group known as the Islamic Salvation Army, and Madani Mirzaq emerged as its leader. The Islamic Salvation Army's ideology was based on the elements of that belonging to the Salafist jihad, and they rejected a return to a democratic system.

The military government was quick to suppress the civil disobedience movement and restrained the political factions, among which were the Islamic Salvation Front, the revival movement, the Muslim Brotherhood movement (started by Nihnah), the Movement for Culture and Democracy (a faction headed by Ayat Ahmad), and the National Liberation Front, which was represented by the last civilian prime minister, Abd al-Hamid

Mihri. There were also many secular, socialist, and communist factions that continued their opposition but were repressed and their leaders left the country. The number of Islamist detainees reached over fifty thousand prisoners who filled jails set up in the Sahara. This led to an increase in the number of armed resistant forces in the mountains; it was reported that their number reached over the tens of thousands! They began to carry out many operations on a daily basis.

News of the jihad in Algeria eclipsed all other headlines in the media during that time, and the Armed Islamic Group became a well-known name, as the most important and the most prominent of the active groups militarily in the confrontation against the government. However, as soon as the group's emir, 'Abd al-Haq al-'Iyayidah, began to emerge, he was quickly arrested by the Moroccan government while he was attempting to purchase arms. He was turned over to the Algerian government and was replaced by another brother, whose name I cannot recall at this time, who was killed, and then replaced in 1993 by the new emir, Abu-'Abdallah Ahmad, who accomplished great things during his era.

The intensity of the military operations escalated, and al-Qari Sa'id was arrested while waging one of the large attacks against the navy in the capital, Algiers. He was able to escape, along with over seven hundred other detainees, from one of Algiers' prisons a few months after that. He then exerted all his efforts to unite the fighting groups into a single entity, but he was killed under mysterious circumstances toward the end of 1994. During that period, the brutality of the government escalated to the point where, in a single incident alone, they assassinated hundreds of political detainees in the Sirkaji prison, which was one of the capital's jail facilities.

In the beginning of 1993, all those in support of jihad in Algeria were calling on the mujahideen to unite in a single entity. Indeed, many jihadist leaders in the Armed Islamic Group exerted immense efforts to accomplish this goal, which was the dream of the second emir of the group, a dream he was not able to live long enough to see happen. Among those who tried to accomplish this goal were the jihadist leaders of the Islamic Salvation Army and many of the local jihadist cells. Abu-'Abdallah Ahmad had taken over as emir following the murder of his predecessor, and it was during his time that the unification happened. He then aired a very moving video, through which he spread joy in the jihadist communities as he showed the sheikhs of the Islamic Salvation Army's leadership pledging allegiance to a young man who seemed young enough to be their son.

The young man was the new emir for the united jihad movement, which was named the Armed Islamic Group. The emir's name was Abu-'Abdallah Ahmad, and the unification led to high hopes of a close and sweeping victory.

The emir for the Islamic Salvation Army, Madani Mirzaq, opposed and rejected the unification. He admonished those who joined it, and he refused to acknowledge any decisions except those made by the two imprisoned sheikhs, 'Abbas Madani and 'Ali Bilhaj. He was determined to follow only these two sheikhs and to keep himself separated from the unification. Nevertheless, many segments and secondary groups from all over Algeria entered into this unification. Thus, the Armed Islamic Group came to represent over 90 percent of the armed mujahideen, whose number had already reached the tens of thousands around the beginning of 1994.

Abu-'Abdallah Ahmad was murdered, just like his predecessor, under mysterious circumstances. A bulletin was issued after that from some of the advisory council members of the Armed Islamic Group announcing Abu-'Abd al-Rahman Amin as the new leader of the group. The bulletin included the pledge of allegiance of all the segments' leaders to Amin. All those who lived abroad and were in support of jihad in Algeria could only offer their support to the group and their prayers. That was around the end of 1994 or the beginning of 1995.

As Abu-'Abd al-Rahman took command of the group, some changes in the politics, the bulletins, and the operations of the Armed Islamic Group began to creep to the surface. Suddenly, the bulletins issued by the group increased in number and the conflict with the civilian sector escalated, as did those with the communities that had even the most remote connection to the entity of the state or the government. The bulletins threatened death to all those mentioned, especially to those in the media. They included everybody from the minister to the newspaper vendor on the street corner. They even included the education sector, reaching all the way to the teachers and the students. They also targeted the Ministry of Petroleum, reaching all the way to the attendants at the gas stations!

They dared to issue fatwas legitimizing the killing of the women and children of those individuals who worked for different government apparatuses. They escalated the level of the confrontations with the civilian militias that were connected to the government and made them a principal target. The level of their excommunication rhetoric escalated in their general speech, and they showed other such extremist tendencies.

In 1995 the Vatican sponsored a convocation in Rome to which it invited the leaders of the Islamic Salvation Front, who were seeking asylum outside of Algeria, as well as the leaders of the Islamic political factions and the secular ones too. The Vatican even invited the leadership of the communist factions. The goal was to establish a political alliance that might solve the Algerian political conflict. However, the military government resisted the offer, and this led to the demise of that strange and suspicious initiative.

Around the end of 1995, Abu-'Abd al-Rahman Amin and his criminal leadership dared to assassinate Sheikh Muhammad al-Sa'id, the mujahid 'Abd al-Wahab al-'Imarah, and other mujahideen who were part of the student group and who had joined for the purpose of unifying the group. They had named them an al-Jaz'arah group [refers to them being a nationalistic group]. It was a name given to them by Mahfudh al-Nihnah in criticism of their curriculum. He claimed that he killed them because of their coup attempt, which was supposed to overthrow his leadership. He also claimed to have killed them because he wanted to preserve the Salafist identity of the group. This is the point at which the truth about the deviations of the group's path began to reveal itself.

Following their crime, this leadership published a book entitled *The Guidance of the Almighty God*, by Abu-'Abd al-Rahman Amin, which he declared was now the curriculum of the Armed Islamic Group. The book was full of ignorance, extremism, excommunication rhetoric, and a deviation from the path of righteousness, which confirmed the veer of the group under its new emir and clarified the extent of the disaster that had struck the leadership of the Armed Islamic Group. 'Abd al-Rahman Amin followed all that by leading his fighters into mass massacres of the civilians in the countryside, surrounding them, claiming that the latter had gotten involved with the military militia. He declared their excommunication and legitimized killing them and taking their women prisoner, in the claim that these individuals are apostates!

The Algerian intelligence services took full advantage of these occurrences (which later turned out to be orchestrated by them) and infiltrated its own spies within the leadership of the group. Actually, it just might have been that Amin was one of these agents. This was later revealed by some of the men who were able to escape and to tell the story so as to preserve and annotate the history of this tragedy.

These massacres occurred during the period of 1996–97. During this period, Algeria witnessed horrors and rivers of blood . . . to the point where people were being killed as they left the mosques after their prayers during the month of Ramadan. The reason claimed for these killings was that these individuals had participated in the elections and were, therefore, considered apostates! The worst massacres occurred in those cities where the Islamic Salvation Front was known to have won the previous elections. That was a way for the government to settle a score it had with those people who had chosen the Islamic political program, as was revealed by the men who lived to tell the tale and show the documents to prove it through different media avenues a few years later. The al-Jazirah television station aired a few highly important interviews related to this issue. Some of these soldiers published their testimonies in book that was later published in France.

As the truth was revealed and as the criminal ideology of the new leadership of the Armed Islamic Group became apparent, all their previous supporters, within Algeria and outside of it, denounced the group. All the individuals and the prominent jihadist organizations, which had previously supported the Armed Islamic Group in its jihadist path, issued numerous bulletins to declare their detachment from the group and its activities. Personally, I was among the first of those who took this stand, as I explained in my testimony in a detailed book. Furthermore, the battalions and the jihadist segments within Algeria all stepped away from the group as the horrific and shameful rivers of blood flowed through the streets of the country. After this, battles between the group and a number of these independent segments erupted.

The mujahideen from the Jama'ah of Jabal al-Arbi'a' (as they were known), who were a group belonging to Sheikh Muhammad al-Sa'id, killed Abu-'Abd al-Rahman Amin and saved the world from his evildoing. He was replaced by another killer, who was a worse criminal, to lead the Armed Islamic Group. His name was 'Antar al-Zawabiri. He continued on the crime path, but, by then, the group had become weaker and its capabilities had diminished. It continued along its criminal journey even after it was isolated in specified areas, until al-Zawabiri was killed in 2003.

The mujahideen became scattered and fragmented, and people distanced themselves from them and became impatient with the jihadist, and even the Islamic, program. By then, the Algerian and outside intelligence services had reached their goals through the massacres they had planned out. At that point, they declared a truce claiming to give amnesty to all those who surrender their weapons. The Islamic Salvation Army, led by Madani Mirzaq, was among the first to respond to what became known as "the Patriotic Harmony" [what is officially known as The Charter for Peace and National Reconciliation]. A number of Muslim scholars who were living abroad volunteered to support the state's call for surrender. Examples of those supporters were Ibn Baz, Ibn 'Uthmayn, and al-Albani, who issued one of his last fatwas declaring that the Algerian crisis was the biggest proof of what he phrased as "disobeying the leaders in these days translates into the disobedience of Islam itself!" A lot of chaos ensued and permeated the Islamic revival arena and that was all because of the Algerian jihadist experience. The latter became the perfect excuse for anyone wanting to prove that the jihad choice is the wrong one to take, and the Algerian experience became the lesson to be learned from and the one cited as an example. Unfortunately, the Algerian intelligence services, all its counterparts that helped it from other countries, and all the work by the different Arab media succeeded in creating a blur between the truth of the jihadist ideology and that of the excommunication principles, the crimes committed, and the massacres and blood baths that took place in Algeria.

These events continued on in Algeria in 1998, and I had left London to head to back to Afghanistan, where it was impossible to follow up on the news and all that going on as I would have liked. I had also distanced myself from that cause and its whirlwind events since 1996 because of the great problems it had caused me. However, I did get to hear about it from some of the great Algerian mujahideen, who had come to Afghanistan during the era of the Taliban, and from some of the people who were interested in that problem. From what I was able to read about it in the bulletins that were issued later, it seemed that the sweeping majority of the armed mujahideen had left the mountains in response to "patriotic harmonization," and a only few small groups were left to continue their confrontations with the regime that was gloating over an immense victory over the Islamists and the mujahideen.

Suddenly a new group calling itself the Salafist Group for Preaching and Combat emerged on the scene, led by its emir, Hasan Hattab. From the bulletins this group issued, it seemed that they had learned some lessons from those horrible events that had occurred. In its bulletins, it focused on rejecting the excommunication and instigating rhetoric and ideology; instead, their goal was to concentrate on confronting the military and security apparatuses of the regime and to make prominent only the general goals so as to establish a state based on sharia. However, most of the jihadist communities were a bit cautious about this because of the horrific shock they had had from the events that had taken place that had been, and were still being, reported by the different news media sources. Among the most noticeable and biggest of these operations reported was the kidnapping of the foreign tourists and the huge sums of ransom money that the group had asked for the tourists' release. Furthermore, the Algerian mujahideen, who had come and established themselves in Afghanistan, tried to organize themselves to restart the work on their cause. They managed to establish a semiorganization that was constantly facing difficulties in reviving a cause such as theirs. Some of the more mature among them began to show signs of success in the accomplishment of their goal, but then events of September 11 occurred and took them, as it did all others, by surprise. Therefore, they had to stop and take their positions in the battle for survival and for the salvation of the principality. Many of them suffered greatly in those battles; a great number of them were martyred, God rest their souls, and others were apprehended. They became victims of the September 11 aftermath

The Jihadist Experiences in Yemen since 1990

I had long believed that Yemen is one of the Arab world's best equipped countries for a jihad movement to take place and be successful. This was especially true after the country's unification. I had written a special study of about forty pages on this issue, which was titled "The Yemeni People's Responsibility toward All That Is Sacred to the Muslims and toward the Muslims' Resources." In this study I proved the suitability of Yemen as a ground for jihad, and I put the idea into practice. Yemen covers a vast territory of about four hundred thousand square kilometers, its coastline extends over two thousand five hundred kilometers, and it also controls the Straits of Bab al-Mandab. Furthermore, it shares a border with Saudi Arabia and other Gulf region countries on one side and, on the other side it borders the Horn of Africa and all it offers as far as ammunition and arms in the East of Africa.

Yemen's population makes up about 70 percent of that of the Arabian Peninsula, twenty-five million out of forty million people. It has a varied topography, and its mountains are very difficult to get through. This type of terrain offers the perfect region for jihadist guerrilla warfare. Another positive factor is the nature of the Yemeni people themselves—they are conservative, religious, and a tribal people who adhere strongly to their old customs and reject the modern civilization along with all the negativity that comes with the industrial world's reality. Ownership of weapons is common among the population, and this fact is closely tied in to their traditions. As a matter of fact, the official census has shown that there are about seventy million weapons in the hands of the tribes and the population in general. This is above and beyond the weapons owned by the government itself. Thus, a simple calculation would show an average of more than three weapons per citizen, including the women, the elderly, and the children in the country!

Moreover, the Islamic revival concept has very strong roots in Yemen and has been present in its culture for many years dating back to the 1950s. The concept is also quite varied and covers all of the revival's schools of thought, including that of the Muslim Brotherhood, the Salafists, the Sururiyyahs, the Suphisms, and many more. There is also the fact that the Yemeni people have been known for their fighting skills and abilities. Throughout its history, Yemen has proved itself an impossible country to occupy, as was proven to such colonialist countries as Portugal, England, the Ottoman Empire, and Egypt (at the time of President Abd-al-Nasser).

During the extended jihadist experience in Afghanistan (1984–92), the Yemeni mujahideen were the second largest group among the Arab youths who came to participate. That was also the case during the Second Term of the Arab Afghans' jihad in Afghanistan (1996–2001). They were famous for their bravery, their equestrian skills, and their steadfastness to their Arab roots. I am always surprised that, to this day, there has not been any large-scale jihadist movement in Yemen! From an economic aspect, sadly over 70 percent of the population lives under the poverty level and in oppression.

Conversely, the majority of the rest of the Arab Peninsula's residents who neighbor Yemen are living in the luxuries with which God has blessed this land from the riches and resources that are the property of all Muslims, especially the inhabitants of the peninsula. It is therefore obvious to all that there are plenty of reasons backed by factors of sharia, economy, population, politics, and geography to set the stage not only for an eruption of a revolution but also for its success. That is why it is very strange that no jihadist movement has taken place there yet, despite the rule of a very weak government, led by an ignorant tyrant for many years who is trying to pass the power on to his son and make him king of what is a socialist republic, and soon to be an American democracy!

The main reason jihad is not happening is that the majority of the Islamic revival's commands are those who do not go to jihad for matters of personal benefit. Also, the majority of the preachers are self-centered individuals and Sultan's scholars who created parliamentary seats and others of personal comfort close to the tyrant ruler. Another reason is the hegemony of the tribal leaders who, for decades or even centuries now, have gotten used to selling out their religion for the comfort of their life on earth. This was clearly proven as the leadership of the Islamic revival and the tribal leaders, who had a major political influence in what was referred to as "the Yemeni Group for Reform" [Islah], brought on the failure of the Islamic popular uprising in what was known as "the Constitution Events" in 1993. They even fought against any jihadist attempts following those events. This crackdown made it very difficult for the new jihadist leaders to accomplish their mission and to establish a structure for the Islamic revival in Yemen.

The problem Yemen faces is the same as that of every Arab and Muslim country, and it can be summarized very briefly as follows: the ignorance and inability of the scholars as well as of the entire population, their diversion from the path of righteousness, and their love of life on earth and their fear of death. God resolve this crisis for all! Getting back to our topic, in the beginning of the 1990s, the Yemeni mujahideen returned from Afghanistan and, during the entire last decade of the twentieth century, there were many jihadist attempts in Yemen. All these attempts failed because of the previously mentioned reasons. One of the most prominent and most serious of these attempts was that of Osama bin Laden (starting in 1990), who tried to establish a jihadist base in Yemen. There was also the movement of what was known as the army of Aden. This was led by the martyred mujahid Sheikh Abu-al-Hasan al-Muhadir. It took place around the middle of 1998.

A Brief Overview of the Jihadist Attempts of Sheikh Osama bin Laden in Yemen

Sheikh Osama bin Laden was originally from the south of Yemen, from Hadhramut. He is one of the sons of Muhammad bin Laden, who had emigrated from Yemen to Saudi Arabia around the time that King 'Abd al-'Aziz came to power. Bin Laden senior took up residence in Saudi Arabia and had a family there, close to Al-Su'ud. The family had great financial and political influence both then and now.

During the period of the Afghani jihad against the Russians, Sheikh Osama bin Laden was very careful to surround himself by an organization in which he focused on jihadist elements from the Arab Peninsula, especially those from Saudi Arabia and from Yemen. During the 1990s, all the preconditions for a jihadist movement against the communist regime before the unification were present and ready to be acted upon. Many Islamist people and tribes from the North of Yemen supported such a movement, and the movement would have also found a lot support from the merchants of Hadhramut, who had great financial power in Saudi Arabia. There would also have been plenty of support from the Islamic revival in general, which held a great deal of animosity toward communism in general and especially in Yemen. Another important factor would have been the existence of a big number of Yemeni mujahideen, of southern origin, during the Arab jihad in Afghanistan.

Osama bin Laden's personal and principal jihadist plan was to have a jihadist movement in the South of Yemen. He began working on this plan in the period of 1989–90 and kept working on it until the unification took place. Despite the fact that many of the mujahideen who were then close to bin Laden, including myself, had encouraged him to carry out this plan immediately, he still hesitated to do so. Bin Laden wanted to convince the leadership of the Islamic revival in Yemen, and especially the organization of the Muslim Brotherhood, such as Sheikh 'Abd al-Majid al-Zindani, who was a prominent leader at the time, to participate in the jihadist movement. However, these individuals did not want to be involved, and, in my opinion, a great chance for this movement was lost.

After the unification of Yemen, bin Laden's plan had turned into an attempt that would focus on the recent issue of the unification of Yemen. The battle over the constitution of a unified Yemen along with the conflicting statements by the Islamists and the secularists presented a chance for the declaration of jihad against 'Ali 'Abdallah Salih and the government of the newly unified Yemeni. Sheikh Osama bin Laden moved in on this opportunity, followed by many among the sheikhs of Yemen, most prominently the famous Sheikh 'Umar Sayf. The latter signed his name on a book that supported that he should be excommunicated for doing so. This book, which was written by a few individuals who were very close to bin Laden, proved that any government that abided by this constitution was not legitimate and jihad could be waged against it. Bin Laden tried to negotiate with the greatest of the sheikhs of Yemen, its Salafist scholars, the Muslim Brotherhood and its leadership, and so forth. He invested large sums of money in the aim of swaying them and some of the tribes to his plan. Sadly, all of them let bin Laden down, and instead they all followed Sheikh 'Ali 'Abdallah Salih, who offered them official positions of power, resources, riches, and different types of help in their personal matters.

Sheikh al-Zindani was the reason for the failure of the million-armed-men demonstration that had headed to the gates of the palace. He was at the head of that demonstration along with leaders from the Muslim Brotherhood organization. He marched along with the general population, entered the palace along with a few other individuals to carry out the negotiations with the president, and then he came out a short while later to tell the armed demonstrators, who were asking for the revocation of the constitution and for the establishment of a sharia-based government, that "All those who believe in God and in Judgment Day must return home." The following day it was announced that Sheikh 'Abd al-Majid al-Zindani was appointed as one of the president's delegates and one of Yemen's five rulers, because he was also appointed to the presidential committee, which was headed by 'Ali 'Abdallah Salih! Thus, he became a member of the polytheist communists, and some of the biggest names among his companions received different positions in the government under the tyrant's constitution, which was legitimized by an un-Godly source.

It was a constitution that had hypocritically stated that the country's religion is Islam and that sharia was the source of all the laws in that constitution! As for Sheikh Muqbil Ibn Hadi al-Wadi'i, his stand was even worse and more damaging. He had written a book in which he described bin Laden as the root of all civil strife in Yemen. He put out recordings to sell on street corners to the people as they left the mosques after their Friday prayers. In those recordings he severely attacked bin Laden and made false claims that the latter had given him money to recruit him to a jihad that aimed to cause civil strife in the country. He claimed he used the money to perform marriage ceremonies and to buy books for the mosques!

Certain young Yemeni mujahideen had claimed that al-Wadi'i was the principal sheikh for the Salafist creed! It seemed then that no one had escaped from his vile doings: he attacked the leadership of the Muslim Brotherhood, those of al-Sururiyyin, those of the Sufist creed, and the mujahideen. Conversely, he would praise 'Ali 'Abdallah Salih, referring to him as "my brother, the president," and would always attest to his commitment to him as a Muslim commander.

I had heard Sheikh Osama speak with some of his guests once and say that if he were to forgive everyone who had ever harmed him in his life, he would never forgive al-Wadi'i. All those who know bin Laden know the extent of his forgiving nature even with those who have caused him harm, so one can only imagine the extent of the harm that the treacherous al-Wadi'i had caused bin Laden.

The majority of the leaders of the mujahideen, whom bin Laden had recruited and trained in Afghanistan, had been swayed by 'Ali 'Abdallah Salih, who had given them positions in the Yemeni army and elsewhere in the military. He had offered them civilian jobs, and they were enjoying a life of riches. Even the most prominent among them, such as al-Fadili and al-Nahdi, had the audacity to work for the intelligence services and for the republican guard, bringing themselves as close as possible to 'Ali 'Abdallah Salih!

It was my belief, as well as that of many of the Yemeni jihadists I had met, that it would have been possible for Islamists to return to the North of Yemen and to enforce the Islamic law of sharia or to at least depose Salih and establish an Islamic state. However, what took place instead was that they returned to the parliament, to their positions in the different ministries of 'Ali 'Abdallah Salih's government, and to the government's secular constitution and apostate rule. The mujahideen became isolated as the majority of them, from the Salafists, the Muslim Brotherhood, and the al-Sururiyyah, followed the leadership of the revival. Many more of them were swayed by 'Ali Salih and went back to take up positions in the military and the government and to gain personal benefits.

By then, Sheikh Osama bin Laden had relocated to Sudan and al Qaida got busy in its financial work and investments in a country they considered to be an Islamist state. Furthermore, some elements of al Qaida participated in the jihad in Somalia, fighting alongside Islamist segments to actively force the American forces to withdraw from the country's treacherous Sahara sand. At the same time, the mujahideen and the followers of Osama bin Laden had also undertaken a few operations of limited resources to stop the Americans, who had started to show signs of wanting to establish a base in Aden. After a few Katyusha rockets were fired on the base construction sites, the Americans changed course and stopped building the base. The mujahideen followers of Osama bin Laden did not have any other mentionable jihadist experiences in Yemen after 1994. But this ended when they got involved in the jihad against America.

In 1997 bin Laden told the *al-Quds al-'Arabi* newspaper that his next station would be the mountains of Yemen. Following that statement, he revived his plan for Yemen, but this time it was based on a different strategy: fighting the root of all evil—America. However, the plan showed disinclination to get involved in any confrontation with America's followers, including the insignificant dwarf, 'Abdallah Salih.

An al Qaida cell carried out a suicide attack on the U.S. Navy guided-missile destroyer, the USS *Cole*, which had docked for a routine fuel stop off the coast of Yemen, in the Aden harbor. This escalated the confrontation level with the Yemeni intelligence services, which had joined America in the war on terror. Many of the mujahideen were arrested, including some of bin Laden's followers. However, as the casualties of the war increased, the government of 'Ali 'Abdallah Salih had to release some of bin Laden's followers, and it was said that Salih made this decision following a threatening letter he received from bin Laden in which the latter reminded the president that al Qaida's war was not with the Yemeni government but that this could very well change.

Around the end of the year 2001, right before September, bin Laden gathered his biggest supporters in Kandahar to tell them that it was time to leave for Yemen. Everyone among the Arab Afghans was surprised about this move, and rumors were milling around in that community; but then the attacks of September 2001 shook the world and a severe crackdown on all the mujahideen in Yemen took place following that, in the claim that that all followers of Prophet Muhammad as well as all enemies of America are related to al Qaida; at least that was according to the American media and to all the antiterrorism programs.

The mujahideen in Yemen suffered the most from these crackdowns; many of the brothers from al Qaida were martyred or jailed in the fight on terrorism in Yemen, which was directed by America and applied by its apostate slaves, who were members of the Yemeni army and intelligence services. Brother Abu-'Ali al Harithi was martyred, along with five other mujahideen, as they rode in a vehicle through a village in Yemen, by a missile fired on their car from an American plane [the CIA had used an RQ-1 Predator remote-controlled pilotless drone to shoot the Hellfire missile that killed the al Qaida operatives]. This was carried out with complete agreement and cooperation from the Yemeni intelligence services. These crackdowns continued and would sometimes escalate into violent battles that would bring news of the martyrdom of one brother or the arrest of another, under the pretense that they were affiliated with al Qaida.

My Relationship with the Yemeni Brothers and My Remarks about the Jihad Experience in Yemen

As I had previously mentioned, I was convinced of the benefit that could be reaped from jihad in Yemen ever since 1989. At that time, I was close to Sheikh Osama bin Laden, who had told me about the course of action for his jihadist plan in Yemen. After the Desert Storm war, which was known as the Kuwait Liberation War, I had tried repeatedly and arduously to convince Sheikh Osama bin Laden of the need to make the move to Yemen because of the suitability of the situation, especially after the arrival of the American forces and their presence on the Arabian Peninsula. Another important reason for my decision was the events that took place because of the constitution. However, he felt that this plan would be hard to carry through without the support of the rest of the revival representatives.

I had known many of the Yemeni mujahideen brothers since the days of the first Afghani jihad. When I returned to Afghanistan in the second term, I was very interested in the experiences that had taken place in Yemen. I made every effort to record its history, along with one of the most prominent young Yemeni mujahideen, the martyr Muuhannad 'Atash. However, he was martyred before we could accomplish this task together.

During the spring of 1998, and after Abu-al-Hasan had left, one of his friends among the mujahideen brothers told me about the experience of al-Muhadir, his aims, and the importance of helping him by advising him and supporting him. He told me that al-Muhadir would use some of my lectures about the history of the Afghani jihad, as well as use my book *The Jihad Experience in Syria* as a resource in the lessons he used to give to his followers. Therefore, the idea was that he would be receptive to my advice. Indeed, I gave this man a letter and an audiotape recording that contained a summary of my thoughts and my advice about the issue of jihad in Yemen. He called me by phone to tell me both were delivered, and I waited for a speedy response that might give us a new jihadist step that would bring us closer to the battlefield. I was hoping to follow him there and to participate in rendering him and his plan victorious, but the media soon broke the news of the disaster I mentioned earlier—his death.

Soon, some of the brothers who had been with Abu-al-Hasan and had witnessed that tragedy arrived in Kabul to tell us the news of that story. Later, I read updates about that experience in some of the Saudi newspapers, which declared that the government had confiscated from Abu-Hasan al-Muhadir's camp some books and tapes that contained my thoughts about annihilating the tyranny of these regimes and those behind them. Among the material confiscated were some tapes for Khalid Zayn al-'Abidin, a name that was a pseudonym I had used when I distributed the audio recordings of my lectures about the Afghani experience. I read that the government had assumed that the pseudonym belonged to the martyr Abu-Hasan al-Muhadir because of the similarity in the last names, which was obviously an erroneous assumption. They also mentioned that they had found a copy of my book *The Jihad Experience in Syria*, a fact that made me happy. I prayed for the martyr and all who died with him and I asked God to grant us all the reward for our efforts in this cause. I prayed we might all be reunited in Heaven and that those who have sold out their faith and religion may receive what they deserve.

During the Second Term of the Arab Afghans in Afghanistan during the Taliban era, some of the Yemeni mujahideen frequented the camp I had established near Kabul. That camp was our training ground and the place from which to spread the ideology of the global resistance, the ideology of the jihadist curriculum, and the history of the movement. I always gave them special treatment because of the value and importance I attributed to that region of the Islamic world as far as the hopes I had for a resistance-type jihad. I published a study titled "The Yemeni People's Responsibility toward All That Is Sacred to the Muslims and toward the Muslims' Resources." I had also recorded many audiotapes on the topic of the jihad in Yemen. I heard that my work had reached that area and that it was studied by the mujahideen and the Islamists. One day we received news of Abu-al-Hasan al-Muhadir's execution and his martyrdom, which affected me immensely. I had never had the chance to get to know the details of the jihad of that brave and heroic mujahid, to whom many of the mujahideen from Yemen and from other places owed a lot. All I could do was to hold a funeral in our camp in his memory after he was executed. It was a celebration of his accomplishments and an occasion of prayers for him by all who attended.

The Jihadist Experiences in Morocco since 1995

The Moroccan Youths' Organization had led an armed jihadist experience against King Hassan II. The organization was headed by Sheikh 'Abd al-Karim Mitba', and the jihadist experience was one of the first to be carried out in the Arab world. It had occurred even before the appearance of the ideological foundations of the current jihadist movement was defined. Morocco, though, is one of the few countries of the Arab and Islamic world, such as those of central Asia, Yemen, Algeria, and Turkey, that has all the components that could lead to a jihadist revolution.

Morocco is a country that is widely spread out, with a terrain that is difficult to cross and that spreads across a vast countryside and treacherous mountainous regions for a distance of over three thousand kilometers. The country is bordered by and controls part of the Straits of Gibraltar. The people of Morocco live under some of the worst conditions of poverty and oppression. Furthermore, they have some of the richest and bravest jihadist history. They are a pious people despite the corruption that has spread to the larger cities because of the economic open-door policy implemented by the government and because of the widespread prostitution that has spread, hidden under the pretense of tourism. Nevertheless, the religion of Islam still has its presence and its sanctity in the country. Morocco has an Islamic consciousness that dates back to the beginning of the 1960s and is based on the majority of the elements of the current-day Islamic revival movement and its different schools of thought, from the Salafist, to the Muslim Brotherhood, to the Sufist movement, to the jihadist.

A decent number of Moroccan mujahideen participated in the Afghani jihad and were able to return to their home country without too many problems, because, at that time, King Hassan II's policy was to attempt to take in that Islamic consciousness and to not provoke it. His policy proved to be very successful in stripping this consciousness from the inside out and in leading the people into the growing pseudo-democratic paths that were emerging in Morocco. The greatest among the country's preachers began to vacillate between the country's prisons, house arrests, and parliamentary seats! Following the Algerian jihadist revolution, after the demise of all the success gained by the Salvation Army, Morocco was one of the principal passageways from which most of the Algerian mujahideen, among the Arab Afghans, were able to cross back into their country. At that time, the Moroccan government had turned a blind eye to this fact because of the Algerian government's support of the Polisario Front, a movement that worked for the independence of Western Sahara from Morocco. Therefore, it formed many cells in the East of Morocco and in the countryside, and it offered a lot of help to the mujahideen in the West of Algeria as far as opening a passageway for them, offering logistic support to them, and helping in the transfer of arms from Europe. That was before the criminal leadership of the Armed Islamic Group took control of that cause, as we had previously discussed.

Thus, between the Moroccan mujahideen's (from the Arab Afghans) experience from one side and the Algerian influence from the other, the nuclei for the Moroccan jihad began to slowly take shape. All the strategic research centers that were following the issues of the Muslims in North Africa and in Europe, especially in France, expected that the Islamic revolution was going to have its start in North Africa from Morocco. I had read a few reports, published in France, that revealed the surprise of that country that jihad in North Africa had actually started in Algeria before Morocco.

Some immature jihadist attempts were made when some tourists were fired at, and there were some rare operations carried out against the Jewish community in Morocco, which controls all the political, economic, and media centers, and which is always trying to push for friendly relations with Israel.

From the middle of the 1990s, there were some serious attempts to form jihadist cells and nuclei of organizations both inside and outside Morocco. The jihadist movement had reached Morocco on the heels of the jihad that had taken place in Algeria. Further, the push for a peaceful relationship with Israel and the Westernization in the country were beginning to get stronger and more obvious after King Muhammad VI took over the throne from his father.

Around the middle of the 1990s, a number of Moroccan youths from the jihadist movement were able to establish the nucleus of an organization that would begin working in Morocco. It seems that the first stages of this plan were started among the Moroccan expatriates in European countries; among them were some of the Moroccan Arab Afghans. It moved from one country to another throughout Europe because of the immense number of Moroccan expatriates in that continent, numbering five million or so! This group established a curriculum and some educational material, which it spread secretly throughout the Moroccan communities of Europe and, to a limited extent, within Morocco. I had seen some of that material, and for the most part, it all followed the general ideology of the jihadist movement that was prevalent during that time.

The Moroccan mujahideen in Afghanistan, like their counterparts from other countries, all supported the Islamic principality. When the September 11 events took place, they got pulled into the self-defense battles and in defending the Islamic principality. They had their share of misfortunes in the process; some were martyred and others were arrested. The rest who were able to escape these fates were able to flee.

Around the end of 2003, the news media reported great explosions that had targeted some western places in Casablanca. These were multiple suicide bomb attacks carried out by a group called Salafist Jihadist. The reports also mentioned that some of the individuals responsible for these suicide bomb attacks were Takfiriyyin [Islamists who pass judgment declaring that an individual or group previously considered Muslims are in fact nonbelievers. It is the practice of passing an excommunication judgment against a Muslim or a group of Muslims].

However, the important fact to mention concerning these events, about which I did not receive any information I was able to verify, is that because of these events, the Moroccan security apparatuses arrested hundreds of men belonging to a group known as the Salafiyyah Jihadiyyah Movement. These men were all either condemned to death or to very long jail sentence by the Moroccan courts. There were also many prominent Salafist preachers and mujahideen in Morocco who were arrested in that crackdown who had no relation whatsoever to the events. This made the government's actions seem to represent an operation that aimed to destroy any possibility of a jihadist movement in that country before it had a chance to start. This was especially relevant when we know that this country was suffering from one of the Arab and Islamic world's worst tyrant governments, which was controlled by the Jews and the Christians.

Personally, I had formed many friendships with a number of the Moroccan brothers since my days in France, Spain, and then Great Britain. That was partly because of the large segment of Moroccans who lived in those countries around the time of the Islamic revival in the West. I knew many excellent cadres among them, known for their great sense of loyalty, the purity of their hearts, and their dedication to jihad. The suffering of their people because of their previous pharaoh, King Hassan II, of his impudent son, the current King Hassan V, and of the latter's entire family and regime, was apparent to the faithful in Morocco and a very influential factor that was instigating them to seek a reformation and a jihadist movement.

I met many of these men during the Arab Afghans' Second Term, especially those belonging to the new organization, the Moroccan Islamic Combatant Group [GICM]. They were a role model for honesty, loyalty, enthusiasm, dedication, and efficiency. I had very high hopes for their promising jihadist experience.

Unfortunately, the aftermath of the September 11 events hit them as it did all the other mujahideen, and many of their cadres became destitute in this world as they fled.

I must not forget to thank and pay my respects to the Moroccan mujahideen who participated admirably in the heroic operation that led to the withdrawal of the Spanish army from Iraq. Despite the fact that I was unable to meet these men personally, the entire Islamic nation is indebted to that squadron of martyrdom seekers who had the honor of resisting the Christian-American alliance. Furthermore, anyone who studies that operation and its heroic end would discover the extent of the abilities of these men, which is an attribute they inherited from their famous ancestors who had carried the banner of jihad for Islam and for the Islamic nation throughout the great and honorable Islamic history.

The Experience of Osama and al Qaida Organization against America since 1996

It is clear that this title is deserving of a book of its own. This is because of the multitude of chapters involved and the importance of its history. It should not be included in passing in such a general book on the different experiences of the jihadist current. However, for the sake of continuity and to completely cover all the important experiences of the second part of the twentieth century, I must review at least a summary of this experience to end the file on these experiences. After that, I may be able to open the file of the experiences of the twenty-first century, which have changed the face of history and of the world as well as the factors involved and the methods used in the battle.

I will review this experience by presenting a brief of the principal sections of it. Before I begin, allow me to say that I had to think long and hard about classifying the experience of al Qaida among those of the jihadist movement, or to classify it among the experiences of the jihadist manifestations against foreign aggression. I almost felt like this was a third type of jihadist manifestation because of its differences in its organization, its curriculum, and its methods. After a long evaluation, I decided to include it among the experiences of the jihadist current for numerous reasons, the most important of which are the following:

- The curriculum adopted by bin Laden and the majority of his followers is a curriculum that could be considered based on the principles of the jihadist movement.

- The second point is that the majority of al Qaida's cadres, founders, trainers, and important men are all from the jihadist cadres who had joined and became members of al Qaida or had been relied upon by the organization in establishing its elements.

- The third issue is that Osama bin Laden had made the confrontation with Al-Su'ud one part of his goals and his direction. His other goal was the confrontation with America, and this is a direction taken by the organizations of the jihadist as far as confronting the tyrant rulers in all the different Arab and Muslim countries. He considered the Saudi royal family to be apostates and relied on the principles of the creed of ruling and on the principles of the Salafist jihadist creed to make this judgment.

- The fourth issue is that Osama was able to drag the entire jihadist movement to the battlefield that he chose and to the ideas that he had for the confrontation. His ideas suggested that instead of confronting the governments and the regimes themselves, they should confront those who support them among the new global system. That made America and its biggest allies the target.

- The last issue is that America has labeled many of the current jihadist manifestations as al Qaida members, whether they like it or not. It uses the name al Qaida as a general one for all elements of the jihadist movement, and it dragged them without a choice into a war with it.

After rethinking this issue long and hard . . . I have decided to omit this section for the following three reasons:

- Al Qaida is still in a war with the enemies of Islam, who are led by America, as are the Arab Afghans of the other jihadist movements and every loyal person of this Islamic nation. Some people might feel that discussing the organization's experience and business might provide something of benefit to the enemy. Personally, I don't believe this would be the case, because this segment would be a study or a general critique of the lessons and of the past experiences. It would not contain any information that could be considered secret. This is especially true because some of the highest ranking men of al Qaida are currently in the enemy's hands. I actually believe that there is benefit for the mujahideen and the Muslims of the world in general, in reviewing the experience. Nevertheless, this was one of the reasons for omitting this segment so as to avoid any disagreements about this issue.

- The experience is still ongoing, thus making its case different than that of other organizational experiences we have discussed and that have ended already. Furthermore, if we were to wait until this experience is finished before we study it, then we would have the benefit of having a more complete picture to research and learn from. I hope we would have achieved the promised victory by then.

- This is a very large experience and is deserving of its own book to do it justice. I hope God will give me the opportunity to write such a book in the future, and I hope to have some of the greatest brothers and sheikhs review it first, because I would like to get their opinions before I publish it. I hope to do all this in the near future . . . and after the complete victory.

I apologize to the readers who wished to study a great experience by our men, the majority of whom have recorded their names in the list of martyrs.

CHAPTER 7
The Intellectual and Doctrinal Foundations of the Jihadist Movement

I will present, in summary, the most important of the jihadist movement's characteristics without interjecting my personal opinion, disregarding some of the trivial secondary ideas adopted by some jihadists,
since such presentation is for the purpose of elaboration only and not for
discussion. Some of the most important jihad ideologies are:

The Rule about Regimes: Jihadists consider the ruling regimes in the
Arab and Islamic world to be defecting regimes because they imposed
their own juridical rules disregarding the rulings of God. Accordingly,
they consider all the rulers in the Arab and Islamic world to be apostate
and infidels.

Consideration of the Associates (Assistants): Jihadists considered those
fighting in defense of these regimes against the jihadists, such as members
of the army, the police, and security forces, to be fighting under the orders
of their imam, and none of them are adjudged with apostasy.

The Rulers Scholars: Jihadists consider those scholars who stand alongside these regimes to be defectors and hypocrites.

The Issue of Democracy: Jihadists consider democracy a philosophical
atheist system in clear contradiction with Islam. Some go as far as considering it a modern religion resembling those old and modern atheist beliefs.
The majority of jihadists consider those democratic Muslims who entered
the parliament or participated in the legislative branch or the executive
branch and accepted ministerial positions as guilty of performing an
atheist act; however they don't adjudge them as apparent apostates and
consider them excused, because their statements are forced, or being ignorant of the nature of these associations.

The Issue of Shiite and Other Non-Sunni Groups: Jihadists consider all these groups part of the Islamic nation as part of the groups mentioned in the Hadith, which informed us that the nation will be divided into seventy-three groups with one granted salvation (that is the Sunni group) and the rest in hellfire. They consider them misguided and deviants.

The Issue of Arab Nationalism: All jihadists consider the call for nationalism and fanaticizing for it to be a pre-Islamic call. The jihadists are nationalists calling for the unity of all Muslims and having a general unified system. Therefore, the majority of them reject the agendas of the national parties, because these parties are joining nationalism with secularism. Jihadists consider the call for nationalism as tearing the nation apart.

The Issue of Independent Countries: Jihadists despise the idea of independent countries and nationalism and of working within the control of these ideas, especially if mingled with the notion of secularism. Thus, they consider as its enemies any preachers suffering from symptoms of apostasy and deviation. There is a contradiction between the preceding two points, as jihadists start in their own countries yet believing in the Islam nation and the call for jihad.

The Palestinian Cause: Jihadists believe that Palestine is part of the Islamic nation, and therefore it should be liberated through militant jihad. As a result, they reject any elements of truce or normalization with the Jews. They consider the majority of the Israelis with the exception of the few thousands of the original Palestinian Jews and their descendants as strangers and invaders who must leave.

The Issue of Religious Minorities in the Arab and Islamic World: Jihadists consider these minorities, with their majority being Christians, to be subject to the preestablished dogmatic Sunni rules of treatment of the people of the book.

The Issue of Confrontation with America and the Fight with the West: None of the jihadist organizations, since their establishment in the 1960s until the inception of the American invasion of Afghanistan in November of 2001, had ever discussed or adopted the issue of militant confrontation with the United States. All were concentrating on confrontations with their local country's governments. In addition, most jihad literary writings minimally addressed the issue of confrontation, especially after the Gulf War and the launching of the new world order and the institution of the war against terrorism. Also, the American support of those governments that suppress Islamists and jihadists failed to create a body of literature that would serve as motivating directives. Sheikh Osama bin Laden repeatedly tried, to no avail, to convince jihadists to divert their work toward America, the snake head as he described it. They were consumed with the notion of fighting their local governments and considered these to be the most immediate danger. They were also occupied with the idea of using militant jihad to establish the Islamic state as the key for all problems. However, the September incidents and its effect on the world, coupled with the American labeling of the Islamic jihad in total as al Qaida, and their chase of all jihadists of every nationality, and their destruction of the infrastructure of the jihad movement, in addition to the following occupation of Iraq . . . since 2001 to the present, the successive deterioration of the intifadah, and [George] Bush's declaration of the Crusades . . . and so forth made confrontation with America and its Western allies the only practical unified goal for jihadists.

It is now important to address errors and problems of the jihad effort. If I am to cite examples, I would start with myself and the experiences I was involved in in order not to sadden any one. Nonetheless, I am generalizing for the greater benefit. I find that the defects in the path on the jihad were of three kinds:

1. Errors in curriculum and ideology;
2. Errors in structure and organization;
3. Errors in development methods and the way they were implemented.

Errors in Methodology and Thinking

Some jihad groups suffered from defects in the curricular ideologies, and these errors became internal obstacles to the movement, as follows:

*   The infiltration of restrictive ideologies to the curriculums of some of the jihadists—while I applaud the positive aspects of a unifying single ideology, I nevertheless point out that sometimes groups were too rigid in presentation of the ideology. The Salafist ideology was chosen by the majority of the jihad groups starting in the late 1980s, and it strongly appealed to the Afghani Arabs. However, many able scholars in the Islamic world rejected jihad and refused to accept jihadist policies of governorship, loyalty, and disavowal of most Arab governments and societies. As the jihad phenomena were devoid of competent scholars, fatal concepts infiltrated the jihad movement that led to disasters. Zealous revolutionaries led to the appearance of extremely ridged

dogmas that allowed the ignorant within the jihad movement to act without restraint and against the interest of the jihad. Repairing this dogmatic damage is of utmost importance in the forthcoming era.

- Jihadists adopting the Salafism forgot we are tasked to charge the nation to perform jihad against the tyrants and their followers even though the majority of the scholars of the nation do not adhere to the Salafist doctrines. There is no doubt that resisting the aggressors requires us to follow Sunni beliefs and that it is beneficial to clear any disagreements to allow all to join in the jihad. Some jihadists, however, draw the jihad movement into fights with other Muslim believers by imposing impossible conditions on them. Some jihad leaders engage in side fights by applying the loyalty and disavowal concepts to numerous Muslims, which restricts their entry into the movement. They should instead have encompassed them to become part of the jihad front or to at least neutralize them. Because of this, numerous jihadists ruined relations with those who could have helped us against our enemies. I recall being engaged in discussions with some jihadists and trying to explain to them the need to unify the Islamic Front for Jihad regardless of the ideological differences. To my sorrow, I discovered that each one was adhering to his beliefs and only his beliefs. One of the astonishing things I heard was a statement of one of Salafist, who said, "Jihad must be under the Salafist banner, and its leaders' curricula and rules should be Salafists. If we accept that non-Salafists participate with us in jihad, we do so as a result of our need. However, they should not have any leading role; we lead them like a herd of cows to perform their jihad duty." I couldn't understand how we are going to participate in jihad with brethrens whom we deal with as cows, through kicks and head hits!
- This approach was so widespread that one jihadist asked me how we can participate in jihad with a man who does not lift his hands while kneeling down in prayers, a man who prays modernly? This personal attack was predicated on the manner I perform my prayers with the Afghan. The martyr 'Abdallah 'Azzam and Sheikh Osama suffered from the same stubbornness of the mujahideen.
- The field of education within the jihad current is one of the most important fields and suffers from many deficiencies, especially after the 1990s, as a result of the security forces' actions against the mujahideen. These chases led to fear and hunger and the need to immigrate all over the earth. Unlike the pioneers' generation that developed between

the years 1965 and 1985, who were able to educate their cadres, the successor mujahideen were unable to implement any comprehensive educational program except on limited occasions. Even then, they depended on existing books and other literary resources that belonged to the awakening schools, although these resources contradict the current jihad prospective in many occasions.

• During the Second Arab Afghani Term jihad under the Taliban, I realized that the jihadists of the third generation are particularly ignorant and suffer from a lack of education even though a stable environment was available under the Taliban ruling. Jihadists, during this 1996–2001 period, concentrated on military training, neglecting other educational programs. The many young men from the general and average classes of Muslims were charged with zeal, loyalty, and emotions, but they suffered from clear lack of religious knowledge and compliance as well as the rules of Islamic dealing and ethics. In addition, the cadres of jihad were suffering from lack of good knowledge in these areas. The lack of proper educational curricula led to severity and the lack of mercy in the leaders of jihad.

• Likewise, the lack of good morals led jihadists to act in a ganglike manner and not as proper jihadists. Also, most jihadists narrowed the Islamic religion to the concepts of jihad and forgot that there are other sides and aspects to Islam. They narrowed Islam to fighting, and fighting to just discharging firearms, forgetting the requirements of patience, preparation, and ethics. I and other veteran jihadists observed the new jihad environment and concluded that a major suffering would return these good souls to the proper character, and this is what came with the September occurrences and what happened afterward.

Errors in System and Structure

The second type of mistakes that appeared in the current jihad is the incompetence and the deficiency of its organizational structure. This problem was revealed after the launching of the big campaign of antiterrorism, which proved it is impossible to continue the jihad work with the existing structure. All the jihadist organizations and groups build their structures on the basis of secrecy, pyramids, and regional orientation.

Problems that were a result of secrecy

- The decision to choose the method of secret work was obligatory and logical when facing a dictatorial oppressor. I am not here to criticize the concept of secrecy in the Islamic work. It is a legitimate concept that has its own proofs and historical precedent starting with the prophet and followed by a lot of trials through the Islamic history. But I am here to point out the big problems that resulted because of the shifting of the security confrontation to a new phase where the upstate regimes became monsters. These barbaric methods caused the jihad groups to go further in secrecy.

- This caused problems in preparation, education, recruitment, expansion, and limited publicity or jihadi ideas and acts and in limiting actions of the movement in producing and performing. Secret work does not allow for education to be completed. And if education is impossible, how can work continue using members who did not learn the methods or the preparation for projects? For education, the secret cells depend on meetings between the responsible person for the cell and his followers, where he prepares them in different ways in what they need to know about methods, techniques, politics, and military preparation and security. These meetings are periodic and most likely weekly, but decrease in frequency with the disruption of the security situation.

- The pioneers of jihad were well prepared, because they were taught before the period of secrecy. They were prepared in the mosques or in the open or partially open Islamic groups, resulting in highly preformed jihad activity. But with the disappearance of the pioneers and the groups that followed them (because the path of jihad consumes its soldiers through death, arrest, or immigration), unqualified cells and cadres join the line, and most of the time they are from the general public and the young generations that most likely were not educated inside one of the Islamic movements.

- Our cadres have been consumed quickly, and the jihadi groups were forced to depend on new cadres who were not educationally prepared by those who already proved their bravery and capability in the combat field. This is leading to the failure of our entire method of engagement.

- The mandatory environment of secrecy and security does not allow the expansion of recruitment. Most of the jihad groups were built before the impact and the combustion of the battle. At that time they prepared their structures and recruited the majority of their members.

After that, the confrontation started, which happened before we had completed our preparations for it, the jihad and organizations found themselves forced to enter into the battle and continue to prepare and build while engaged in fighting. They started losing cadres and members, which meant they needed new recruitment, and that meant they needed publicity. They also needed time to observe the candidates to be sure of their abilities and the reasons they were joining. But secrecy and the security problems do not allow for this, and so they weaken recruiting.

- After being torn apart or consumed gradually in battle, jihadi organizations failed to widen their recruitment base and, without exception, the number of the jihad cadres and members decreased or failed to expand. For example, the number of jihadists in Syria did not exceed fifteen hundred active jihadists in addition to supporters in a country of almost twelve million. And in Egypt, a nation of more than sixty million people, the jihad organization did not exceed two thousand members. And in some countries like Tunisia, the numbers was in the tens.

Problems caused by the pyramid structure

- All the Islamic political and jihadists organizations were built using the pyramid structure. This is because most of the time the call starts with a few people who decide the bases of their methodology and goals and the work program, and they pledge for one of them to be their emir, and the first group will be his leaders and board of councilors. Thus, the top of the pyramid is created. The recruitment and mobilization continue, and every one of them takes responsibility of an organization or a cell or a group, and the system continues. Thus, the whole is shaped in what is known as the organized pyramid.

- That method in the dynamic structure holds a strong attribute to power and control, because the orders are given and the programs decided, and then goes down from highest to the lowest. Reports, information, advice, and suggestions go back and forth fast and easily. However this kind of structure contains a security flaw.

- The security organizations and dictatorial governments and the atheist forces that fight the jihad phenomenon have proven their readiness to use every method of violence and physical and mental torturing, even using drugs and medicine to obtain information! The majority of the mujahideen could not resist and confessed most of the information they knew, even adding to it to please the savage animals who were standing by ready to extort any and all articles of information from their memory.

- A few hours was enough to extort information that allowed the security organizations to widen the circle of detention. Then it is repeated and repeated again until the security forces have uncovered the greater part of the secret organization in a very short time. Thus, the pyramid structure became like a blown plastic bag that contains a liquid, which, by pinching a hole, sooner or later you cause it to empty its contents. This pyramid crisis was not solved during the crusade of violence, torture, kidnapping, and submission and has led to deterioration of the organizations and to their fragmentation and weakness.

Regional problems

- Most, if not all, of the jihad organizations are regional in their work and goals. This is a result of the political and social conditions that were common before the spreading of the globalization in all elements of human activities, even including the jihad organizations themselves. There were few countries that provided large areas supported by geographical roughness in addition to large populations, wide borders, and openings that provide the right environment and opportunity for successful jihad gang battles. Even these large countries, like Egypt and Saudi Arabia, are not suitable for the success.

- As we mentioned, the organization's principal leaders were forced to leave their countries and immigrate under the pressure of the security campaigns. They settled far from their fields and cause, and they communicated through messengers or through international communication! This situation created weakness within organizations, because it supplied the security forces with penetration points. Also, this naturally created active military leaders who stayed in the local area and leaders abroad who were often in conflict. The field leadership often found itself in a position where it was required to move and act, but it was restricted by two obligations: the pledge to obey the leadership abroad and the extreme need for the money it sent.

- Jihad organizations were limited in number and did not have a sufficient amount of money. So they were forced to turn to out-of-the-country sources. This created a big problem, because these sources failed to meet needs. The launching of projects and the bills for mili-

tary spending and the compensation of the martyr families complicated the situation. Jihad organizations were forced to depend on the
support of Islamic groups from other countries or some of the charitable people who are backing the jihad in countries other than their
own. Most of the people who support this movement are from the Gulf
Cooperation Council, especially Saudi Arabia and Kuwait.

- The organizations were forced to accept help from special-interest governments and regimes. I don't want to discuss details of the number
  of problems that were caused by this situation. The jihad organization
  started its operation under the motto of charity for God. But the result
  was that the jihad programs exhausted all the resources available to it.
  The irregularity of the flow of the resources drove the organization to
  bankruptcy. And this was one of the main reasons for our failure.

The problem of the weakness of internal security within the jihad current

- The principle of working in a secret organization that acts like a gang
  is that it is a foreign concept to Arab and Islamic societies. In open
  Islamic and Arabic societies, education depends on interaction with
  the public, oration, and open preaching. People exchange news through
  rumors and public confrontations. The hiding methods and secretive (underground) gangs, conducting operations in mafia-like style
  (keeping accurate appointments, short meetings, strict short orders,
  and the strict execution without applying personal initiatives, punishment of the culpable, and also elimination of the corrupt within the
  gangsters' work) are unacceptable within our society.
- Jihadi organizations could not behave in this fashion except as very
  small cadre units. The general characteristics of our society led to disasters because of its disharmony. On top of these problems, there existed
  the lack of security and the inability of the active jihad elements to
  adapt their methods. I observed the most of the mujahideen heroes,
  who were marvelous performers in field confrontations, failed when
  tasked to perform secret missions. Numerous cells were destroyed
  during various operations because of rumors, inability to keep secrets,
  inappropriate movements, lack of respect for communication security,
  and, eventually, the Internet. I resolved that these methods do not suit
  our people and that we have to find alternative methods to them.

Errors in methods/style of work

To be brief, I will innumerate these errors as follows:

- Inability to set work strategies because of the lack of foundations and turning the work into a group of daily chores and haphazard decisions.
- Engaging in side fights with classes of the Islamic awakening school, which harm various sects of the population and its political and social components needlessly in addition, a lack of unified fighting direction toward the main enemy represented by tyrant governments and the foreign aggressor.
- Being dragged into forced, lengthy confrontations with governmental security apparatus that turned into a war of attrition where all parties involved are of the same nation—all this while the foreign aggressor stayed intact and unconcerned about the fights that consume our sons.
- The failure in most cases to determine keys for the struggle and slogans for the confrontation that would unify the people against the governments that the jihadists confront, which enabled the Sultan's scholars to undermine the basis of our movement by defeating its underlying concepts. Jihadists could have used hunger, injustice, and the people being denied their dignity as rallying cries, along with the occupation of the holy places, and the West's political and economic plundering of our lands. However, the jihadists, especially after the infiltration of Salafist ideology into its curriculum, failed to seize the opportunity, preferring to engage in difficult religious discussions.
- The methods of oration of most of jihadists were not popular. Means of communication were poor and limited. In addition, most oration was delivered with viciousness and arrogance that supported sarcastic media campaigns against jihad characters.

Other miscellaneous errors

- The lack of leading scholars within the jihad.
- The low standard of juridical science in general within the current jihad, which led to the birth of young cadre leaders of small jihadists groups with very limited knowledge.
- The low standard of religious, behavioral, and ethical upbringing of those young people who joined jihad recently, reflecting the lack of upbringing curriculums.
- Widespread ignorance on all levels, coupled with the lack of good morals and behavior. This was not only the condition of the young

people who joined jihad, but also of some of the leaders who commanded important tasks.

- Limiting the educational programs to military sciences and the absence of the proper preparation programs, including those relating to juridical science and political guidance.
- The appearance of the strictness during the recent jihad incidents, with the adherence to violence and radicalism even in the most trivial matters.
- Widespread arrogance, the disappearance of creativity.
- The deterioration of order, compassion, and the lack of self-criticism.
- The prevalence of the "at whim mujahideen," those that have no group association or emir to guide them.
- The prevalence of the concept of mujahideen that never engaged in jihad—those appearing in the forefront and encouraging jihad through being vocal and aggressive in their calls.
- The prevalence of those who prepared for jihad, yet who refused to participate.
- Working on behalf of others in areas of conflicting national and international interests.
- Forgetting the detainees.
- The lack of the ability to deter all sorts of enemies.

CHAPTER 8
Sharia-based Political Decision Making of the Movement

The Three Qur'anic Axioms

Muslims must yield to three fundamental legal boundaries for all decisions, actions, and activities. These legal boundaries are:

1. Legitimacy trials (what is permissible or forbidden)
2. Political trials for benefit and harm (what is beneficial or harmful)
3. Realistic and achievable trials (what is possible or impossible)
   For example, if a Muslim merchant wanted to conduct a business deal, he would be compelled to study and abide by these three perspectives:
   - Is this business deal legitimate or forbidden; is it a respectable sale or is it risky, fraudulent, cheating, or deceptive?
   - Is this business deal beneficial to him commercially and financially, or is it harmful?
   - Is this business deal materially and realistically possible?

Likewise, if a Muslim wants to get married and is choosing a bride: First, is this wife permissible, that is, is she a Muslim or a woman of the Book, or is she considered forbidden? Second, will he benefit or be harmed by ties to her? Finally, can he carry out this marriage or are there obstacles that make it impossible? These legal boundaries are of the utmost importance in the political arena, especially regarding matters of fate such as resistance, including the legitimacy of political, military, and informational decisions.

This field is one of the most sensitive fields that should be considered by the jihadist leadership, because it is the driving force behind the resistance. Making wrong decisions, especially in the military domain, such as the poor choice of a target or involving the resistance in battles of lesser importance will result in the loss of its identity and public support. The same should also be applied to political decisions and media efforts. All decisions of this sort and all active members of the resistance should yield to these legal boundaries.

And one is compelled to ask himself:

First: Is that which he wants to do forbidden or permissible? If he does not know, he should follow the saying of the Almighty, "Ask the believers (people who do know) if you do not know." Refer to one who is confident in his knowledge of sharia or one who is confident in his religion [the believers], for this is a question of responsibility for blood, honor, and money.

Second: He must think about the aspects of his work and all that it entails; is it beneficial or harmful to the cause of the resistance? This matter is more difficult than the former because of the intricacies between what is beneficial and what is harmful. It would not be enough if the ruling was ostensibly permissible and lawful for it to actually be so, because if it is proven by political calculations and the opinion of experts that this work will result in damage, then such actions are not permissible according to the general rule of anything that could be damaging is not permissible. However, if you do not have the knowledge, refer to those believers who are trusted in political affairs, those who are trustworthy in their religion, and the experts in war and shrewd policy. If the matter proves to be permissible and beneficial, then consider the third point.

Third: Consider the possibility of executing such a work. This is best appreciated by those who are determined to undertake it, especially if they consulted with the experts, within the stipulations of consultation (engage the services of the strong and the trustworthy). So it is clear, according to religious law and logic, that one cannot carry out any action or decision without considering these three legal boundaries, which include sharia, the politics of interest, and the reality of the action. The action should eventually be permissible, beneficial, and possible.

Doctrine (Creed) and Sharia (Jurisprudence)

It is the duty of the leaders of the resistance groups and cells to prepare an educational program for the mujahideen within their groups. The program should include a short book that explains the details of the doctrine and the practices of the people of tradition and congregation.

For the purpose of strengthening the belief in the hearts of the muja-hideen, I usually recommend that they read the work of martyr Sayyid Qutub, and the work of Sheikh 'Abd al-Qadir Ibn 'Abd al-'Aziz. Also, I rec-ommend the work of Sheikh 'Abdallah 'Azzam, for he is considered to be a complete school of thought and knowledge. I also recommend listening to lectures and recordings by important figures from the awakening move-ment in the Land of the Two Holy Shrines [Saudi Arabia]. These record-ings are considered to be excellent educational material on jihad.

However, it is necessary to pay special attention to the work of some of those individuals right after they were released from prison and during the war on terrorism campaign, because some of them went through severe relapses, may God forgive them.

This does not lessen the value of their publications, but the duty of choosing the right material for the youths and for the resistance cells is the responsibility of the leaders who have enough knowledge to select the best material for the purpose.

The Sharia or Jurisprudence

The resistance mujahid should learn three main points from the sharia, which are very important and valuable for the mujahid. They are:
1. The sharia rulings regarding worship—This includes the jurispru-dence for ablution, prayers, fasting, giving alms if a person has wealth, and pilgrimage of the person who is capable of performing this ritual. Each resistance cell must prepare a short jurisprudence study for its members similar to the way these acts of worship are practiced by the majority in the area in which the cell is located. This is a clear and easy point, and there is no need for further explanation.
2. Sharia teachings pertaining to the aspects of life—The mujahid must learn the religious rules governing his behavior. For example, if he is married, he must learn women's jurisprudence in order to be able to educate his wife; if he is a merchant, he should learn selling and buying

rules and jurisprudence, including what to deal with and the amount of charity he should pay. This subject must be studied and learned by Muslims so that they can live a pious life.

3. Jurisprudence of jihad and its rulings—The resistance mujahid and the mujahid who is determined to travel the true path for the sake of God must learn the duty of jihad and must realize that jihad today is a mandatory obligation prescribed for every Muslim. The mujahid should be convinced that he is doing the right thing, and he should realize the importance of jihad. When the mujahid learns the rules of jihad, he also will discover the rewards prepared for him and for the martyrs in the hereafter, by the will and grace of God, when they fulfill their duty. He must also understand the consequences that will result from neglecting this duty as well as the losses this neglect will cost him, his family, his people, and his nation. The mujahid must also understand the hardship, humiliation, and suffering he will bring upon the people, which will include loss of lives, honor, and wealth.

Once the person is ready to perform jihad, then he must learn the rules and the jurisprudence; his jihad will affect rights, belongings, and lives. It will also deal with permissible and nonpermissible issues. Therefore, he must not be confused, and he must know the rules and understand what is considered right and what is considered wrong.

Most important, the mujahid must understand the goals and the ethics of jihad. These are areas that will take too long to explain. It is the duty of the mujahid to learn as much as he can and as much as will be of benefit to him, his position, and his responsibilities.

Each jihad group, cell, or organization must have a person they can ask and seek guidance from whenever they need it or whenever they do not understand something.

I have included the basis of these principles below:

*   Governments ruling Muslim nations today are apostates for changing the divine commands and for using laws other than the ones prescribed by God. Also, they are considered apostates for befriending the infidels.
*   It is a prescribed duty for every Muslim to fight a leader who committed apostasy.
*   Muslim lands are occupied by enemies, and fighting them is the duty of every Muslim.

- Sharia laws unanimously state that anyone aiding the infidels against Muslim is an infidel and apostate and must be killed.
- Sharia laws state that it is permissible to kill anyone who transgresses on Muslims, their religion, their honor, or their belongings, even if this person is Muslim.
- Sharia laws state that the blood, the money, the belongings, and the honors of Muslims are protected, that the presence of the invader infidels in our land is not permissible, and that their blood and belongings are considered free.
- It is a prescribed duty to help and aid other Muslims who are under the aggression of the infidels, regardless of whether or not these Muslims have committed any sins. Jihad is a duty prescribed for all Muslims.
- The issue of democracy and the participation of Islamists in it is forbidden.
- Sectarian conflict within the Sunni group is forbidden.

I would like to briefly mention some of the religious rules in regard to some important issues that might face the mujahid today:

Jihad against the Distant Enemy—With Allah's help, the enemy who is farther away will become afraid when he sees the closer enemy defeated.

The Ruling on Seeking Permission for Jihad—What if the enemy was not in his country and was not massing troops against the mujahideen, or the mujahideen had sufficient personnel to defeat the enemy in his own land? In this case, jihad is not required; rather it is optional. If jihad is optional, then permission from parents and a spouse are required. However, if the enemy attacked a group of Muslims or mujahideen or a piece of Muslim land, then, as we have mentioned before, jihad becomes a requirement in that country. In this case, no permission is needed from parents, spouse, or creditors. This condition remains in effect until the enemy is expelled from Muslim lands. In this scenario, jihad is required. As a result, jihad ranks higher than submitting to one's parents (even though that is a requirement too). The reason jihad is a higher priority in this case is because it is undertaken to protect the religion, which, in turn, protects all the Muslims, including a person's parents. Thus, protecting the religion is a higher priority than protecting oneself.

The Example of Imposing Enforcement and Adequacy—Let's suppose a group of families went picnicking on a beach. There were among them men who knew how to swim very well. They saw a boy drowning. He was screaming, "Save me, please!" but none of the good swimmers went to save him, except one. However, his own father stopped him from doing so. Would any legal scholar say that this man should have listened to his father and let the boy drown? This is the example of Afghanistan (and of other occupied countries such as Iraq and Palestine, Kashmir, and so forth). They are calling for help, and some men want to help save them. But some controversial voices are being raised, asking them, "Do you want to do this without your father's permission?" To save the child from drowning is the duty of all the swimmers who see him drowning. Before anybody moves, all swimmers should be called upon to save him. If a person acts to save the child, then no fault rests with the others. However, if nobody moves to save him, then the fault lies on all the swimmers. In such instances, the father's permission is not needed. Also, if the father were to stop his son from saving the drowning person, then the son does not have to obey.

Getting Permission from the Sheikh and the Educator—No Muslim scholars ever wrote that the sheikh or the educator has the right to limit the worship of his students. Every Muslim can perform jihad without obtaining permission from his sheikh or his educator, because the Lord's permission is the highest priority, and he not only permitted but ordered jihad. If a student wanted to study engineering, medicine, or history in Western countries or in America, where disorder is like the dark night and where there is lively entertainment and adultery, I will say, "If this student went there, the sheikh and others would not object to this. But if he went for the purpose of jihad, you would see everybody talking against him."

Getting Permission for the Enforced Jihad—It's clear to us that no permission is required for a person carrying enforced jihad. Also, no father or master should be asked permission to conduct the morning prayer before sunrise. Also, nobody should be asked for permission to carry out jihad. For if the father and the son slept in the same place and the son wanted to perform early morning prayer while his father was sleeping, would anybody say the son should ask his father for permission to pray? And let's assume the father prevented the son from praying so he wouldn't bother others who were sleeping. Should the son obey his father? The answer is clear—there should be no obedience to a creature if it is a sin against the creator.

Would We Carry on Jihad without Having One Emir—Yes, we will perform jihad without having an emir. Nobody said that not uniting Muslims under one emir will end the jihad's task. We saw Muslims fight the Crusaders and the Tatars when their emirs where at odds and when in every country there was one or more emirs.

Fighting as an Individual If the People Shirk from Their Military Obligations—The Prophet of Allah commands:

1. To fight even if only by oneself;
2. To rouse the believers.

The Almighty reminds us of the wisdom of fighting to stop the infidels, because the infidels are not afraid of our presence except when fighting. By abandoning the fight, polytheism will increase and persecution and victory will be on the side of infidelity.

Is It Permissible to Invade alongside the Immoral and Corrupt?—Yes, one should invade alongside the righteous and immoral, or any imam. The Prophet said: Jihad is your duty with every emir whether he is immoral or righteous. If jihad is abandoned with the immoral emir, it would end the road of jihad and allow the infidels to prevail over the Muslims, leading to faithlessness and great corruption.

Killing Infidel Civilians, Looting Their Money, Killing Women, Children, and the Elderly—We noted before that Muslims don't kill anyone except those who want to kill them, or those who assist the unbelievers and the enemies of Islam with money or influence. There is no need to kill women unless they have fought, nor children, nor the monks, unless they mixed with the unbelievers. Torturing humans and the weak is something Islam does not need.

The scholars' opinions are at odds on this and are subject to different ideologies:

First Ideology: women and children should not be killed in any case. Even if the infidels were to use their children and women as human shields, they should not be fired upon. If they protect themselves in their fortresses with their progeny, they should not be bombarded by the catapult and other things.

Second Ideology: Weakness in fighting is not counted unless the women and children mixed in with the fighters and so we can't fight without killing them. It is not permitted to kill women and children in a war or in other places if they didn't fight, because the Prophet forbade their killing. The other issue is the impermissibility of killing women today if they do not participate in war and do not join the army and do not adopt communist principles, or any other principle that they will be willing to die for. But now the situation has changed; a woman in such cases is not much different from a man.

Ibn Al-'Arabi said, "Don't kill women unless they fight; the Qu'ran has forbidden killing them, if they didn't fight. If they fought, then they should be killed."

Killing a Monk (Priest, Evangelist, and So Forth)—As for the monk, the permissibility or impermissibility of killing him depends on whether he mixes with the people. If he mixes with people, he should be killed. If he is in isolation, praying to his Lord, then he should be left alone.

Killing the Infidels' Elders, the Sick, the Blind, and the Insane—There were two opinions in killing of the unbelievers:

1. Those who grouped the elderly with children and women. The Muslim scholars said the reason for not killing them is the same as the one for not killing the children. They are of no use to the infidels and constitute no danger to Muslims.
2. Others, such as the scholar Al-Shafi'iya, allowed killing them because of the general proposition saying, "Kill the unbelievers wherever you see them." Because he is an infidel, there is no use for his life, and he should be killed like the young one.

To summarize the issue: Whoever is useful for the unbelievers or others should be killed—whether he is an old man, a monk, or a crippled person. The assembly of Muslim scholars agreed that whatever is useful for Muslims and harmful to the infidels during war or when preparing for it is permissible whether it means killing a human being or an animal or destroying buildings. War means the start and finish of eliminating disorder and spreading the call to raise Allah's religion.

Killing Communist Women in Afghanistan—As for the communist women in Afghanistan, they should be killed whether they participated in the war, provided advice, did not participate, whether they separated or mixed, or whether they were one or a group, because they have beliefs against Islam and they harm Islam and Muslims.

Using Guns, Planes, Mortars, and Rockets in Shelling—We indicated that fighting for Islam is intended to eliminate the hurdles that obstruct its call and to destroy the political regimes that prevent Islam from reaching the people. If we can deliver this without killing or fighting, then this is what Muslims wish. However, if this cannot be accomplished, then all barriers should be removed by any means possible. And if we cannot reach the tyrants that rule the earth unless we kill humans and demolish installations, then we should do it! Because we have been forced to do this.

The Ruling on Martyrdom (Suicide) Operations—Suicide is haram [haram means forbidden by Islamic Law], because the soul does not belong to its owner but rather to almighty Allah. He is not allowed to do whatever he wants with his soul except what pleases Allah. The suicidal deserve hellfire. However, a human sacrificing himself to serve Islam, raising Muslim morale, or hating the enemy for the sake of almighty Allah is not considered suicide.

An Important Question: What is the ruling on a man who with a suicide belt tied to his body throws himself in the midst of a group of infidels or tanks and blows up himself and all of them? And what is the ruling on an individual who attacks an enemy by himself on their own ground?

The Fatwa: The Muslim scholars have permitted the sacrifice of oneself for the sake of Islam's victory, and this is not considered to be a suicide. There is a difference between suicide and self-sacrificing. Suicide is killing the soul by fleeing from life's pains and troubles. Self-sacrificing is exerting the soul for the sake of protecting Allah's religion and the triumph of the religious laws without pain and grief.

As for a single man attacking the enemy on his own ground, a man should only do this if he is seeking salvation and benefit to Muslims:
1. And if he is not seeking salvation, but he is enticing Muslims so they do the same thing he has done, killing and spiting the enemy, then it is good if Allah wills it. Even if he does not seek salvation, it is not bad that he attacked the enemy.
2. If he is doing it because he is imitating others who have done so, that is also good, and I hope he gets his reward at the end of times.
3. And if he is not seeking salvation but he terrorizes the enemy, that is good too, because this is the best of all spites and has benefits for Muslims.

The Ruling of the Enemy's Prisoners—The ruling on the enemy's prisoners varies in gender and age and religion. There are three types of prisoners:

First, women and children: these should not be killed during war if they are alone. After they become captives, they should not be killed either, for they become slaves.

Second, scholarly men and the educated people: on these the Muslim scholars had mixed opinions. Most agree that the imam has the choice between killing the captives and enslaving them. As for extending kindness toward the captives without a monetary compensation, it is forbidden. As for ransom, it is agreed that captives can be released for a great amount of ransom money or if Muslims need the ransom money. However, freeing an unbeliever so he can return and make war with Muslims is always a sin. Committing a sin for the sake of money is not permitted.

The Predominant Opinion on the Issue of Prisoners—There is no doubt the most prevalent opinion is that the imam has the choice in matters concerning prisoners in what benefits Muslims, be it killing the prisoners, showing them mercy, or exchanging prisoners for ransom or for Muslim prisoners.

The Impermissibility of Selling the Enemy Anything That Might Strengthen Him against Muslims—As for the business of developing deals between Muslims and infidels during a war, when the religious scholars (jurisprudents) established the basis for trading, they established it on the basis of what was good for the Muslims and to press the infidels. For example, Imam Malik allows importing from infidel countries and allows war merchants to enter Islamic countries carrying their merchandise. This strengthens Muslims. Conversely, Imam Malik forbids exports to infidel countries that strengthen the infidels. Meanwhile, the purchasing of infidel products internationally now strengthens the infidels by providing hard currency to the exporting countries.

Exporting weapons to infidel countries is forbidden as is exporting petroleum that is used to manufacture weapons and war machines. The Muslim scholars even forbid exports of silk and silk garments, because silk is used to manufacture war machinery. Exports of iron that is used to manufacture weapons is forbidden. In these modern times, it also is forbidden to sell copper and cobalt, radium, and uranium (because atomic bombs are made from them).

The Summary of the Issue of Infidels Using Muslims as Human Shields

First, infidels will take some Muslim prisoners, or will keep them with them so that the Muslim mujahideen will not shoot at them for fear of killing their Muslim brothers. The mujahideen should not refrain from attacking them, because the Muslims may be defeated if they do so or if the harm resulting from refraining to shoot at them is greater than if they were to shoot at Muslim prisoners and detainees.

Second, the issue of those who are forced to fight among the infidels (such as the recruited Muslims in the infidels' army). The scholars ruled that it is permissible to kill them if one is not able to identify or distinguish them among the infidel army. Allah would not oppress the mujahideen if they kill those Muslims, for they will be judged according to their intentions.

But the recent developments occurring these days bring up a very sensitive, difficult, and important issue. The occupying forces entered our countries and engaged in face-to-face combat and confrontation with the mujahideen, making the situation in Iraq, Afghanistan, Palestine, Kashmir, Chechnya, and others difficult. The presence of the occupying enemy is also very different: military, security, and civilians mix among the Muslim populations inside the cities and housing complexes, rendering guerrilla warfare and "hit and run" tactics the main way to confront them. Explosive ordinance devices became popular with the mujahideen, regardless of whether they exploded at a distance, by suicide bombing, or by other means.

This raises the same issue regarding the presence of apostates—those who are loyal to Allah's enemies, the invaders who are against Allah—and their military and security guards among the Muslim in residential areas, and in commercial (market) places. In these cases, targeting those apostates and infidels, enemies of Allah, with the different types of explosives will cause the loss of innocent Muslim lives as well as the destruction of their properties. I believe that making light of this issue and giving the free hand to the mujahideen with no scrutiny, guidance, or restrictions is flawed and puts the mujahideen in a position where they are responsible for the bloodshed of innocent Muslims, the destruction of their property, and the rape of their women.

I am not saying to completely stop fighting the infidels who mix with Muslims, because this will allow them to get hold of our country and destroy the Muslim religion; this is the goal of the enemies of Allah. And I would certainly not call for that. The mujahideen should study every operation according to the Muslim sharia, the same way they study it from a security and military perspective. The key factor, from our perspective in this case, is who among Muslims is going to be killed with the explosive operations of the mujahideen. They (Muslims) should be avoided by any means possible. The mujahideen should weigh the benefit and importance of the operation, the relative unintentional harm inflicted on Muslims, and the damage that the operation will inflict on the infidels, and how that damage will affect them (the infidels).

In some operations, we found out that some bombs planted in crowded Muslim markets will only kill a few infidel military patrol personnel. A car bomb in front of the American consulate parked outside the fence surrounding the front yard will only harm offices that employ no Americans. . . . No one in his right mind would think that such operations would harm one single American! Only a small number among the targeted enemy will be injured or killed, and none might even be harmed. Conversely, many Muslims, including children, women, and other innocent people will be killed and/or injured, and, in addition, much damage will be done to property! This result is known to every smart man. So it requires a little calculation and study of the area and weighing the possibility of Muslim presence there. I believe this should not be happening.

There is a big difference that should be taken into consideration, between using explosives in infidel countries and their capitals, like Tel Aviv, Washington, and London, and using them in the capitals and homelands of Muslim countries. Attacking the immoral and the infidel does not provide an excuse to hurt those staunch in faith.

If the mujahid is sure that the target will cause considerable damage to the infidel, which will defeat the enemy and give victory to Muslims—for example, the target will be an important enemy leader, or the operation will inflict serious damage hindering the capabilities of the enemies—and the mujahideen tried their best to keep the Muslims far away from the operation area, even picking the right time when Muslims are not present . . . if all these precautions are taken . . . and an accident happened where some Muslims were hurt unintentionally, then I ask Allah to forgive the mujahideen, for they tried with the good intentions.

When discussing the loss of Muslim lives, the explanation I heard from the mujahideen implied their disdain for some Muslims. They argued that the Muslims who are hit by these operations are immoral or are lazy and not participating in jihad and other explanations that may or may not be correct. But such talk is not valid. They are Muslims, and Islam gives them protection, and so they should be avoided. No scholar would say that their blood is permissible. Muslim blood should not be wasted unless it is said in the books. Though I noticed that in some situations, the psychological condition that some mujahideen reach, caused by the pressure from the enemies and caused by people not defending Allah's religion, may lead them to such disdain. This is very dangerous and it should not be allowed to happen.

The Ruling on Residing in the Lands of the Polytheists—It is not permissible to live in the unbelievers' land, except in an emergency and under extreme conditions. This ruling is to protect religion, honor, and property. So, a Muslim should choose the safest place to reside according to what will protect his religion, honor, and property. The prohibition against residing in the land of infidels and unbelievers is a general ruling that is agreed upon among the Muslim scholars and all their sects, for the harm it entails to religion. Such harm includes following the unbelievers' traditions and mixing with them, which in time will lead to familiarity and which is forbidden by Allah, as is mixing young generations with their children and learning their many rotten traditions. It also leads to a drift away from Islamic traditions and the customs, and the lack of mosques to remind people of Allah. Besides, the infidels are trying to hurt Muslims and are attacking them.

But I was fated, out of necessity, to live a long time in the European lands.

During the years 1983–97, because of security reasons, others and I were forced to migrate from the oppression of tyrant regimes. I lived in these countries and studied and worked in many fields of trade, including journalism. It was my fate to live in France for three years, for about eight years in Spain, and more than three years in England. I visited many European countries, like Germany, the Scandinavian countries, Italy, Belgium, Holland, and others. And I worked among many Islamic awakening groups there.

I have personally witnessed that what the Prophet prohibited, that is living in infidels' lands and among unbelievers, is truly a Prophetic miracle. I witnessed the conditions of Muslims (in the land of infidels), the moral and immoral among them, even the ones who claim they are part of the Islamic awakening, including those mujahideen who went to Europe! These countries have an effect on those Muslims who live in the land of infidels and on their children, with no exception. Of course, the difference in the level of immorality varies reaching total apostasy.

I do not have time to explain to you here what I saw and heard about the bad conditions of Muslims, their traditions and religion, and what happened to them there. If time allows, I will record that in a special letter. The majority of those called Muslims in the land of infidels—they count for tens of millions in Europe by itself, perhaps more than 45 million, and the same in America, Canada, Australia, and other lands—do not pray, do not contribute to charities, or follow Islamic sharia. They have little left from their father's religion except a few manners and traditions that are melting slowly with their children and grandchildren. Their women and daughters go outside uncovered and mix with Muslims and infidels, studying in their schools. Their youths are spoiled; they drink alcohol and many of them eat pork. Adultery is common among them, also among their women, and many men are marrying infidel women (most of whom should not be slept with because they are not believers of any Holy Books and they have no religion; like most of the Western youths; they are proud of this).

Thus new generations know not of their Arab fathers' language or of Muslims, and they live their mothers' way of life! Girls are marrying infidel men in civil marriages, and some found lost scholars to help in this kind of forbidden marriage, along with other kinds of illegal marriages, and adulteries. Many Muslim girls are meeting other men and friends, with the knowledge of their fathers, who are unable to stop them for fear that their daughters may flee from the house! And other Muslim girls became cheap professional prostitutes, especially in mid-European countries! In addition to participating in European festivals and holidays and the normal daily life of eating, drinking, and dressing, you will not see a difference between an infidel and a Muslim.

Those whom I asked about their religious answered enthusiastically, "We are Muslims!" This is the situation of the majority. I tried to imagine the number of people who pray on Friday in the countries I lived in; most of them do not pray five times. If I am not mistaken, the percentage of Muslims who pray on Friday is no more than 1 or 2 percent, at best! As for the committed people who attend mosques and Islamic centers, we can tell their ideology and situations by following their satellite programs where they broadcast their news, like Iqra' Channel and others. In summary, I believe that Muslims (in the lands of infidels) have found for themselves a European-American religion out of necessity and moderation. I can simply testify—out of knowledge—that what remains in their new Western Islamic religion of the religion of Muhammad is nothing but some traditions and prayers. The role of most Islamic centers and mosques is to provide (Halal) meat and prepare the Friday prayer and marriage contracts, funerals, lectures, and some parties and ceremonies.

They have found for themselves a Western Islamic way that fits the calling for moderation! For the minority that is holding on to their traditions and religion from the other ones that have moved away from them, most have no way or strength except by the almighty Allah. Apostate thinking has spread among the ones that are called "Islamic thinkers," and some who are scholars in the West, trying to bring religions closer, with religious "forgiveness," cultural dialogues, Christian-Muslim dialogue, and what they call the dialogue with the others and the denial of terrorism in religion. They are spreading Islamic fatwas that need to be looked at individually and scrutinized and answered. One strange example I have heard about is those called Muslim thinkers—the ones who have "plucked" beards, and white collars, or what is called a Western tie or "civilization halter," as one of our sheikhs called it. He said the sun will come out from the West before the hour, which means Americans and Europeans will become Muslims, *and* the Islamic sun will appear from the West! The Americans and other Westerners will carry the Islamic call and come to our lands to conquer it in the name of Islam, and because they have military power, they will keep the Islamic banner! This is similar to the Tatar case, when they came to conquer; they became Muslims, and Tamerlane returned with his Muslim Tatar grandchildren and conquered our lands and others in the name of Islam!

Can you imagine how stupid their thinking is, how they do not follow the details of the Hadith and its witnesses. None of these ideas has any basis in truth and shows a lack of knowledge about history and the infidelity of the Tatars, whom they are testifying about, after they claimed Islam. They polluted (made rotten) the lands and the jihad of our Muslim ancestors against them. This is the state of their thinking when they are corrupt and left to discuss incoherent concepts. As for today's political trivia, they call for socializing with Westerners, joining their political parties, establishing lobbies to pressure governments, and imitating their social traditions, as well as other disastrous practices.

Also, those—a very few Muslims and jihadist are among them—who took their religion with them and requested political asylum in some of the Western countries are the rare few who live in a foreign environment.

Since the modern Crusader campaign began in 1990 and along with it the so-called global war on terrorism, conditions of Muslims in the West have started to change. This became more evident after the events of September 11, 2001; after the American occupation of Iraq; after the

Americans and their allies announced projects in the greater Middle East; and after their overt statements on Crusading. A wave of anti-Muslim sentiment and apartheid became very clear in Western communities in Europe, America, and elsewhere, with attacks on mosques, the burning of Islamic centers, bombings, and attacks on Muslims and their children and their women, especially those who covered their heads with the hijab. These attacks were not only waged by those fundamentalists and racists, who are many and increasing in numbers because of the war and what the mujahideen are doing, but also attacks on Muslims have occurred because it has become the policy of Western governments.

All the Western countries have passed new laws that place restrictions on Muslims, claiming they (the laws) are antiterrorism and antifundamentalism measures. A law was passed in France that prevents women from wearing the hijab. Similar laws are being studied in other countries. Laws have been passed to monitor preaching in mosques and to dismiss preachers who do not abide by the government's strict instructions. Most young people who pray in mosques are monitored, and many of them have been called in by the authorities and investigated. The intelligence community has recruited thousands to watch people attending prayers at mosques. This is in Europe.

As for America, the measures are stricter and harsher and more aggressive; hate is mixed with security measures. As all of you know, these stories are repeated in daily news broadcasts.

It is worth warning you that these developments and pressures have begun to push many Muslims living in the West to do what is forbidden and to issue statements that jeopardize their religious beliefs, to prevent them from being accused. Accusations of terrorism and fundamentalism have caused some of them to deny their religion by not covering with the hijab, by not attending the mosque, or by denying their religious beliefs. Some of them have reached the point where they speak against their religious beliefs for the same reasons. The most ridiculous thing of all is what Muslim imams and directors are doing. These heads of Muslim communities are holding back because of threatening pressure. It has reached the point that they are showing loyalty to the infidels and distancing themselves from the faithful, especially from the mujahideen who strive for the sake of Allah. They openly curse at them in the media. Those of us who monitor the media have been very surprised by their statements and practices. If you search for the reasons for this, you will see very clearly that these (Muslims) are living in infidel lands for the love of the worldly plea-sures and that they reject their religion and their children's religion toward infidelity as a price for that end (worldly pleasures). Living this way was forbidden before the infidels who rule these countries applied pressure and acted aggressively. It is even more so (forbidden) after all these campaigns of oppression. The truth is that most of them have accepted the worldly pleasures and are happy.

Before concluding this section, we still have to remind and warn Muslims about two important issues:

First, everyone should know that whoever has religion in his heart, has obedience to Allah and his Messenger according to the sharia, should know that it is not permissible to live in the lands of the infidels unless it is necessary and that he should return to his own land (the land of Muslims) even if there is oppression, poverty, and other difficulties. If he is unable to return to his country for fear of persecution by the governments of his country, then he should seek refuge in other Muslim lands. The migration should be from the lands of the infidels to Islamic lands if this is possible. If this is not possible, he should go to lands where his religion is safe and his honor and properties are safe. He should pick the best option and the less corrupt option. As for the world and its money, Allah is the provider. Working, trading, or looking for daily bread is not an excuse for living in the lands of infidels, especially in the circumstances these days. Living in the lands of infidels is not permissible unless that is the only choice, or for a legitimate reason pertaining to jihad against the infidels in their country in defense of Muslim land.

Second, we should warn Muslims who live in Western lands and other countries at war with Muslims and are allied with America in the inva-sion of our lands that the war has started, it will continue for a long time, and its ferocity is increasing. The members of the mujahideen and the resistance have begun to deter America and its allies, in both our lands and theirs. Turmoil should be seen as normal as the infidels seek to take revenge and pressure them. I don't think a wise man will ask the muja-hideen for the sake Allah to leave the enemies of Allah alone. Whoever has joined and protected the infidels in their lands for pleasure and has become one of them is a traitor and is corrupt. So don't let the task cease because the majority have disobeyed their Lord and have broken the Prophet's clear commands.

The Definition of a Martyr—It is agreed: a martyr who is not washed and not prayed over, he is one who died fighting the infidels, whether an infidel killed him, a Muslim's weapon shot him by mistake, his own weapon killed him, he fell from a horse, or his animal kicked him. He died, or was stepped on by Muslim animals, or something else. Or he was shot by an arrow that might have been shot by Muslims or infidels. Or he was found dead at the beginning of the war and no reason was found for his death and whether there was blood on him or not. Whether he died immediately or died from wounds over a period of time after the war, whether he ate or drank and whether or not he recited his will, all this is agreed by us.

The Conditions of Martyrdom—The battle should be for the sake of Allah.

- Patience—if you were killed unintentionally while being patient and ready, Allah will forgive you all your sins, except in religion. Whoever is patient and goes against the enemy won't feel pain in his heart, hatred of death and separation from his family. Patience in worship is acting according to its conditions.
- No looting.

CHAPTER 9
Media and Incitement in the Call to Resistance

Once again we would like to evaluate our past experiences and lessons derived from these ventures to deduce the perceived wisdom we might glean from these experiences. It should be possible for us to examine the advocacy experiences at the following levels:

1. Audience (beneficiary) receiving the message—This is the particular Muslim audience to which the advocate can address his message.
2. Content of message—This is the motivational communication and the endorsement the mediator conveys for the purpose of launching jihad.
3. Style of message—This is the tenor, construction, and method of the mediator's presentation of his message.
4. Delivery system of message—This is delivery system the mediator has adopted to deliver his message to the public to motivate them for jihad.

Message Beneficiary and/or Audience: Throughout our history, advocates of jihad would communicate their message of jihad to the *ummah* at large, including its rulers, the ruled, the poor and the rich, the able and the competent, the weak and the irresolute, all echelons of society, and all constituents of the Muhammedan *ummah*.

Content of the Message: The general content and tenor of the message is to motivate and induce the Muhammedan *ummah* for jihad. This motivational content would become a reminder of the beneficence and grace of Allah Almighty to lead the people to a better life on the path of righteous. It would also cover the potential victory achieved from jihad and the expansion of the Muslim empire that would result.

If the purpose of jihad is to defend the *ummah* against the raids of enemies or tribes, the message would focus on arousing the patriotic fervor of
the Muslims to defend their honor, integrity, and land and the lives of the
inhabitants of the *ummah*. The message would also come as a reminder of
the ill consequences, such as humiliation, hegemony of the enemy, human
casualties, and destruction, of neglecting this religious obligation.

Style of the Message: The style is calculated to promote the faithful to
be vigilant and mindful of the Islamic faith. Furthermore, it is designed
to propel the troops' desire for Allah Almighty's beneficence and grace; to
spur the manhood, mettle, and audacity of the *ummah*; to become a more
crucial value in Islam. The style should draw on the literary and poetic
diction and oratory that were prevalent during the early history and for-
mative years of the faith.

Delivery of Message: The spiritual vehicle of delivery, as well as the
venue, is of great importance for delivering the underlying spirit and sub-
liminal value of the message. This is represented in the mosque, which
is the essential venue for scholars and preachers where their views and
sermons can be heard.

Our approach to communications in the current jihad has not been true
to the above precepts, and it is bereft of any popular dimension that would
be geared toward the hearts and minds of the Muslim public at large. Our
content is also almost void of clues to other dimensions that are supposed
to be included in the message, such as the politicoeconomic dimension
and the daily afflictions and discomforts of the Muslim community.

In general, the jihadist message is vainglorious, egotistical, and over-
bearing; it may even be uncompromising, threatening, impassionate, and
rigid. It is lacking in sentiment and is nonappealing to the masses and
their psychological spirit. Again, it was unilateral and elitist.

Our messages must be focused on a fundamental and underlying idea
that is religiously deep seated within the public and customarily comprehensible to them as a universal spiritual fact. That truth is represented in
preventing foreign aggression and defending the Muslims and their homeland against such an aggressor. Also, it not only entails the provision of
support and aid to the Muslims engaged in the event, but as a gospel of the
faith, it also mandates joining the Muslims in that event, financially supporting them, and mortally aiding them as a mandatory requisite.

Our message style needs to be lucid, streamlined, and cogent. It
must be a passionate and inspiring message that combines not only the

promise of victory and rewards but also Allah's beneficence and grace for attempting to face foreign enemies and his retribution for dereliction and delinquency.

Initially, and in the early 1980s, the accepted medium of delivery was through mainstream publications, magazines, and electronic media such as recording cassettes.

In this endeavor, Sheikh 'Abd al-Rahman 'Azzam was instrumental in establishing a reputable school of public information and communication that is worthy of examination, development, and drawing upon its successes. The practice of jihad by Muslims in Bosnia Herzegovina and their informative adopted doctrines have contributed a valuable dimension, namely the use of CDs and VCRs as a recording medium, and thereby managed to address serious deficiencies. This was followed by the jihadist drive in Chechnya that was instantly on line to emulate and develop experience and was able to promote the recording medium as well as the Internet, to the next level: the videotape.

This has launched the jihad into higher levels of success that have made the presence and movement tangible everywhere.

The public information and communication success in the area of jihad was monumental and spectacular. This was clearly seen in the support of the *ummah* to various jihadist aspects in which hundreds of thousands of men and women, rich and poor alike were volunteering to provide aid and material sustenance to the jihad theater. A careful examination of these experiences in jihad and the lessons learned from them, with the grace of Allah, enable us to formulate and establish the fundamentals of an advocacy and information theory for the companies of the global Islamic resistance movement and its inclusive and integrated advocacy drive. Among the important lessons learned from our past experiences are:

- Religious and spiritual dimension—defend and preserve the Islamic creed, shrines, and the tenets, or "pillars," of the faith.
- Economic dimension—defend and preserve sources of wealth, the homeland, and sinews of existence.
- Political dimension—defend and preserve civilization.
- Sentimental dimension—defend and preserve the value system, morals, traditions, and customs inherited, such as honor and dignity.
- It is imperative to use simple, comprehensible, and popular language that appeals to the general public as the basic lingua franca among the masses of the *ummah* and to steer away from extensive and detailed

legal opinions and religious analysis. The message would then focus on arousing the patriotic fervor of the Muslim troops so that they march in defense of their honor, integrity, land, and the lives of the inhabitants of the *ummah.*

- Endorse variant forms of popular communication to get messages to the populace. In this day and age, where electronic advances are quite sophisticated and the power of communication and knowledge is applied to the Internet and the satellite television stations, both are powerful engines for communicating with the public at large. Compact discs are another variant form that can carry the message. In these popular means of message delivery, the divine wisdom of Allah Almighty can be attested for by those who are keen on delivering the message and communicating with the people. Let us not forget that large-scale publication expenses are exorbitantly high and exceed the budgets and capabilities of most organizations, not to mention the inconceivable option of disseminating a particular jihadist ideology. The answer to overcome that difficulty lies in the Internet and the satellite television stations that have and are visiting the critical mass of households, rich and poor. What is missing now is the good faith, will, determination, integrity, and a profound strength of character and loyalty in actively and effectively publicizing on a large scale.
- The role played by the mosques, as well as that of the weekly seminars or conferences held in this venue, should not be overlooked. Special emphasis should be awarded to Friday prayers and sermons. This is a great access of publication and propagation that Allah has provided to the descendants of His prophets and messengers, and yet the majority of the *ummah* preachers have wasted this valuable asset to curry favor with the ruling elite.

Content of Message—The message should delineate its content: fend off foreign enemies. This is a mandatory obligation for every male and female Muslim. The details of the content should be tailored according to every cast of the society: the general public is to be addressed in generic terms and various species of the *ummah* are to be addressed with specific messages.
- Call attention to the body of Qur'anic textual material, as well as that of the Muhammedan archetype and paradigm that brings to the fore the theme of combat and jihad, its rewards for those who engage in the act, and punishments for those who refrain from it.

- Call attention to the body of fatwas produced by the coterie of contemporary and late Muslim scholars that are relevant to the religious obligation and jurisprudence of jihad, particularly within the context of self-defense, and all related canons.
- Bring attention to the body of anecdotes and narratives from the Prophet's biography, Islamic history, and provocative war stories that bring to memory the war glories of Muslims that incite jihad.
- Emphasize and play up the history of the Crusade expeditions, its course of events, and its literature. History is just repeating itself in most of today's events.
- Intensify and highlight contemporary colonial Crusade expeditions since the turn of the sixteenth century, particularly those campaigns launched by major colonial powers since the eighteenth century, as well as anecdotal history of our forefather's jihad against contemporary foreign aggression and the ideological struggle in all countries of the Islamic and Arab world.
- Emphasize and feature anecdotal history of aggression and destruction perpetrated by modern historical colonial powers in a detailed fashion, particularly as accounted for in their academic and documented sources.
- Emphasize and highlight the history of modern-day conspiracies against the Islamic world by the Orientalist structures and movements and their relationships, as well as that of intellectual invasion, with respect to colonial powers and the course of colonialism.
- Punctuate the role played by intellectual and doctrinal Westernization by contemporary secular movements, its parties, its intelligentsia, its advocates for them from among the citizens of the Islamic and Arab world, and their subservient role in furthering colonialism and bringing about the destruction of the *ummah*.
- Highlight and bring to the fore the events and roles played by the Jewish-Zionist onslaught against the Islamic world since the Balfour Declaration and the ensuing immigration waves to Palestine, the establishment of the state of Israel, the Arab-Israeli conflict and its history and what has come to be known as "peace with the Jews," the normalization of relations with the Jewish state, and the relevant social, cultural, economic, political, and military cooperation programs and their destructive influences on the Islamic world.
- Highlight and bring into relief the events, scope, and means of the contemporary American onslaught against the Islamic world that

took place since the formulation and launching of the new world order. Highlighting informational material on America; its decadent and degrading areas as related to civilization, life, and science; and its offensive drive throughout the world since its creation (i.e., the United States) during World War II, highlighting the role and scope of contemporary European and Western allies to the United States, and particularly those in the NATO membership to expose the mendacity and pugnacious policies toward Muslims and their participation in the ongoing decisive onslaught.

- Give emphasis to, and feature the history of, stalwart operatives, martyrs, and other achievements in preserving the Islamic faith; scenes from, and denominations of, the Islamic resurgence movement; as well as its history in every country as delineated by reliable sources there and increasing the awareness of the *ummah* with its history.
- Give prominence to, and publish the contemporary history and all forms of, resistance to literature and arts that would be conducive to rekindle the ethos and morale of jihad.
- Stay vigilant and alert to contemporary American cultural invasions and the means employed to socially and intellectually corrupt Muslim society through the Internet and television channels. Remain prudent to all attempts made by the fifth column and advocates for contemporary American Islam by the enemies of the faith and those who harbor enmity toward its culture and ideals in the name of moderation.
- Feature and disseminate a culture of security through the circulation of relevant publications, sensitize the Muslim community and increase its awareness with regard to the enemy's means to face the resistance, and penetrate the *ummah* and our society.
- Feature and disseminate a culture of militarism through the circulation of relevant publications, as well as the different schools of military science and warfare, guerrilla warfare, and its ordinances and armaments used in that field. Exchange information and trade experiences that are relevant to that expertise.
- Feature and disseminate the military and political dimensions of American campaigns, and particularly in the area(s) of military discipline and professionalism, political intrigues, economic plundering, and manipulation and with respect to social, cultural, and civilizational destruction and the means of combating it.

- Feature and disseminate atrocities perpetrated at the hands of American campaigns and their allies with a view to enliven zeal and passion among the *ummah* congregation.
- Call to attention the body of fatwas produced by contemporary and late Muslim scholars and e-mail them as en mass attachments nationwide.
- Mail threatening messages to institutions and people that cooperate with Zionist and American expeditions.
- Mail instigating messages as well as supporting documents thereto to all concerned sectors of the *ummah*.
- Mail messages of admonition to people who cooperate with Zionist and American expeditions.

Recommendations

1. Beware not to neglect keeping intention, loyalty, and accountability under watch at all times.
2. Beware not to disregard the cultivation of the jihadist doctrine in all of its facets in the hearts and minds of mujahideen.
3. Beware not to disregard a comprehensive education, particularly in regard to devotion to the sharia and moral behavior.
4. Beware not to wrongly accuse Muslims of faithlessness and beware not to follow those who aid in the faithlessness of Muslims.
5. Beware not to mix armed jihad with the jihad of argument and manifestation.
6. Beware of confrontation with the scholars of prevailing governments, leading to the unintentional straying of the resurgence leadership from the path.
7. Beware and exercise vigorous caution not to shed the blood of Muslims in the course of the battle against the infidels and apostates.
8. Beware not to disregard the [religious] rulings of jihad and the rules of conduct and moral practices of Islam vis-à-vis friends and foes.
9. Beware not to cause the resistance and the mujahideen to lose the public opinion of Muslims.
10. Beware not to target neutral parties in this confrontation, even if they are infidels.
11. Beware not to change the structure of the brigades of the call to resistance into central hierarchical organizations.

12. Beware not to issue statements or communiqués by any brigade on behalf of the call for global Islamic resistance. This task is reserved to the Central Guidance Office.

13. Beware not to be affiliated to or become involved with the institutions of the occupiers or the satanic rulers [The Arabic word "taghut" is used here, which means Satan; a reference to Arab leaders] who rule contrary to God's revelations, in the name of the interest of the call for global Islamic resistance and resisting the occupation and the satanic rulers.

14. Beware of an overt jihad, centralized in open battlefronts, or clearly delineated domain, unless it is unavoidable, as long as the American military force is not abolished and their surveillance is [not?] terminated, especially in the air.

15. Be vigilant in communications security in all its forms: telephones, radio, and Internet.

16. Beware of rumors and revealing secrets; divulge information only on a need-to-know basis.

17. Beware not to forgo the religious obligation of battle and convince oneself that calling for jihad is enough.

18. Beware not to get preoccupied with controversies and ideological battles among Muslims. In particular, avoid that which is outside the realm of the confrontation.

Index

Abaykan, Abd al-Muhsin al-, 44
'Abidin, Khalid Zayn al-, 153. *See also* Suri, Abu Musab al-
Abu-Ya'li, Mustafa, 134–35, 137, 138, 139
Afghan Arabs. *See* Arab Afghans
Afghanistan: Arab organizations working in, 23; assault by U.S. on, 39–40, 94, 97; effect of 9/11 on jihadist movement in, 97–100, 127; generations of jihadists born in, 11, 84; immigration into, 88–90; influence of Afghan jihad, 82–85; Islamic state in, 10, 39, 76, 88–91; jihad in, 11; jihad in, number of participants, 82, 83; jihad in, support for, 77–80, 82–84, 133; jihad in, U.S. aggression against, 97–100; jihad in, U.S. support for, 72–74; jihadist organizations in, 89–90, 91–93, 106–7, 131–32; losses from Afghan jihad, 74–75, 133–34; mujahideen success in, 65; training camps in, viii, 10, 88, 93, 114, 153; training of mujahideen in, 77–78; triumph of U.S. in, 27; victory in, U.S. role in, 74–75; war with Soviet Union, 11, 81
Africa, 40, 86
agriculture interests, 38
aims of believing elite, 6–7
Albright, Madeline, 38–39
Algeria: failures of jihadist movement in, 11–12, 21, 56; jihadist movement in, 64, 93, 112, 130, 134–45, 154–55; massacre

of civilians in, 21, 142–43
Algerian Afghans (Algerian Arab Afghans), 136, 138
Amin, Abu-'Abd al-Rahman, 141, 142, 143
Ansar, Al-, 87
Ansar al-Islam, 27
Ansar al-Jihad, 11–12
apostates, 52, 59–60
Arab Afghans: attitudes and beliefs of, 84–85; birth of movement, 84; Desert Storm and, 12–13, 18; Islamic revival through, 73; methods of destruction used against, 27–28; number of participants, 76; price to preserve Islam paid by, 28; relationship with U.S., 75–76; schools of, 11; second phase of, 22; security sweep against, 18, 39; Taliban toppling and, 24; as terrorist organization, 95; training of, U.S. role in, 75–76
Arab governments. *See* Middle East and Arab governments
Arabian Peninsula. *See* Middle East and Arabian Peninsula
Arafat, Yasir, 61
Armed Islamic Group (Algeria, GIA), 21, 87, 130, 134, 139, 140–43
Armed Islamic Group (Libya), 86, 87, 92
Asad, Bashar al-, 43
Assad, Hafiz al-, 38–39
Atta, Mohammad, viii
'Azzam, 'Abdallah, 49, 75, 76, 77, 78, 82–83, 93, 173

Baa'th Social Party, 68

"Balance of Power in the New World Order" (al-Suri), 17

Balfour Declaration, 33

Banna, Hassan al-, 68

belief: believers and unbelievers, 51–54; faithlessness of leaders, 53–54; infidels and unbelief, 48

Bergen, Peter, viii

bin Laden, Osama: Afghan jihad role, 77–80, 83; Afghanistan as base for, 89; 'Azzam's influence on, 77; confrontation methods of, 25, 26; connections to Saudi intelligence of, 76–77; connections to U.S. of, 75, 76–77, 81; failure to find by U.S., 77; family of, 147–48; forgiving nature of, 150; global jihad push, 23; ideological shift of, 78–80; ideology embraced by, 22; jihad against U.S., 150–51; jihad against U.S., call for, 23, 90, 106; jihad against U.S., support for, 133; jihad against U.S., writings about, 157–59; jihadist goals of, 78, 81, 158; Libyans working with, 129; media campaign against, 81, 90; relationship with al-Suri, vii, viii; as symbol for Arab jihadists, 90–91; U.S. as enemy of, 79, 80; Yemen activities of, 148–52

Bosnia, 11, 57, 65, 86, 191

"Brigades of the Global Islamic Resistance" (al-Suri), 23

Burma, 57

Bush, George H. W., 76

Bush, George W., 24–25, 60, 96, 162

caliphate, 30–31

Call for Global Islamic Resistance (al-Suri), ix–xi

"Call for the Sake of Establishing the Global Islamic Resistance" (al-Suri), 18–20

Central Intelligence Agency (CIA), 75, 76

Chechnya: elimination of mujahideen in, 40; jihad refugees in, 86; jihadist movement in, 11, 57, 191; military achievements of, 65

chemical weapons, viii

children, aggression against, 177

China, 81, 91–92

CIA (Central Intelligence Agency), 75, 76

civilizations, clash of, 24–25

Cole attack, 57, 93, 151

communist women, 178

Crusader campaigns, 3, 55–56

Crusader-Jewish campaign: equations about battles against, 57–60; goals of, 3, 16; illegality of attacking, 15, 61; jihad against, lack of support for, 22–23; occupation of Arabian Peninsula by, 13, 32, 49; resistance to, 5–8, 56–57, 63–64; sharia legitimacy of, 14; support for, 1, 4–5, 16, 18, 60. *See also* enemies and infidels

culture: Americanization of Muslims, 61–62, 125, 184–85, 186–87; cultural annihilation of Muslims, 3–5, 7, 13; ethnic cleansing, 24, 37; Western influence on, 34–35

death, "no escape from" quote, 26

defensive jihad, 49

democracy, 34–35, 160

Desert Storm, 12–15, 16, 18, 19, 37, 38

East Turkistan jihadist movement, 57, 90, 91–92, 99

economic jihad, 19

Egypt: Afghan jihad, support for, 72, 73, 83; cooperation with Iran by, 121; jihadist movement in, 68, 79, 92, 102–8, 112–21, 166; wheat production in, 38

embassies bombings, 57, 93

enemies and infidels: battle against, obligation of, 26, 48–51; business dealings with, 180; collapse of, 80; confrontation methods against, 25–26; cooperation with, 48; equations about battles with, 57–60; friendships with, 52–53; killing of, 177–78; Muslims fighting with, 181–82; Muslims living in land of, 183–87; sharia rulings and, 48–49

equations about battles with enemy, 57–60

Eritrea, 51, 57, 65

ethnic cleansing, 24, 37

Europe: battle against, obligation of, 26; Crusader campaigns support, 60; goals of against Muslims, 3; jihad against, 81; jihad against U.S., support for by, 81; jihad refugees in, 85; prisoners in, 51; racist attacks against Muslims in, 41;

war of ideas against Islam, 2
excommunication judgements, 112, 141,
142–43

Fahd, King, 79
Faisal, King, 39
faithlessness of leaders, 53–54
Fajr, Al-, 87, 128, 134
fatwas, 15, 79, 113, 179
fearlessness in jihad, 7
fight, will to, 8
Fighting Jama'ah Isalmiyyah, 127–34
Fighting Youths organization, 109–10, 111
Foreigner Groups Camp, 93
France, 44, 81, 135, 136

generations of jihadists, 10–11
genocide, 37
Ghanushi, Rashid al-, 122, 123, 125, 126
"Global Islamic Resistance" (al-Suri), 23
global resistance call, 18–20; audience of,
    189; content of message, 189–90,
    191–95; delivery system for, 190, 191,
    192; recommendations for, 195–96;
    style of message, 190–91, 192
global war on terrorism. *See* war on
    terrorism
God's laws, replacement of, 31
Granada, 20
Great Britain, 3, 32, 43, 60
Guantanamo Bay detention center, 51, 98
Guidance of the Almighty God (Amin),
    142
Gul, Hamid, 73
Gulf Cooperation Council, 72

Hadid, Marwan, 108–10
Haq, Ziya al-, 39
Holland, 41
Huntington, Samuel, 24, 95
Hussein, Saddam, 19, 33, 42
hypocrites, 1, 20, 60

immigration laws, 41
independent countries, 161
individual jihad, 19, 67
Indonesia, 28, 57, 65, 86
International Monetary Fund, 38
Iran, 43, 99, 115, 121
Iraq: invasion of, 27, 43, 94; military

achievements of, 65; occupation of, 42;
    Spanish army withdrawal from, 157;
    triumph of U.S. in, 27; weapons of mass
    destruction in, 42
Islam: fundamentals of, 52–53; principles
    of, understanding of, ix x; revival of in
    Afghanistan, 73; teaching of ideology
    of, 69–70; war against, 1, 2, 24–25,
    40–42, 96–97
Islamic Awakening, 6, 17, 79
Islamic Current, 122–24
Islamic National Movement, 138
Islamic religious sentiment, 8
Islamic resistance. *See* jihad and jihadist
    movement
Islamic Salvation Army, 139, 144
Islamic Salvation Front, 135–37, 138–39,
    142, 143
Islamic state: in Afghanistan, 10, 39, 76,
    88–91; defeat of, 39, 58–59; victory of,
    58–59
Israel: battle against, obligation of, 26;
    goals of against Muslims, 3; normal-
    ization of relations with, 42; support
    of U.S. for, 32–33, 96; surrender of
    Palestine to, 13. *See also* Crusader-
    Jewish campaign

Jabal Hatat, 28
Jama'ah al-Isalmiyyah Organization, al-,
    104–5, 106, 112–21
Jaza'ri, Aby Bakr al-, 14
Jerusalem, 13, 32, 33, 76
Jihad, Al-, 82
jihad al-masri, Al-, 79
jihad and jihadist movement: assault
    by U.S. on, x, 1, 16, 25, 27–28, 39–40,
    46–47, 97–100; axes of, 5–8, 134; call for
    resistance, 18–20; call for resistance,
    audience of, 189; call for resistance,
    content of message, 189–90, 191–95; call
    for resistance, delivery system for, 190,
    191, 192; call for resistance, recommen-
    dations for, 195–96; call for resistance,
    style of message, 190–91, 192; com-
    mitment to, 5–6; components of, 67;
    confrontation methods against U.S., 28;
    definition, 66–67; disarray within, 1–2;
    dispersion of jihadists, 85–87; as duty
    for Muslims, 6, 25, 29, 48–51; effect of

9/11 on, 24, 57, 94–100, 107, 127; effect
of war on terrorism on, 46–47, 85–87,
100, 131; elements of, 56–57; equations
about battles with enemy, 57–60; errors
and problems of, 162–70; failures of, ix,
11–12, 21, 56; fearlessness in, 7; foundation for current movement, 68–72;
God's support for, 29, 47; groups supporting, goals of, 22; groups supporting,
lack of, 15, 16–17; ideology behind,
160–62; ideology behind, lectures on,
23; ideology behind, popularity of,
84; ideology behind, spread of, 69–70,
86–87; ideology behind, understanding
of, ix–x; importance of understanding,
x; important attacks, 70–71; important
jihad movements, 71–72; individual
jihad, 19, 67; influence of Afghan jihad
on, 82–85; jihadist experiences, writings about, 101–2, 157–59; justification
for by scholars, xi; leaders for, 2, 100,
169; legal boundaries for decisions,
171–72; legality of, 61; levels of, 8–9;
media campaign against, 90; military
achievements of, 64–65; new world
order and, 17; nonviolent civil resistance,
7–8, 64; number of participants in, 5,
10, 76, 82, 83; operations of, ix; organization and structure of, 22, 164–70;
political achievements, 65–66; price
to preserve Islam paid by, 28; recruitment for, 165–66; resistance, axes of,
5–8; secular reasons for, 66–67; security
sweep against, 18, 28, 39, 87, 100, 106,
131; security within, 168; sharia rulings
for, 174–80; slander against, 8; status of,
63; success and achievements of, ix, 6,
57, 64–66; support for, 19, 20, 167–68;
targets of jihad, x, 19–20, 161–62, 167,
182–83; as terrorist organizations,
95; threats to movement, 1–5, 46–47;
training and education for, ix–x, 2, 6–7,
8–9, 11, 64, 163–64, 169–70; types of
jihad, 49; *ulema* for, 9; youth interest in,
9. *See also* Arab Afghans; mujahideen
Jihad Experience in Syria (al-Suri), 152, 153
Jihad Group (Egypt), 87
"Jihad Is the Solution, but Why? How?"
(al-Suri), 23
jihadist creed, 8–9

jihadist generations, 10–11
jihadists, 67
Jordan, 42, 43, 93
jurisprudence, 173–80

Kashmir, 45, 51, 57, 65
Khaldan Camp, 93
Kissinger, Henry, 24, 95
Kurdish militia, 28
Kurdistan, 84
Kuwait, 12–14, 43, 77, 79–80

Lebanon, 56, 83
legal boundaries for decisions, 171–72
Libya, 56, 83, 127–34
life, sharia rulings on, 173–74
livelihood, legitimate and illegitimate
means, 33
London bus bombings (2005), vii

Mahdi, 25
martyrs and martyrdom operations:
in Afghanistan, 76; as curriculum
examples, 64; reward for, 46, 47; sharia
rulings for, 179, 188
Mecca, 13, 32
Mecca conference, 14–15
media: campaigns against bin Laden, 81,
90; effect on Muslims, 34, 61–62; por-
trayal of Afghan jihad by, 74
Medina, 13, 32
Middle East and Arab governments:
control of by U.S. and allies, 38–39;
cooperation with U.S. by, 1, 4–5, 41–43,
46–47; Desert Storm support and participation, 13, 14–15; faithlessness of,
52–54; Muslim fortunes robbed by,
36–37; sharia rulings and, 48, 85
Middle East and Arabian Peninsula:
history of, 55; occupation of, 9–10, 13,
32, 49, 100; political map of, 3, 42; U.S.
goals for, 3–4, 42
military achievements, 64–65
military aim, 6–7
mineral and petroleum interests, 35–36
Moroccan Islamic Combatant Group, 157
Morocco: jihadist movement in, 92, 102,
154–57; security sweeps in, 28, 100
Mubarak, Hosni, 106, 107, 114, 117
Muhadir, Abu-Hasan al-, 152–53

mujahideen: in Chechnya, 40; commitment of, 79; definition, 66–67; dissolution of, 17; founding of, 79; generations of, 10–11; goals of, 67; illegality of activities of, 61; killing and imprisonment of, 40, 98–100; leaders of, 100; methods of destruction used against, 27–28; military achievements of, 64–65; number of participants, 82, 83; in Pakistan, 12–13, 18, 40; price to preserve Islam paid by, 28; recruitment of, 76; religious and political training of, 19; rewards for, 67; secular interests of, 132–33; security sweep against, 18, 39, 131; sharia rulings for, 173–80; statements against by *ulema*, 18; successes against Russians, 65, 83; training and education of, 18–19, 77–78, 169–70, 173–80. *See also* Arab Afghans
Mujhadoon, Al-, 87
Musharraf, Pervez, 39, 40, 52
Muslim Brotherhood: Algerian operations of, 138; ideology behind, 69; influence of, 79; jihadist movement in Syria and, 69, 108, 109–11; killing and imprisonment of, 102; operations of, 15, 68; al-Suri's activities with, vii, 11
"Muslim Condition" (al-Suri), 23
Muslims: Americanization of, 61–62, 125, 184–85, 186–87; cultural annihilation of, 3–5, 7, 13; education of, 1–2, 7; equations about battles with enemy, 57–60; excommunication judgment against, 112, 141, 142–43; fear in life of, 37; fighting with infidels, 181–82; global war against, 16; holy sites for, 32; as human shields, 180; jihad as duty of, 6, 25, 29, 48–51; killing campaigns against, 37; killing of by Muslims, 181–83; leaders of, faithlessness of, 53–54; legal boundaries for decisions, 171–72; livelihood of, 33–34; living in unbelievers' land, 183–87; militarization of, 76; political life, 34–35; poverty of, 35; racist attacks against, 41; religious life, breakdown of, 30–35; restrictions placed on, 185–86; social and moral life of, 34; status of, 39–47; support for war on terrorism, 95; U.S. goals against, 3–4, 42, 96–97; worldly

blessings of, loss of, 35–39
My Personal Testimony on the Jihad in Algeria 1989–1996 (al-Suri), 12

Nasar, Mustafa Setmarian, vii. *See also* Suri, Abu Musab al-
Nasser, 'Abd-al-, 68, 102, 113
National Liberation Front, 135, 139
nationalism, 161
new world order, 14, 16–17
new year celebrations, 45
Nixon, Richard, 24, 95–96
nonviolent civil resistance, 7–8, 64
Northern Alliance, 98

oil interests, 35–36, 97
Omar, Mullah Mohammad, viii, 23, 28, 88, 92, 93
Oslo Convention, 61
Ottoman Caliphate, 31, 32

pacificism, 64
Pakistan: Afghan jihad, support for, 72, 73; control of by U.S., 39; cooperation with U.S. by, 40, 42, 52, 98–99; intelligence operations, 78; mujahideen in, 12–13, 18, 40; Peshawar, 82; sharia movement in, 56
Pakistani mujahideen, 90
Palestine: intifada, 56, 90; Jews migration to, 32–33; jihadist movement in, 93; liberation of, 76, 161; normalization of relations with Israel and, 42; surrender of, 13
Paris subway bombings (1995), viii
Patriotic Harmony, 144
peaceful resistance, 7–8
Peshawar, 82
petroleum interests, 35–36, 97
Philippines, 40, 51, 57, 65, 86
Polisario Front, 155
political achievements, 65–66
Political Freedoms in Islam (al-Ghanushi), 125
political life, 34–35, 63–64
political-intellectual aim, 6
poverty, 35
prisoners, 46, 51, 179–80
prostitution, 38
pyramid structure, 166–67

Qadhafi, Mu'ammar al-, 127, 129, 130, 131
Qaida, al: Afghanistan as base for, 89,
    92; basis for, 79; cooperation of Al-
    Jama'ah with, 115; establishment of,
    77, 104; global jihad push, 23; interest
    in by terror groups, x; jihadist experi-
    ences, writings about, 157–59; methods
    of destruction used against, 27–28;
    operations against U.S. by, 57; price to
    preserve Islam paid by, 28; radicalism
    that helped create, 79; responsibility for
    September 11 attacks, 94; strength of,
    10; training for, 77–78, 79
Qari, Sa'id al-, 136–37, 139, 140
Qarni, Ayid al-, 43–44
Qatar, 42
Qutub, Sayyid, 68–69, 102–3, 108, 173

Rahman, 'Umar 'Abd al-, 113, 114, 116,
    117, 118
Rambo, 74
recordings of lectures, 23, 152, 153, 191
reformist schools, 15
regimes, 160
religious life, breakdown of, 30–35
religious minorities, 161
religious-cultural aim, 6
resistance. See global resistance call; jihad
    and jihadist movement
revolutionary jihadist climate, 6, 7
Road Map to Peace, 61
Roosevelt, Franklin D., 39
Rum, 2
Russia: elimination of mujahideen by, 40;
    jihad against U.S., support for by, 81;
    losses from Afghan jihad, 74–75; muja-
    hideen success against, 65, 83; prisoners
    in, 51; war with Afghanistan, 81

Sadat, Anwar, 112, 113, 119
Sahwa, Al-, 79, 84
Salafist Group for Preaching and Combat,
    144–45
Salafist Jihadist, 156
Salafist movement, 15, 137, 138, 162–63
Salafiyyah Jihadiyyah Movement, 156
Salih, 'Ali 'Abdallah, 148, 149, 150, 151
Saud, Abd al-Aziz Al-, 32
Saudi Arabia: Afghan jihad, support for,
    72; bin Laden's connection to, 76–77;

British control of, 32; cooperation with
    U.S. by, 32, 80, 99; intelligence opera-
    tions, 76–77, 78; legitimacy of govern-
    ment, 79–80, 158; Muslim fortunes
    robbed by, 36–37; refuge offered by, 70;
    resistance movement in, 56–57; secu-
    rity sweeps in, 28; sharia in, 31; sins of,
    32–33; teaching of Islamic ideology in,
    69–70
Saudi Islamic Awakening (Al-Sahwa), 79,
    84
Schwartzkopf, Norman, 18
secrecy, 165–66
security apparatus, 5, 28
security sweeps, 18, 28, 39, 87, 100, 106,
    131
September 11 attacks: assault on
    Afghanistan after, 39–40, 94; blame for,
    90; effect on jihadist movement, 24, 57,
    94–100, 107, 127; exploitation of events
    of, 6; jihadist generation born of, 10, 11,
    23; responsibility for, 94; success of, 26;
    al-Suri's role in, viii
sharia: classification of people in, 51–52;
    faithlessness of leaders and, 53; jihad
    as duty ruling, 48–49; justifying jihad
    through, 20; legitimacy of Crusader
    campaign and, 14; peaceful resistance,
    illegality of, 7–8, 63–64; removal of
    from modern life, 30, 31; ruling on
    martyrdom, 179, 188; rulings for muja-
    hideen, 173–80; as source for legislation,
    31; as source of problems for Muslims, 31
Shiite groups, 161
Signs on the Road (Qutub), 69
slander, 8
sleeper cells, viii
Somalia, 57, 65
Soviet Union: collapse of, 80; mujahideen
    brought in to destroy, 75, 76; war with
    Afghanistan, 11
Spain: Madrid conference, 13–14, 61;
    Madrid train bombings (2003), vii;
    al-Suri's activities in, 18; withdrawal of
    army from Iraq, 157
Steinberg, Jeffrey, 24–25
Stinger missiles, 74
Sudan: bin Laden in, 78, 80; Libyans
    removal from, 129; refuge offered by,
    85–86, 105–6, 129; wheat production

in, 38
Sufi movement, 15
Sultan's scholars. *See ulema*
Sunni *ulema*, 14, 18, 19
Suri, Abu Musab al-: Afghanistan activities, 21–24; anonymity of, xi; capture of, vii; events linked to, vii; jihadist movement activities of, vii, viii, 11–12, 111; journalist career of, vii–viii; lecture recordings by, 23, 152, 153; London activities, 21, 87; relationship with bin Laden, vii, viii, 81; relationship with Zarqawi, viii–ix; reward for capture of, vii; training camp established by, 23, 153; writings of, viii, ix–xi, 12, 18, 87, 134, 152, 153; Yemen activities of, 152–53
Syria: jihadist movement in, 64, 68, 75, 83, 84, 108–11, 166; response to Iraq invasion, 43; al-Suri's activities in, 11; transfer of power in, 38–39

Tajikistan, 57, 64, 88
Takfiriyyin, 112, 156
Taliban: beginning of, 88; Islamic state in Afghanistan under, 10, 88–91; price to preserve Islam paid by, 28; refuge offered by, 22; support for, 132; toppling of, 24, 39, 56, 98; U.S. war against, 94
targets of jihad, x, 19–20, 161–62, 167, 182–83
Thailand, 86
Third Crusader Campaign, 3
Tora Bora, 27, 127
Tunisia, 93, 122–27
Turkey, 42, 86
Turkish mujahideen, 92
Turkistan, 57, 88–89, 91–92
Turkistani, Hasan Abu Muhammad al-, 92, 99

ulema: cooperation message of, 5; cooperation with Crusader campaign by, 16, 18, 43–45, 60–62; evils of, 61–62; fatwas issued by, 79; as hypocrites, 1, 20, 43–44, 60; for jihadi movement, 9; legitimacy of, 80; revolution against, 18, 20; silence on jihadist sacrifice, 10; Sunni *ulema*, 14, 18, 19
ummah: believers and unbelievers, 51–54;

call for resistance activities by, 19–20; commitment to resistance by, 5–6; complacency of, 26, 45–46; participation in jihadi movement by, 10, 26; price of war for, 26; recruitment of, 5, 29; resistance by, 5–6; threats to, 1–5
unbelievers, 51–54
United States: Afghan jihad, role in, 74–75; Afghan jihad, support for, 72–74; assault on Afghanistan by, 39–40, 94, 97; assault on jihadist infrastructure, x, 1, 16, 25, 27–28, 39–40, 46–47, 97–100; battle against, obligation of, 26; collapse of, 80; dominance of, 28, 95–97; as enemy, 79, 80; evils of, 94–95; goals of against Muslims, 3–4, 42, 96–97; jihad against, 19–20, 81, 161–62; methods of destruction used by, 27–28; military strength of, 27–28, 55; occupation of Arabian Peninsula by, 9–10, 32; opposition to, 41; political goals of, 95–97; relationship with Saudi Arabia, 32, 80; religion of Congress members, 44; support for by Arab leaders, 1, 4–5, 41–43, 46–47; support for Israel by, 32–33, 96; victory of, 27; war against Islam by, 1, 2, 24–25, 40–42, 96–97; war against Taliban, 94. *See also* enemies and infidels
usury, 33
Uzbek mujahideen, 89–90, 91, 99
Uzbekistan, 57, 88

Victory without War (Nixon), 95–96
voluntary jihad, 49

Wadi'i, Muqbil Ibn Hadi al-, 149–50
Wahabi school, 79
war against enemies: as battle of destiny, 26–27; organization and structure for, 26; price of war for *ummah*, 26; unbalanced battlefield, 55
war on terrorism: Arab support for, 43; basis for, 97; effect on jihadi training camps, x; effect on jihadist movement, 46–47, 85–87, 100, 131; elimination of Islam through, 40–41; jihadist organizations as terrorists, 95
weapons, viii, 27–28, 74, 151
West Bank, 42

wheat production, 38
Why They Executed Me (Qutub), 102
will to fight, 8
women: aggression against, 37–38, 177–78;
    duties of during jihad, 7; fatwa for
    killing, 141; permissibility of marriage,
    171; prostitution of, 38; veil wearing
    by, 34
worldly blessings, loss of, 35–39
worship, 173

Yemen: bin Laden's activities in, 77, 78,
    148–52; culture in, 146; elimination of
    mujahideen in, 40, 99; jihad refugees
    in, 86; jihadist movement in, 28, 56,
    145–53; location of, 145; population of,
    145; topography of, 145–46; unification
    of, 148–49

Zarqawi, Abu Musab al-, viii–ix
Zawahiri, Ayman Al-, 103–4, 106–8, 133
Zindani, Abd al-Majid al-, 148, 149
Zionist-Crusader campaign. *See* Crusader-
    Jewish campaign

About the Editor

Having served more than a dozen years on active duty as an infantry officer and recently retired from the Army Reserve, Jim Lacey is a widely published analyst at the Institute for Defense Analyses in Washington, D.C., where he has written several studies on the war in Iraq and on the Global War on Terrorism. He also teaches graduate-level courses in military history and global issues at Johns Hopkins University. Lacey was an embedded journalist with *Time* magazine during the invasion of Iraq, where he traveled with the 101st Airborne Division. He has written extensively for many other magazines, and his opinion columns have been published in the *National Review*, *The Weekly Standard*, the *New York Post*, the *New York Sun*, and many other publications.

Lacey is the author of newly released *Takedown: The 3rd Infantry Division's Twenty-One Day Assault on Baghdad* (Naval Institute Press, 2006). Another book, *Fresh from the Fight: The Invasion and Occupation of Iraq: An Anthology of National War College Studies by American Combat Commanders*, will be released in summer 2007 by Zenith Press. Two other books, *Concluding Peace* (Cambridge University Press) and *Pershing* (Palgrave-Macmillan) are scheduled for publication in summer 2008.

The Naval Institute Press is the book-publishing arm of the U.S. Naval Institute, a private, nonprofit, membership society for sea service professionals and others who share an interest in naval and maritime affairs. Established in 1873 at the U.S. Naval Academy in Annapolis, Maryland, where its offices remain today, the Naval Institute has members worldwide.

Members of the Naval Institute support the education programs of the society and receive the influential monthly magazine *Proceedings* or the colorful bimonthly magazine *Naval History* and discounts on fine nautical prints and on ship and aircraft photos. They also have access to the transcripts of the Institute's Oral History Program and get discounted admission to any of the Institute-sponsored seminars offered around the country.

The Naval Institute's book-publishing program, begun in 1898 with basic guides to naval practices, has broadened its scope to include books of more general interest. Now the Naval Institute Press publishes about seventy titles each year, ranging from how-to books on boating and navigation to battle histories, biographies, ship and aircraft guides, and novels. Institute members receive significant discounts on the Press's more than eight hundred books in print.

Full-time students are eligible for special half-price membership rates. Life memberships are also available.

For a free catalog describing Naval Institute Press books currently available, and for further information about joining the U.S. Naval Institute, please write to:

Member Services
U.S. Naval Institute
291 Wood Road
Annapolis, MD 21402-5034
Telephone: (800) 233-8764
Fax: (410) 571-1703
Web address: www.usni.org